NEGLECTED

DAMAGED

GRACED

SCARS ON THE INSIDE

An Autopsychography

———————

Emmanuel S. John

Neglected Damaged Graced: Scars on the inside.

Copyright © 2023 by Emmanuel S. John, (Books for Head Publishing)

ISBN
Paper #978-0-9851898-8-4
Ebook #978-0-9851898-5-3

Printed in USA by Lightning Source (Ingram)

DEDICATION

This book is dedicated to the victims of emotional damage. To anyone emotionally wounded or scarred by another person's selfishness, self-centeredness, carelessness or perversion. To human resilience, compassion, generosity and Grace. To all of the people that extend themselves to others, in small ways, every day.

PURPOSE

I wrote Neglected Damaged Graced because I believe we can all play a role in the reduction of human suffering. I didn't write it so that you could know me or so that I could be known. I wrote it because some of you are me and I wanted to give us a voice. I wrote it because I know that some of the wounds in me match some of the wounds in you. I wrote it so that people like us won't feel as hopeless and alone as I once did.

When I started writing this book I wasn't thinking that I would make a lot of money, I probably won't. I took on the emotional burden because I hate seeing people suffer needlessly and because I want to do my part. I believe this book's contents will ease your emotional pain and heal some of the damage that others may have carelessly or selfishly inflicted upon you.

I wrote this book as a wake-up call to the therapeutic community and to society as a whole. We have become so focused on the word trauma that the majority of our emotional wounds are being left untreated. If we want to fully heal the wounds that scar us emotionally we must treat the elements of our damage. We must do more than treat the reaction to traumatic events; we must treat its root causes.

It's been my experience that most episodes of neglect and abuse needlessly go untreated for far too long. When left to fester, these emotional injuries can become permanent emotional scars. These scars taint our self-concepts and worldviews. The distortions in reality that they cause often result in a lifetime of preventable dysfunction. These stains on the psyche manifest as both emotional and behavioral problems that can result in unhealthy and even dangerous choices.

Recognizing the effects of emotional damage isn't that difficult. We all see it when we hear the past history of some person that committed some heinous act in the public square. We shake our heads and wonder why people let it happen. Sadly, sometimes without realizing it, we're

1

often the very people letting it happen; worse than that, some of us are contributing to it. I believe we become culpable when we see neglect, damage and abuse occurring and do nothing about it.

I won't be asking you to change the world, because you can't do it alone. Instead, I am asking for us all to be more Grace-full. I'm merely asking that we all be more attentive to the positive impact we can have as individuals. In this book, I'm going to show you how even the smallest of acts and considerations, can be huge stepping stones for survival and healing. I will show you how your seemingly small deeds can prevent horrific outcomes. I'll prove to you that you have an untapped powerful form of Grace hidden within you.

Simply stated; I want you to help me reduce suffering. I want you to help me create a level of awareness that wakes us all from our naiveté of just how great of an impact our small acts can have. I'm going to show you how simple acts of Grace on a personal level, at key moments, can prevent catastrophic suffering. I'm telling you my story so that you can see how we can be either the darkness in someone's heart or the light at the end of their tunnel.

In this book you will hear about the people who have neglected me, abused me and damaged me. They are people I once despised but now, while I may still have reactions to them, I don't want them to suffer either. I've learned the hard way that their suffering doesn't heal my wounds and that wanting it only made me more ill.

Through momentary acts of individual "Grace," I've healed enough to move beyond vengeance and justice. This allows me to now give Grace to others. To be clear I'm not speaking of religious Grace per se; I'm speaking about the Grace that made all the good parts of religion possible. I see Grace as a form of love that is being underutilized by mankind.

I'm certain that what is in this book will help people, even the ones that hurt me, even my abusers. My goal is to move us past ill will and spite so that we can all heal and be more loving. My hope is you'll be convinced that if I can recover from all my damage, then you can recover from all your damage too. When that moment occurs you'll understand the exact purpose of this book and why I spent 3+ years writing it.

If you are an offender, an abuser, or even if you may be predisposed to be one, then my goal is to help you see the scars that such acts leave behind. I want you to see how a minute of selfish indiscretion can result in an eternity of dysfunction, deep-seated pain, suffering and emotional scarring. Please don't allow your damage to last an eternity for others.

If you're a professional that works with wounded and damaged patients I want you to get out of the trauma box. I want you to understand that damage occurs that won't qualify as PTSD and that stretching the diagnosis is missing the mark. I want you to understand that sometimes the "little scars" can be even more dangerous and disastrous if left untreated. I want you to understand that by healing the damaged parts we can actually prevent more traumas from occurring. If we don't teach people how to treat the damaged parts in one another, then we'll be treating trauma forever.

SCARS

If you've made it through your childhood, life and loves without any serious emotional wounds then count your blessings; a lot of us didn't. After only a few short years on this Earth, many of us have scars on both the outside and the inside too; I know I do. Like you, I have some typical injury-related scars from life hazards like bike wrecks, car accidents and broken glass but I no longer feel those scars. I do however still feel the emotional scars that are hidden deep down where no one can see. Sadly, our internal damage isn't treated as readily as the external wounds usually are; if it were it wouldn't scar us as badly.

Unlike our external scars, internal scars seem to move around a bit. They pop up in the worst places; often when we least expect them, usually during difficult emotional exchanges or times of high stress. Sometimes these wounds are obvious to others but more often than not they're usually only visible to those few people we let in close enough to feel them too.

For most people, it's hard to see the scars of strangers on the street. The truth is that sometimes we can't even see our own until they leech out to the surface during some awkward emotional encounter. When emotional scars do surface they're usually not very pretty and they're often fairly uncomfortable for everyone. Our impulse is to ignore and forget about them as soon as possible. While that may bring quick relief it doesn't heal them, it only pushes them down deeper where they're harder to treat.

We aren't always aware of our wounds and sometimes, by some Universal Grace, we're able to forget they're there. Unfortunately, we only realize they're still present when we re-feel them. After they do present they quickly retreat back under the surface so fast we struggle to understand their nature. We feel our internal scars most acutely when they leave us feeling alone, incompetent, or unwanted. They're often activated by relatively trivial events. Some internal scars appear as subtle facets of our personalities that present when we are criticized, hurt, or mistreated. Some people express their scars violently while others internalize theirs in sadness and fear.

Many of the people I have known my entire life are unaware of the majority of my emotional scars yet there they are in plain sight to me at nearly every emotional turn. (This is what I refer to when I say I wear my scars on the inside.) While emotional scars are usually more visible from the inside out, there are times when others can see them and we can't. Personally, I try very hard to manage my damage so that it doesn't impact others. People that can't manage their emotional wounds are usually not much fun to be around. They can be emotionally toxic and even physically dangerous.

I know I'm not the only one with scars on the inside. Many of you reading this book probably have some serious emotional damage too. These scars usually present as dysfunctional aspects of ourselves that we are not very proud of; parts of ourselves that we are not very eager to have other people notice. I refer to our feelings of embarrassment about our damage as Shame Stains.

Tragically most of our major wounds are created by the very people that were supposed to protect us from this damage. Every family has dysfunction and therefore everyone has some type of emotional scarring. The difference being that some wounds are just a lot deeper than others.

Some people know their scars and some people don't. Tragically, when people are not aware of their scars it creates hardship and dysfunction for the people around them. Sometimes unknown scars are so deep they can actually scar others for life (hurt people, hurt people). Neglecting our wounds often means negatively affecting others.

Our scars can have many origins; some we notice, some we don't. Some fade over the years and some just won't. Some are from neglect, abuse, accidental injury and traumas, while others are sometimes even self-inflicted. All these scars form as the result of damage taken to our psyche. For some people, their scars are the literal bane of their existence. For others, they are the origins of their fears, addictions, obsessions and compulsions. My plan is to show you how some of these scars form and how they present so that you can begin to treat them, thereby limiting your own (and others') needless suffering.

Thankfully there is a form of Grace that allows us to operate as if our scars aren't present. By treating the scars we do find and limiting their role in our lives, we create a form of Grace that everyone benefits from. We can even Grace others by not shaming them for their wounds and by forgiving their failings.

Once these wounds are realized the question then arises; what can we do about these emotional wounds and scars? Is there hope for those of us that have taken damage? The short answer is yes, there is hope. The best outcomes however, occur when we treat them before they become traumatic. Waiting until the damage becomes trauma is a form of neglect. We heal damage with Insight, Sunlight, Love (including self-love) and Grace.

Some of the greatest healing events I've experienced occurred when other people shared their similar struggles with me or when they expressed concern for my personal hardships. While their loving acts may not have completely healed my scars they did, at least for a short time, reduce the emotional pain, dysfunction and loneliness associated with them. I believe their acts healed me enough in those brief moments to save me from becoming another catastrophic statistic. I am certain that were it not for random acts of Grace in key moments of my life, I would not have lived past age 21.

My hope in sharing the story of my damage is to spare you or someone you love the suffering that I've had to needlessly endure. My goal is to use the awareness of my scars and how they have presented in the past, to lessen the emotional pain and isolation that your scars may be causing you or your loved ones. My vision is that you'll then do the same for others. I call that "Perpetuating Grace."

It's not enough for me to just help others see their scars. I want to help you realize that your scars are present so that you can see how they affect your choices, perspectives, feelings, behaviors and reactions. I am going to share my scars with you to show you precisely how some of this damage occurs and how it can affect a person's worldview. It's been my experience that we feel less broken when we realize that most of our own negative actions are simply the result of damage we have incurred. (This awareness reduces shame.)

I'm sharing the gory details of my story with the hope that it will help some of you see that these scars, as sad and as horrific as they sometimes are, are a part of what makes me me and you you. While I don't recommend them they do add to our uniqueness and they can even evolve into great gifts of compassion that we can then Grace others with.

When we share our scars with another we all feel less alone. By sharing my ugly stuff some of you will undoubtedly gain a sense of unity in a shared struggle. Some of you will just gain more empathy for the scarred people close to you. These awarenesses will help us all reduce suffering in a world that has far too much of it.

The real key to healing is to understand that there is value in our life struggles; not just for us but for others too. There is value in realizing our wounds, learning from them, embracing them and refusing to be ashamed of them regardless of their origins. Scars are merely evidence that we have survived; that we are survivors. Our wounds only define us if we let them or if we're not paying attention.

One of the most healing things that I have personally experienced and witnessed in my life is seeing my scars help lessen the suffering of others; even if it's just a bit and just for a moment. That respite is another form of Grace. If I'm being truly honest here, you're only safe from people like me, because people just like me shared their pain, showed me their scars and explained to me how they healed some of their damage. I know that sounds a little melodramatic but wait, you haven't seen my scars yet.

CHAPTER ONE

BEFORE THE COMING OF EMMANUEL

My family history is quite storied. By that, I mean that some of it is true and some of it is probably just partially made-up stories that were passed on to my sister and me. The reality is that it doesn't matter whether the stories we are told as children are true or not. They still help form our identities and personalities simply because we believe them. Typically, the ancestral stories we are all told fail to mention the less-than-desirable truths while others are intentionally buried.

As children, we are dependent on what we learn about ourselves and our families from our families. Prior generations like mine didn't have an Internet, we had grandma and grandpa. What we are told forms our worldview regardless of the truth. The information we are given affects our emotional outlook and how we form culturally as people. Thanks to modern technology in the form of a DNA test, I can at least confirm that my "people" are in fact from where I was told they were from. I have to confess that aside from the immigration dates they pretty much nailed it, eventually.

OUR FATHER

Our father always told us that he was half Greek and half Turkish. The genetic origins appear to be right but the portions are skewed as there are a few other ethnicities mixed in too. The story my father told me as a child was that my Grandfather was from Rhodes Greece. He moved to America with my Grandmother after they met in Cyprus. That's the story that I grew up with until adulthood. The story was that my grandfather and grandmother met in Cyprus where the Greeks hated the Turks and the Turks hated the Greeks. He painted a picture of how they were cast out by their families in a Mediterranean Romeo and Juliet type saga. They chose love over family and came to America to pursue their romantic destinies. Sadly I'm afraid it wasn't actually that pretty or that poetic. After some genetic profiling the love story he told seems to be that of his paternal grandparents that never made it to the US.

A more realistic account says my paternal grandmother was born here and that they met after my grandfather's arrival. My DNA supports my grandfather actually having been from an area between Greece and Turkey, with a little Italian mixed in. The fact that our last name was originally Diakogianis helped to support this narrative considerably. My father believed that my grandmother was a complex mix of nationalities. According to him, her family was Gypsy/Roma (possibly Hungarian-Slovak Romani) from Europe. One thing is for sure, she could be a little mysterious at times and always passionate about what she believed. My Grandfather Emmanuel Diakogianis was dead long before I was born so I never got to speak with him. My grandmother always seemed tough as nails; she would have to have been to pair up with my namesake.

EMMANUEL DIAKOGIANIS AND GRAND MA

My grandfather was described to me as a mean son of a bitch. My father believed he was once a for-hire hitman that moved around the Mediterranean quite a bit throughout his youth and early adulthood. (My father's own Mediterranean connections supported his account.) My father described him as the kind of person that could walk up behind you, grab your chin, cut your throat, and hold you as you bled out. (Later in life I would feel that part of him in me but I never saw it in my father.) While people from the community may have talked nice about my grandfather they probably did so for their own welfare. My father didn't believe his father was capable of feeling empathy. My father worked very hard to be the antithesis of his father. Despite all of his father's shortcomings, my father was still proud of his ancestry. He believed it was his father's Turkish blood that made him so ruthless.

I was told my grandfather happily changed our last name to John during the immigration process because he was fleeing private and government forces in Greece and Turkey. When they wanted to anglicize his last name at the port my grandfather happily took on the name John, as in Dee-a-co-Jee-ohn-ese (Jee-ohn). It was a government-issued alias given to him at the dock that he was overjoyed to have. While many immigrants believed the new names made them more American, there is no doubt that the name change would have aided his attempt to disappear into the melting-pot fabric of America following the turn of the previous century.

My father's account of history suggested that his father was on the run from a family seeking revenge. My father's behavior backed this up as he was always attentive to what might be going on in the background; as if someone might pop out of the darkness and attain said revenge. From a little child, he taught me how to observe an entire room when I entered it, to never sit with my back to the door and to always have an exit strategy. (He always did.)

My father shared with me the damage he endured as a child. He told me of the horrific torture and punishment methods his father used. The stories proved his father was not just mean but a child abuser too. My father experienced punishments like being forced to kneel on dried beans in the corner of the kitchen for as long as six hours at a time lest he be beaten. He was once made to eat nearly 2 pounds of pipe tobacco when he was caught smoking. He was repeatedly forced to balance books on his head for hours when he did something stupid and to sit out in the cold if he lost his coat or hat. Sometimes he was even starved for days when he wasn't grateful for or complained about the food he was given (there were others). Obviously, my father had some scars of his own but he hid them well; I'm sure the alcohol helped.

After my grandfather's death and before my birth my grandmother remarried a quiet and warm man we called Grand-pop Eddie. He was a Polish man, known for walking miles to work every morning to Crown Cork and Seal in Baltimore. Eddie was a disciplined man that never missed a day of work and he never fell ill. He used to walk his Scotty dog named Fella so predictably that you could set your watch by him.

The whole neighborhood knew what time it was when he was walking to work or when he was walking that dog. Eddie was always very kind to me as a child and my father respected him for how he treated my grandmother. In addition to being a stay-at-home wife my paternal grandmother was at one time a bookie for the illegal numbers racket back before the lottery existed. You know the game, the one organized and operated by people of Mediterranean descent. (Some say she was very money focused.)

THE WHITER SIDE

Odd jobs weren't limited to my father's side of the family. My maternal grandmother got in on the action too. She took bets during the war while being a "Rosie the Riveter" building planes at Martin Marietta and later as a professional oyster shucker. When all the men went off to war the women went off to work doing many of the men's jobs; not just the legal ones.

My maternal grandmother (Busha) had it hard. She was born to a Jewish mother in Southern Russia. Her mother died at age 2 when they both caught one of the many pandemics of the time. Since men didn't raise children on their own in those days she was shipped off to live with her father's Christian sister. (Her Jewishness was never spoken about again.)

My mother's father was a typical Blue Collar guy that worked his entire life for the city of Baltimore. He worked eight to four every day then came home to his slippers and a cold beer. He was of Polish, Czech and German descent. He was a Witkowski.

Growing up I often referred to my maternal grandparents as being German and Polish because the Russian Jewish history wasn't relayed to me until I was around age 40. It seems that the German/Polish guy married the Russian Jewish girl just before that part of Europe became German against Jew and Russian against German. My grandfather lost support from his family for marrying the Jew (both of their families had migrated to the States before WWII, sometime around 1927).

PARENTAL UNITS

My father was an endearing character to say the least; a very gentle man that I never saw angered. He was a Blues singer during his glory days that went by the moniker of Mr. Blues. While quite controversial by today's standards his band went by the name "Ray John and the Nigger Band." They were so successful that they actually cut a 45 record in an era when it was quite hard to do. In those days an all-black band couldn't legally play in a white club. It's possible that my father was the first non-black affirmative action or "token non-black guy" ever hired in America. I say it like that because, by today's standards, you'd consider my father to be white but not in those days. In the 1940s 50s and 60s Greeks and Italians were far from white. In those days dark haired brown-eyed Mediterranean people were just not seen as equal; especially the poor immigrant versions.

I still picture my father as a dark-haired and dark-complected Mediterranean guy looking at you sideways with an unfiltered cigarette protruding from the corner of his mouth while keeping one eye half shut to avoid the smoke. That is unless he was singing or dressed for the club/bar; then he was a slicked-back greaser that looked like a mix between Dezi Arnez and Johnny Cash (before Dezi and Johnny had a look).

Looking back and trying to piece together some history it appears that my father was actually a kind of Frank Sinatra-esk type before Frank was a type. He was certainly a mob darling (friend of the mob). Rumor has it that my father once sang on the same stage as ole Blue Eyes himself at "The Champagne Ballroom" in a part of Southern Baltimore known coincidentally enough as Brooklyn Park. This was well before Frank made it big in NYC.

THE FAMILY

My father had an older sister, a wonderful woman to me and one of those stay-at-home moms that everyone should at least get a glimpse of while growing up. She was however also a product of her parents. She was known as one of those women that nobody messed with or wanted to cross. Despite her toughness, she was a dedicated mother to her children. I have fond memories of walking to their house on Oldham Street to join them for dinner at the same time every night of the week.

If I ventured out early enough on a Friday or Saturday afternoon I could help my Aunt and Grandmother scrub the soot from their white marble steps in front of their row houses. In those days the good moms cleaned them weekly so that their families had clean cool marble steps to sit upon on hot summer nights. (It was their form of bling! Clean steps meant you kept a good home.)

On those hot summer evenings, the entire neighborhood of Greek town would commune on the streets to people-watch, drink a little and socialize a lot. It seemed to me like the entire neighborhood was taking a census every weekend. Some people walked from house to house catching up on the recent gossip while others stood fast. Their steps were the first social networking platform I ever knew.

On Fridays, there was always a steady flow of traffic as the people from the docks came to cash their checks at the corner liquor store named O'Conner's. In Baltimore, the Irish could always be trusted to provide the carryout booze.

I loved those hot summer evenings. I couldn't wait to see all the fancy 50s and 60s cars. (Our family didn't have many vehicles then.) At times the cars would be double and even triple-parked in the street. It was like all the rules were suspended so people could cash their checks and get their booze. One after the other they would get their checks cashed, buy some booze in brown bags and talk about their destinations for the night, right out in the middle of the street. Black, White, Mediterranean, it didn't matter who you were in Greektown; that's how we grew up in the city. If there was ever a problem it was usually between people from the same ethnic group and it was usually over someone's spouse or girlfriend. There wasn't much race/culture mixing in those days; unless you count my parents.

Some people would split off and head to the docks for night fishing and crabbing while others headed out to the GoGo bars and neighborhood dives. It was obvious that a certain number of those men from the docks were duty-bound to head home after cashing their checks. We would watch as they got their beer and buddy fixes right out in the street. (There was no such thing as drunk driving.) Pretty sure some folks purchased a little weed here and there too. I think that's why my father sometimes disappeared when certain people showed up; he always had business to attend to.

In those days if you wanted air conditioning you usually had to go to a movie theatre, store, bar or restaurant. It was either that or retire to your cool basement family room that may or may not have had an expensive new AC unit in the basement window. Most of us poor people just had those old metal oscillating fans; the ones without the safety grate.

Unlike his father my father was a warm and funny man; a man with many friends. He was always welcomed into all different types of groups and cultures. My father was an alcoholic but confusingly to some, he was also one of the most loving and nurturing people that I have ever known. It was obvious that people really liked and respected him.

For years I thought my father knew every person in Baltimore. We couldn't walk down the street without people waving or happily greeting him. Sometimes they came running from the next block or across the street just to talk to him. He knew people in every store and every bar. It seemed like we had to stop at every establishment in town because he had business to conduct with them all.

I later found out that one of his roles was as the payout guy for the same numbers racket my grandmothers booked for. I watched my father do a little collecting too but that didn't seem to be his thing. He was usually distributing the winnings to the people that "hit the numbers." (I'm pretty sure he was training me to take his place one day because he made sure everyone knew who I was. I think I was good cover too.) All the store and bar owners treated me like I was going to be a part of their future. I like to think that he and I were treated well for who we were but

I'm pretty sure some of their respect was monetary in nature. Either way, their reverence for him was obvious. I always preferred being with my father because it was very different than the way I felt with my mother.

My father was often surrounded by very large, tough and intimidating people of all ages. People seemed to congregate near him naturally; there was always someone else around. He was never really alone unless he was with us kids but even then his large and fast-talking friends always stood by. My father always seemed to be the leader, the one in charge.

By and large, delivering their winnings for having picked the right 3 digits (later 4) usually meant that people were happy to see us. It was like they'd become conditioned to smile whenever we entered. It wasn't until much later in life that I was to learn just how cherished my father was when he was alive. I actually had to use his name once to stop someone from putting a hit on me. It seems I had slept with the wrong guy's wife (I'll tell you about that later). I'm still not sure if my father was ever a "made guy" or not. My suspicions about my father being connected however were validated when the connected guy that wanted to kill me told me he was given a hard no out of respect for my father. We were ordered to work it out like men.

My father "owned" and lived in a three-building rooming house for most of my childhood. Based on our conversations over the years I'm pretty sure that the people visiting from Greece and Italy were there on "business." There were lots of mysterious men, some from other countries and some from the neighborhood: all with dark eyes and dark pasts. Some of them I was allowed to talk to and some I wasn't: Some barely spoke English. Mostly they'd just express warm gestures and niceties as I passed them in the hallway to the shared bathroom.

MAKING MOM-ORIES

Despite her wonderful mother and hard-working father, my mother turned out to be a real piece of work; a troubled woman to say the least. I know it's hard for some moms reading this to hear a son talk this way but as I suggested before, you haven't seen my scars yet. You're certain to be appalled once you have. Confusingly, my alcoholic father was the real nurturer of the pair, while my ACOA mother (adult child of an alcoholic) left some of the deepest wounds.

When I do process the events of the past it seems that my maternal unit was probably responsible for more emotional scarring and damage than the thing that sexually abused me at age 11. At least that POS left the illusion that I was wanted. (Yeah, I know, like I said, I got scars.) I'll tell you a little about mummy dearest now; the abuser in time.

To this day my sister still refers to our maternal unit as E-1; as in Evil One. She truly believes that if you mention her name or reference her directly, that misfortune will befall you in short order. The crazy part is that my sister believes this while not really being much of a religious or spiritual person. (We'll discuss my sister's scars and emotional artistry later too.)

My mother's parents were an interesting pair. My grandfather Joseph Witkowski married my grandmother Victoria Roth after both of their families immigrated to the US through the ports of Baltimore. My grandfather was obviously Polish by name but there was a lot of mixing in northern Europe during that era. The DNA people confirmed that he was German and Polish and she was Russian and Jewish.

The Jewish part was one very dark and well-hidden little family gem that I didn't find out about until after 9-11. You see my wonderful "Busha" (Polish for grandma) was actually born to a Jewish (Ashkenazi) mother in Russia thereby making her Jewish by birth. (As mentioned this little piece of cultural identity was swept under the carpet of time so I grew up "not Jewish.")

As mentioned earlier my grandmother and her mother got very ill during one of Europe's mass die-offs and her Jewish mother passed away. She went to live with her Aunt Aggie and her Jewish-ness was hidden away in shame.

I haphazardly learned of my Jewish heritage when I told my sister I was working for the "Associated Jewish Federation of Baltimore" and she retorted, "Well, you know we're Jewish right?" I believe I said, "Get the fuck out of here!" She confirmed her statement by referencing a complete family genealogy she had done for a school project. (Quaint little conversations like this are how you learn about your true identity and heritage in a dysfunctional family.)

It was a wonderful experience working at the Jewish Federation. I really enjoyed learning about my family history and culture from inside the Jewish community. It brought me closer to one of my favorite people, my dearly departed Busha.

My maternal grandparents got married and raised their three children in an area of Baltimore City known as Canton. Canton is a neighborhood located between Little Italy and Greektown. It was the same neighborhood where nearly every Polish and German immigrant into Baltimore got off the boat from Europe. A port so busy that it often exceeded the immigration numbers coming through Ellis Island during the same period. Like many immigrants to NYC, my family didn't go far from the docks either; their family home was literally within sight of the port of Baltimore where they arrived.

Except during WWII my maternal grandfather worked for the City of Baltimore his entire life. My Busha was a stay-at-home mom except during the war when she helped with the war effort by building planes and taking some side bets. My grandfather fought Hitler in the very same area that he and his family had migrated from. Poetically he was there trying to free my grandmother's people from the death camps.

My mother's paternal grandmother died in 1971; it was the first funeral I ever attended, my first open casket. The church was packed with family that I'd never see again because a large portion of my grandfather's family wasn't thrilled about his choice of a Jewish wife at the time. (Did you notice I called them "his" family?) After they made me kiss the dead stranger I never saw any of them again.

Europe is known for its beautiful women and on the outside my mother was very attractive. She could have truly been a very successful model during the 50s & 60s. In fact, one day when I was around age 15, I found some pictures of Marilyn Monroe in the family picture drawer and asked my sister about them. Her response was, "That's not Marilyn Monroe stupid that's ma." I remember being a little stunned by how pretty she was. Seems she was indeed an aspiring model on par with Monroe, Taylor and Mansfield. Like many women of that era, our mother was all about looking good and being pretty to find her value in society. She openly resented my sister and me for ruining her life. She blamed us for ruining her body and thereby her chances at stardom. (More about E-1 later.)

EMMANUEL S. JOHN

CHAPTER TWO
WANTED DEAD OR ALIVE?

HOMECOMING

Thus we arrive at the point when little baby Emmanuel comes home from the Sinai; Sinai Hospital that is. While babies don't think much you'd think that a baby was expecting to be wanted by its mother; the truth was mine just didn't. What she was bringing home was a baby she wanted aborted; she would later let me know that I was only alive because abortion was illegal. (Wait until you're done reading to decide if it was a good or bad law.)

In every moment of my earliest memories my father wanted me. Like most men my father always wanted a boy to carry on his name. I knew I was much more than that to him because he made it clear every day I was with him that he adored me. While he loved my sister the sad reality was that females just weren't as valued as males were at the time. Perhaps this is even more so among fathers from Mediterranean and Middle-Eastern cultures. It wasn't that they didn't love their little girls, they did; they were just firm believers that males carried on the family lineage. The fact that our last name was actually changed by government immigration officials didn't seem to matter; we all knew our real name.

It wasn't just my mother that didn't want me. My sister actually started plotting my demise from day one. Being a baby I was obviously oblivious to her disdain and resentment towards me for being born but I would know it soon enough. While not cognitively aware I quickly began to feel her apathy towards me via her emotional alienation; something I continue to feel to this day. It was like having a roommate that you never really got to know. The only times I remember her playing with me was when my father and I were playing cars and she was jealous. The sad truth is that our mother didn't have enough love for the daughter she had.

21

By default, being the newborn I would be taking away what little energy and attention she did have to offer.

Not that I needed the verification but just a couple of years ago I saw a social media post my sister made with pictures of the two of us shortly after my birth. In the post, she openly admitted that she wanted me dead from the day I arrived. She confessed that she spent many years trying to figure out how to kill me and make it look like an accident (she obviously had some of our grandfather in her too).

Her social media conversation continued on with several of her friends. It was obvious they were taken aback by her frankness but still not an ounce of reproach on her part. I don't think she meant any malice with the post at the time but what do I know? She was just being the only insensitive sister I'd ever known. Like her mother, she's clueless about the emotional impact she has on others. The truth is I can't recall ever feeling an ounce of empathy from her during our childhood. She always felt like an enemy: Not just brother and sister fighting kind of enemies though, more like the cover your ass and watch your back type. There was never any alliance of any kind in our youth; no friend only foe.

It's now more than 60 years later and her 6-decade-old emotional scars are very present. Her scars are a great example of how emotional wounds sometimes leak out so they can be seen in the light of day. Her limited childhood insight left her thinking I was taking our mother's attention away when in reality she was astutely sensing there wasn't enough to go around.

I mention this social media experience here because I think it's a great example of how we are constantly uncovering scars that we didn't even know we had. My sister continued on in those comments quite emphatic that she never wanted me in the house. It wasn't until around age 20 that I was to see any true compassion from her.

I'm not aware of my sister ever actually trying to kill me but then again she's not big on talking about her failures. I certainly wouldn't put it past her. I think that the only reason that she never tried to kill me (again, at least I don't think she tried) is because she desperately wanted our father's approval as she certainly couldn't get any from E-1. I personally think my father gave her plenty of love and attention; probably more than most men were giving their daughters at the time.

Despite all his love it's important to consider that my sister was emotionally programmed and damaged by E-1's rantings like, "He doesn't care about you, and he doesn't love you." I realize now that by being 4½ years older my sister had to emotionally weather the early years of misery on her own. I'm sure my sister was never really given a fair shot at not resenting and even hating the men in her life. Through her actions, E-1 began teaching her how to monetize men early on. My parents split up when I was 18 months old (my sister 6). I'm sure she heard and comprehended all kinds of hate spewing and disdain about half of her genetic code.

Not surprisingly my sister was always the tough Tomboy type; perhaps trying to be the son our father wanted until I came along. I'm pretty sure she needed that tough exterior to survive our mother. Looking back I don't think I've ever seen her cry.

I believe my sister is still currently a lesbian but she was never big on molds either. I say "I think she's a lesbian" because since the death of her wife Sidney, some of her statements suggest she may be open to relationships with men now. I don't even go down that road with her; people have to find their own way and no one should be labeled straight or otherwise. I do however believe that our mother's apathy and lack of empathy left my sister starving for female support and nurturing.

My sister did work quite hard at trying to have relationships with the other females in our family. I hope the Grace she did find healed at least some of those wounds but it's hard to tell because they're hidden so deep down inside. She's really good at building thick emotional walls.

I personally have no conscious memory of my mother and father in the same house. E-1 always claimed she left him because he was a drunk but finding drunken men continued for most of her life. Her affinity for alcoholics may or may not have been the result of trying to love her own alcoholic father. Regardless, I don't think my father's drinking was the real problem. The real problem was that my father's drinking got in the way of him making big money. You see she only "got with him," because she thought he was going to be the first Frank Sinatra or maybe even the first Jerry Lee Lewis. She was convinced that his fame would bring on her fame as a model; if not she would at least be able to suck up some of the attention and limelight that she yearned for till her death.

While my mother stayed in great shape her modeling career actually did die with my sister's birth. When my parents married my mother came to live on the "other side of the tracks" with our father. I mean that literally and figuratively as we lived on the other side of the tracks where Greektown and Canton are divided by the old train yards to the port. Apparently after a big drunken fight one night my mother called her father (who was no fan of my dark-skinned dad) and they came to fetch us from the hells of Greektown.

I'm not denying that my father was an alcoholic or one of those musician types, he was. Performers and actors were all seen as lowlifes in those days so my grandfather happily came in a borrowed car to retrieve his daughter and her two kids. We never lived together as a family again.

Being only 18 months old I have no conscious memory of these events. We went to live with my grandparents on Stripper Street in Baltimore (at least that's what we all called it). If you think she was mad before we left she was just getting started. Now she was forced to retreat back to the family home she tried to escape by marrying our father in the first place. Back to the same house she was born in within sight of the ports where her "backward" parents arrived.

This home was the place of some of my first real memories. At that time Canton was predominantly the home of Polish and German immigrants. It was a part of Baltimore (between Greektown and Little Italy) where you heard so many different languages on the street that you never knew who was what. It wasn't until my 40s that I found out the actual pronunciation of the street was Streeper Street. The prior name was more fitting than you know. (I'll tell you how my sister and I took on the sex industry later.)

For my sister and me, our lives were a constant fight for both love and resources. My sister and I were never factored into our mother's dreams and goals. Instead, we were always in the way and she never let us forget it. Some of my earliest memories (mom-ories as I call them) were her screaming at the top of her lungs from another room (starting around age 4), "If it wasn't for you god damned kids I'd have a great life." That went on for years until around age 9 when we eventually started reminding her of her role in the baby-making process. One day my sister (14) yelled back "Well then you shouldn't have fucked our father. That's how that shit works lady."

Wait, what's with the shocked face? Where did you think we were going with this, to the Cleaver's house? We had some serious family values alright. Fighting hard is what you have to do to survive emotionally toxic people; you fight or flee and there was no escape at that age. Instead my sister and I lived like tortured prisoners for years; it never let up and she never relented.

I want to make something very clear here. This book is not about attacking my mother from some place of bitter resentment. It wasn't until after I let go of her shortcomings and forgave her for her failures and the neglect, that I was able to see any of this clearly. It took years for those wounds to heal, decades before I could even think about the way things were in any detail. (The truth is it wasn't until I was editing this book that I realized I never even mention the physical abuse we endured as well. Since that is not what this book is about I've omitted it intentionally.)

My mother quickly tired of the poor immigrant neighborhood; it wasn't a good look. She packed up my sister and me in her slick new Chevy II Nova for a move uptown to one of those newfangled apartment complexes with a big pool and a laundry room. It was closer to the nightlife that she wanted and closer to the men of means that she had her gold-digging sights set on. We ended up moving in right next door to her also "recently divorced from a Greek guy" party buddy girlfriend known to us as Ms. Carol. Carol had two sons and a daughter. Her youngest son's father was actually cousins with my uncle on the Greek side so we started referring to each other as cousins. (In case you're not aware "cousins" is a poor people designation used to suggest family-like associations, experiences and shared struggles.)

Shortly after the move to the new modern apartments in Hamilton my sister and I got our first real "momory," perhaps "tramory." We were introduced to "Uncle Jim" with a loud banging on the door in the middle of the night. ("Uncle" was a designation given to a mom's boyfriend in those days; seemingly to forge closeness and acceptance. It does however still seem a little creepy and incestuous; kids calling their mom's boyfriend Uncle, but they were confusing times, especially for us). We hadn't met "Uncle Jim" before the move North because E-1 didn't want her prospects to know she had kids: She was way too embarrassed by her parents to bring them to Canton.

Uncle Jim made one hell of a first impression. I still remember his bloody face he somehow attained while trying to kick in our front door. Supposedly he just found out that E-1 slept with one of his richer friends. (She jokingly told me the background in my late 30's. No mention of the childhood trauma though. No hint of curiosity about what it must have been like for her children to have bloody people kicking in their front door in the middle of the night in a strange neighborhood.) As I listened to her recount the event it became even more clear she had no capacity for empathy; no way to comprehend how her actions affected anyone else. All she could ever express was self-pity and a sense of victimization.

Apparently, the apartment in Hamilton was still too close to the poor people and the white trash in the city (known to her as family) so around 1970 she moved us to a place called Cockeysville, Maryland. It was a much more affluent area or as some might call it, middle class. Despite her attempts to upgrade us, there still seemed to be an obvious status difference between the people that lived in the houses and us broken-home folks that lived in the apartments.

GOD WHO?

The move further uptown made one thing clear to me as a child. Once I saw how other people got to live (that weren't just families on TV) I became convinced that God only really loved and cared about the rich people. Rich kids had food to eat, went to private schools and they all seemed to go to church every Sunday too. I just figured that we didn't go to church because we weren't rich. When I say rich I'm referring to the people that actually got to live in houses with both moms and dads. The really wealthy people even had pools and dogs.

I figured it out. God had just chosen some people to love and the others were left to fend for themselves. That's why some people had nice things and some didn't. The "didn't-s" were forced to fight each other for the leftovers. Fights like who got the first sip off the single shared bottle of soda or the little bit of love and attention that might be offered. As a 7-year-old I figured that since people with two parents got more love they didn't have to hate each other because there was enough of everything to go around. (Pretty sure my negative, jaded and cynical thinking at age 7 is a sign of damage.)

Even as elementary school kids, we all knew who was gonna get a car by age 16 and who wasn't. At age 7 I viewed God as the adult version of Santa; if you were good people you got good things. Divorced people obviously weren't good "God" people. You were either born into the right family or you weren't. If your parents screwed up you paid for their mistakes. It was that, "Sins of the father cast down upon the son" thing.

I remember also thinking that maybe we just moved so much that God couldn't find us. I had already lived in 4 places by the time I was 6. By age 7 I was fully convinced that we weren't ever going to be one of the chosen people no matter how many rich guys our mother made into uncles.

By the time we moved to Cockeysville E-1 had already dumped ole Uncle Jim and found herself with of all people another Greek. His name was, wait for it, Hercules. Yep, you can't write this stuff, but you can recall it as the trauma reactivates. Herk (as we called him) was GREAT!! For those old enough to remember the Hercules cartoons we used to say, "Hey Herk Hey Herk!" The truth was we all knew that Ma had hooked a big fish. Herk was rich. He owned a freight company called Panda Freight with the actual name on the trucks; trucks we would see driving down the highway.

Hercules wasn't just rich; he knew how to win kids over. Every time we saw Herk, both of us got $20 bills. That was a lot of money in 1971 when the minimum wage was about $1.50 an hour. I think he knew we needed it and that she wasn't any good at holding onto it. It's possible the cash-giving was motivated by guilt knowing we were often left alone to fend for ourselves so he could have a date.

We liked Herk because he gave us money but he was also Greek so that helped a lot (because Greeks were cooler than other people). In fact, he was a stereotypical "Greek Boy" (man) that lived with his mother until the day she died. Herk was connected too, but not just to mobsters, it was worse than that, he was connected to lawyers, judges and politicians. If you know any Greek Lawyer/Judge families in Baltimore you know their names. I'll leave them out of this as they were always stand-up people to us. (I will say that watching the Luskin's fireworks from Gus's house with the pool in Towson was full of good memories.)

When it came to "Herk Cash" I have to admit that in hindsight it seems like we were our mother's pimp and he was just paying us to leave the room. I think that by giving us money he felt he could take her away on trips around the world without us hating him. "Here you go kids, $20 each; we'll see you on Sunday." (Honestly, I know this will sound harsh too but I think he overpaid.)

As fate would have it rich boyfriends for Ma ushered in a new era for the John kids. I like to warmly refer to this era as the abandonment era. Not just emotional abandonment, that actually started years earlier, she could do that while she was still in the room. This was real physical and actual abandonment. She would dump us anywhere she could in order to go jet-setting around the world for a week or a month. She would be off on adventures bragging to us via postcards from Spain, Madrid, England, Portugal, Italy, Germany, Greece, Switzerland and even a Safari in Africa. All while we spent a few weeks with strangers we hadn't met until an hour before she left.

From what I can piece together my Busha and Grand Pop stopped watching us in an effort to reduce her gallivanting. It was either that or she was just embarrassed about how little time she spent with her kids. I'm not sure about the guilt though because that requires some level of empathy. Chances are E-1 probably just got passive-aggressive about it, leaving us with complete strangers claiming it was their fault for not helping her. If you haven't noticed yet blaming others when she was faced with harsh realities was her best trick. (It's also criteria for Borderline Personality Disorder.)

Obviously my mother had some serious emotional problems. I am convinced that she was in fact a Borderline Personality Disorder in its purest form but she was also an ACOA. Her bitterness and diminished self-worth (damage) cost everyone around her. It's quite possible her esteem problems began while growing up as the only female and middle child of an alcoholic father; a dynamic that left her desperate for the male approval she never attained.

Aside from his drinking, my grandfather was a very quiet man that seemed comfortable leaving the children's care exclusively up to my grandmother. It seems my mother was taught one very damaging script by her alcoholic father that was still with her at her death. Her script being that "there will never be enough; not enough of you, not enough of them and not enough of what you need to be OK." That was probably her deepest scar and due to her lack of Grace she passed it on to us. Since she wasn't aware of her scars she blamed us for her lack of everything; a sad little reality that fostered self-worth, self-concept and permanent value issues deep within our hearts.

Today I'm a firm believer that children don't even have to actually be important to their parents to prevent this scar; they just have to believe they're valued. When it came to our maternal unit we were never given a chance to believe it. It seemed like she did it on purpose but in reality, she just didn't care enough to notice it. That was the cornerstone of our neglect; she either didn't or couldn't care.

CHAPTER THREE

A WENCH IN THE WORKS

HUNGRY?

Before we moved to Cockeysville MD my mother's best party girlfriend Carol and her kids moved there first. It's possible that Carol's reaching for status created some sort of competition for my mother; that or it was my mother's idea but the Sapp's lease ended sooner. Not sure who followed who but the two of them became inseparable. Being a former model my mother was prettier than Carol who was more of a full-figured woman. (Ma never had a friend that was more attractive than she was.)

Once my sister reached about age 12 our mother decided that it would be OK to take short trips without leaving us anywhere. This meant that we were frequently left home alone without any adult supervision for days at a time (textbook neglect). When Carol and her went on trips together they would tell us kids (5 in total) to help each other out. We were told that if anything bad happened to go to the other family's apartment. (By bad I think they meant if they forgot to pay the utilities or a hurricane came.) The Sapp family's apartment was about 125 yards down the street. Our safe house was the very same apartment where the kids once started a fire when Carol was away: A fire that nearly burned down the entire building.

When Ma would go on her date trips with some dude, she would do us one big favor before she left. She would use some of her boyfriend's money to go grocery shopping. (I'm pretty sure that she kept half of that money for herself.) With a few exceptions we seemed to get the same groceries regardless of what trip she was taking or for how long.

The Sapp kids got a similar package deal too only I remember them getting peanut butter. We would get 4 loaves of box bread (4 for a dollar,) one of those big packages of bologna, some government cheese from our grandparents, 10 Kool-Aid packs, a bag of sugar, hot dogs, eggs, milk, butter and about 4-8 boxes of Mac and Cheese. Sometimes there would be a big piece of ham and a 6 pack of Coke thrown in but that was more of a guilt package for longer trips. I know that when we saw the soda and ham we knew she'd be gone longer.

The above supplies were usually enough food reserves for about a 3-7 day trip for her. When she did get home she would seldom be running out to get more food because she would've spent all her money while away, usually on something fashion related. We did however get shot glasses from the various countries she visited. She wouldn't buy gifts from the actual places she visited; she would instead stop at the airport duty-free shops and pick something up before coming home. (Did you notice that she was giving shot glasses to little children?)

For obvious reasons, my sister and I would learn how to both ration and horde food fairly well. We're both still very good at it thanks to that damage. What I really mean to say is that we both have major food anxieties.

During those same years, I remember her bringing home lots of those tin foil swans from the fancy restaurants she would go to on her dates. My sister and I would go running to the door, not to see her but to see what was in the doggie bags. I know it sounds desperate but they ate good food at really nice places. Sometimes we'd get in actual fights over the food, like two little dogs fighting for the same scrap of meat.

It probably won't surprise you to hear that E-1 always ordered Surf and Turf. Some people understand that reference, for those that don't; it was a "white trash girl" tactic to order the most expensive thing on the menu. Waiters and rich men would giggle together when any "poor girl" ordered it. The girls with class wouldn't order it for just that reason. Many people still refer to the "Surf and Turf" as the "Poor Girl's Special." The smart girls avoided that by choosing the second most expensive thing on the menu but everyone knew that trick too. While Herk always gave us cash he caught on to the doggie bag thing so he started ordering extra food for the table just for us. Like most Greeks, he was a family guy and sharing food is an expression of love in Greek culture.

What I remember most about her trips away was that the food would often run out before she would come home. The Sapp kids had the same problem but the two boys David and George had an innovative solution. They would simply go to the store and steal more food. (Ever seen a little kid walking around a grocery store alone chewing food? We invented that too.)

Before we reached the point of stealing the 5 of us kids would pool our resources and share until all the food was gone from both houses. That's why I remember the Sapp's peanut butter because we always had the leftover bread. When the bread got stale we made peanut butter on toast. In those days the bread and rolls weren't hard to get though. Most of the food store chains at the time would get their bread deliveries at about 4am. They would place them in front of the stores on large rolling racks. Since we were up all night playing we would just walk up and take what we needed.

To this day I can do all kinds of interesting things with bread to fill my stomach. (Lots of "Wish sandwiches.") As a child, I remember comparing it to the bread and water rations prisoners would get in the old movies if they were bad. (Yep, another sad consequence was thinking that because we didn't have food that we must be bad or not deserving. All those feelings are a form of shame but to feel bad because you're hungry leaves major self-concept scars and a huge hole in the soul.)

By the Grace of something the Sapp boys were good at stealing real meat from inside the store; those boys had talent. It started with Steak-umms (for the free bread) but eventually they started stealing real steaks. Obviously, we all knew how to cook already; you had to if you wanted hot food.

After the Sapp boys figured out how to eat in the store they taught us. We'd walk around eat this, eat that, grab some grapes, make a sandwich, have a pickle or even a few cookies. (If you've ever seen open food in the store that's from hungry people; we didn't invent that.)

Honestly, when I look back the stores had to have known what we were doing. I think they just felt so sorry for us that they let us do it. (I didn't think I was stealing because I wasn't taking anything outside of the store.)

It was during those years that we also learned how to hustle groceries. That's when you go to the supermarket and ask the women leaving; "Do you need help with your bags Mam?" We made some good tip money back then because the carts were always fenced in and you had to leave your cart at the store to go get your car. If we helped them they didn't have to get out of the car again. We learned which expensive cars to watch for and we'd wait for those people to come out. After a while, we even developed repeat customers. (Sadly the Sapp boys didn't live long, David died in a DWI accident at 19 and George was gone by 25; his body was found in the woods years after he went missing. It was either suicide or murder. They were some of the statistics that Grace spared me from.)

It was around this time that my father got me my first shoeshine kit. I would hang out at the stores and shine men's shoes for money. It was my first real business. For some reason, none of the white kids thought this was a cool thing to do but they did like the idea of the money. I learned how to sell, hustle and manage inventory. (Thankfully the perverts weren't too brazen at the shopping center.)

I realized later in life that I had become a food hoarder when I was a kid. I still have food anxieties to this day. I can have a thousand dollars in my wallet and still worry about not having enough of something. I also learned to hide and stash food during this time. My sister and I would separate the food we did get into halves to make sure we both got our fair share. It wasn't until around age 40 that I realized I had these food issues among all the other anxieties. It wasn't until I was writing this book that I realized that our mother almost never ate the food in the house. It was probably not good enough for her; she knew she was going out to eat.

Since food is a basic survival need the food scar has been a really hard wound to heal. I believe that the preoccupation with food scar will be with me until my death. On the upside, I know a lot about food and nutrition.

CLASS ON THE INSIDE

The emotional pain became physical when I was in the 3rd grade. I began having serious stomach aches and diarrhea while in school. I know now that it was a mixture of the lack of healthy food, our self-centered mother, Ms. Tate my mean third-grade teacher and wondering if E-1 might decide to not come home from one of her trips.

My teacher Ms. Tate HATED ME; she was brutal. She looked like the old stereotypical spinster schoolmarm. I know she met with my mother once and I don't think it went well because shortly after that Ms. Tate began to rage on me far and above any other kid in the class. It seems they both had a thing for Mr. Richard the school social worker. Of course Ma ended up dating him for a bit so she won and I lost.

My sister has fond memories of Mr. Richard being nice to us. I remember his face but that's all, I think we played catch once. Despite his role, Mr. Richard didn't help me with Ms. Tate. In fact, he seemed to stay clear. Ms. Tate certainly crossed the line with me; some of her actions would be considered physical assault by today's standards.

Picture a bitter dark haired woman with a sour-looking puss and an outdated Bee-Hive hairdo, black plastic frame glasses and her lips so tightly pursed together it would make her face wrinkle despite her only being around 35 (think Earnestine from Laugh-In but meaner). She always reminded me of the mean old stepmother from the fairy-tales. Now take a second and try to imagine her quickly walking between the rows of desks toward you in her cheap black low-rise pumps, taking short quick steps because her skirt was too tight around her knees. She then grabs you by the skin on your neck between her thumb and forefinger, twisting it and using it to lift you up out of your chair (at age 8-9). Imagine her then dragging you down the aisle in front of everybody (still twisting your neck skin) and then out the classroom door to make you sit on the floor in the hallway for hours at a time. (Her skin grabs repeatedly left big red welts on my neck.)

That memory is so vivid I can actually see the classroom, the color of the chalkboard, and the side panels decorated in yellow and green. (I think they call that PTSD now, not sure if it qualifies for Big T trauma but it was certainly damage.) It happened at least once a week for most of that school year (no wonder I hated school).

During that same year I was admitted to GBMC Hospital where I stayed for 10 days. They ran test after test but they couldn't find anything physically wrong with me. No one ever guessed that it could be emotional; that I was a third grader with an anxiety disorder. (FYI, my mother still went out to the clubs while I was hospitalized; another free sitter for her.)

Essentially, I was a child without a parent to confide in about the physical and emotional abuse I was experiencing in school almost daily. We didn't change classes in those days so I was captive in there with her all day. It was like being taken hostage at school. My stomach would get upset and it would give me diarrhea. I would be forced to hold it until the bathroom break we took as a class because she wouldn't let me go to the restroom. I remember the feeling of turning pail and feeling like I was going to pass out.

Now imagine that third grader also being left at home with a 13-year-old that hated him his entire life. A third grader without enough food to eat, lacking emotional support and still being expected to do everything he was supposed to do just like all the other little kids. All the while fearing total permanent abandonment be it from the death of his mother in a foreign country or her just deciding to never come home because she hated her kids. (It actually still unsettles me to write about those days.)

Today I know these emotional circumstances affect a child's sense of well-being and security. It can make that child grow into an adult that is either overly eager to please others in order to be valued, wanted and cared about or one that decides to make other people suffer too. Children who experience these struggles will one day come to a crossroads. Either people's feelings will really matter or their feelings will become irrelevant. "If no one cares about me and my feelings why should I care about theirs?" A script that says; "That's how life works; feelings are irrelevant." This type of damage and the accompanying emotional scripts are key ingredients in the formation of a sociopath. Children that learn feelings don't matter stop trying to read them in others; they stop developing their empathy.

When you're not taught that feelings do matter and when no one acknowledges them you learn to shut them off all together. Simple logic would then suggest to the developing brain that hurting people is in fact a part of life because that is what has happened to them. It leaves that child with a choice; try real hard to be liked or get angry, give up on being liked and give them a real reason to not like you or even fear you. (Sound familiar in today's social landscape?)

Looking back on my experience I would feel very sad for that child today. The stain is so deep that knowing about the dysfunction does nothing to help heal it. Seeing the scar only sets the stage for healing. Most people are afraid to dig into them; afraid of allowing these scars to surface. When scarred people witness what they went through in another it triggers their damage. They have an emotional response to it. If they witness these types of abuse it can potentially trigger them to hurt the offender/s in order to save the child: a way of saving themselves by proxy. If the school hurt them they could rationalize that by attacking the "school" they could actually be saving children in the future.

While these scars can be hard for me to see these scars are certainly not hard for me to feel. Who could imagine that 10 years later that diminished sense of self-worth would present to others as ego, arrogance, cockiness and narcissism; just like it does for so many scarred people. These forms of abuse and neglect occur daily yet still we wonder why we see so many kids having behavior and attention problems.

Looking back over those years it's hard for me to see any Grace but perhaps some did occur. Someone at the school figured out we weren't eating right at home. That led to the John and Sapp kids being the impetus for the school's first free lunch program. Maybe it was Mr. Richards doing or maybe it was just the Grace of the lunch ladies who had been buying our lunches for us when all we could afford was a 3¢ milk. The other kids tried to bully us about it but we just did what all poor kids do when they realize they have less than others. They spin it to make it look like they have an advantage others don't. We just boasted that we didn't have to bring our lunch or pay for it; that their parents were buying us lunch with their taxes. HAHA!! (It worked great but it buried those "lack of privilege" scars so deep down that they became nearly invisible. Not feeling them means not healing them.)

THE GOOD COP

Growing up we were known by the school system as "walkers" because we didn't ride the bus. In those days elementary school kids could walk up to 1½ miles, the Junior High and High School kids, up to 2 miles. On my walk home from school, there was a nice couple in their 30s that lived in one of the ground-floor apartments. When I was in the second grade I would stop by to pet their Beagle dog "Barney" almost every day. Eventually, the wife started asking me questions about my family life (pretty sure they noticed something lacking in me).

Over time they started emotionally mentoring me as I ate the awesome pop sickles they'd offer while petting Barney. As time passed my sister and I began to hang out in their apartment with them. It was no shock that E-1 said it was OK after they called to ask permission. To her they were just another free sitter. (Perhaps nature does abhor a vacuum?)

Over the next year, the husband John (a police officer) started teaching me to play chess. We would play while his wife watched on. I took to it very naturally; so much so that several years later I tied the Harford County chess champion 15 draws in a row without knowing who

I was playing. (The encounter was a setup by my father after I continued to beat him. He thought he would teach me a lesson in humility.)

I remember fantasizing that the lady (Sandra) could be my mother if anything did happen to E-1. I now believe it was the attention, charity and Grace of people like John and Sandra that kept me from falling apart at the time. Their small loving acts added that little spark of light necessary to keep the dreams and hopes of a young child alive. They mattered.

I'm also convinced now that if you can get enough of these little sparks of Grace you can endure almost anything. That is what we all have to offer one another. I believe that's how Grace works: just a few little sparks here and there, when absolutely necessary, to keep the flame of hope alive in us. When I refer to our need to "Perpetuate Grace" I'm talking about committing these seemingly very small random acts of love and kindness when it's not our responsibility. These acts can make all the difference in someone's life, especially a child's. I'm certain they made all the difference in mine.

OUR FATHER WHO...

Not sure how it got started but my sister and I often referred to our father as OUR FATHER. For some strange reason, it always sounded like OUR FATHER WHO ART IN HEAVEN; at least it did to E-1. At the same time, we started saying "your mother" when talking to each other about ma. Our father was an alcoholic, no doubt about it, but as mentioned earlier he was also one of the most nurturing people that I've ever known. Compared to E-1 he even seemed a little divine. Except for some visitation, custody and support issues you never doubted that you were the most important thing in the world to him. Even when he was drunk and even if his actions didn't always match up, you still believed it, inherently.

This is what I spoke about previously when I suggested that "I've come to believe that all that matters to a child is they believe they are wanted." Children's minds are about perception, not intellectualization.

What really makes one a good parent emotionally is the ability to make a child feel wanted, important, valued and relevant. Kids aren't "judge-y," they don't need proof. Belief works for them even if your actions don't support it. This phenomenon is why children still love their dysfunctional adults; because they believe they're of value to them (facts are irrelevant). This same mechanism also allows children to believe in the Tooth Fairy, Santa and the Easter Bunny.

The truth is that Our Father was often even more loving when he was drunk. When he was drunk he would tell us that we were the most important kids in the entire world: We were hugged so tight it was almost suffocating. You know how when someone is really drunk and they keep hugging on you, almost to that awkward moment? Yeah well, kids don't know it's the booze; it's just dad hugging you. It was great, especially in contrast to E-1. I still like the smell of Old Grand Dad bourbon because of it. Why wouldn't I love it; it always made him seem even more sincere.

Did "Our Father" ever come up short? Yep! Like many kids from poor divorced families of the day, we often heard that our father was going to jail and that he didn't care about us because he never sent money. At the time it seemed like a big deal because we were hungry but looking back I think he knew she was overly invested in that money and that she would've spent it on herself.

We all knew that her having money didn't mean that we'd have food. Our father knew about her disappearing trips because he was another sitter for her. She would actually drive us all the way to Greektown so she could have her weekend gallivanting with the support and gas money he did give her. I'm certain she never drove us down there so that we could see him. I would repeatedly hear her on the phone telling Carol that she was going to "dump the kids off at Ray's house" and then meet her out somewhere. (FYI, your children hear everything you say.) Sometimes she'd actually lie to us and say he was in jail as an excuse to not have to drive us to Greektown. She'd just leave us home alone instead. (Imagine the anxiety created in a child that falsely believes their father, the only one that expressed love, was in jail.) Sometimes E-1 withheld us from him just out of spite.

Sure, he could've had a car but drunks with cars are never a good idea. That was actually his reason for not having one. When she was in one of her moods she'd say, "He doesn't love you, if he did he would help us." When he did give her money she would just show up the next time in new clothes. Beauty parlors and department stores are where most of the household money went. She was convinced and she convinced us, that her looking good would pay off for all of us one day.

He should have paid the support anyway but I don't think it would have changed anything in the food department. Truth is I don't know if I even believe her claims against him not paying. He always had lots of cash and he never actually went to jail. In fact, he would often give us food to bring home. He was a great cook and she never had a problem eating what he made for us. I promise you that he's not being let off the hook for his failures.

During my early childhood, our father worked as a Merchant Marine so there were always long periods of him making money but that meant that he'd be gone for long periods of time. Not making money meant he was home and we liked him being home better. We were children and we didn't care about economics, we just wanted to see our father; the one with the great hugs. (While in the Merchant Marines, he imported a lot of drugs from Asia; often duffle bags full as he bypassed customs.)

Our father didn't hide or deny his problem with booze. I remember him telling me that he didn't want a car because he was afraid that he would drive it after he started drinking, maybe hurt us or someone else. He drank a lot! On average about a fifth of Old Granddad a day or more. He was 5'9" and 165 pounds on a fat day.

There is no doubt that his drinking did separate him from his children and his children from their otherwise loving father. I never saw him struggle to pay his bills though and he always had a roll in his pocket. All his other bills got paid but if he withheld money from her that's on him.

Everyone knew Ma was money hungry, no doubt about it. I'm pretty sure she took cash from her dates' wallets because that's just who she was. If she thought you owed her something (even if you didn't) there were no limits to what she'd do. She dated greedy people and criminal elements so in her eyes no one was really a victim in their exchanges. Years later I would come to grips with the fact that my mother was one of those "chicks at the club" that did things with men in their cars.

Trust me; I hid that awareness scar really deep for a very long time. Not surprisingly those girls were always intriguing to me as a young man out for an evening. I spent many decades trying to prove my worth to my mother by proxy. What's shocking is how those scars resulted in me ending up with girls in a car at a club. You'd think I'd hate them but instead emotional scars get spooky like that. I'm pretty sure it's because I learned how to bond to that personality type from birth. My programming suggested the important men were in those cars at the club. My quest for relevancy was me trying to be one of those people that Ma found more important than us. I can promise you one thing. I never let those girls put me before their children. I even sent a few packing when they tried.

Once again OUR FATHER was no saint, he always had women around and he was usually the center of attention. He was one of those guys that had so much personality that it actually masked the reality of his shortcomings, especially with his children. In full disclosure when I would stay with him we would always go to the local bars and usually sit there until closing. I loved how when we would walk down the street people would often see him and think he was Johnny Cash; even more so when sitting on a bar stool. Eventually, he just started signing the autographs saying the people felt better thinking they met him. He would even give them the old train whistle woo-a-woo to send them on their way after they bought him a drink. While we all thought Greektown was the center of the Universe I still don't understand why those people thought Johnny Cash would be in a dive bar in Baltimore.

GRACED

While at the local bars, I would get nickels, dimes and quarters from the people (mostly men) to play songs on the jukebox. Like many children I would start dancing around and singing songs; songs like Knock Three Times and Cupid, acting them out as I went along. There weren't any TV's in the bars back then so I was often the only entertainment. For a kid with abandonment issues that craved attention, it was really cool. I also got that much-needed reinforcement my mother always cherished called cash. That's right I was dancing in bars for cash, with a Cash look-a-like, as early as age 4 or 5.

In hindsight, it seems that some of those men gave me money to get in good favor with my father. Eventually, I started getting so much money that I would come home from the bar with pockets full of change. (Not once did he ever ask for any of it.) I always left his house with lots of money; four to five dollars in the time of 2 cent Good Humor ice creams, was a lot of money.

I remember our walks home from the bars very fondly. He would always bring home a new piece of glassware. He would jokingly accuse me of staggering and making him stagger as we walked home with our arms around one another stepping over the cracks not to break my mother's back. Pretty sure I passive-aggressively hit the cracks sometimes thinking that we would get a call saying she was injured.

I recall the sidewalk lines and trying to keep us both in the squares and along the straight lines. The sidewalks were about 3 squares wide. I would try to keep us in the middle square, away from the marble steps on the right and the cars on the left. Sometimes we hit the cars on his side but we never hit the steps on mine. He taught me that a gentleman always walked on the street side when with a lady, to protect her. While he didn't say it I think he was doing that for me. It meant something then. Fortunately, we only had to walk a couple of blocks.

I now know that the emotional dichotomy that was our father and mother was very abnormal. On one side was our mother that went to work every day and provided a roof over our heads but who was a very hurtful and bitter person. On the other side OUR FATHER, a gangster

43

alcoholic that was an amazing nurturer but couldn't pay his child support on time. He was a warm, kind and loving man despite his condition; a man who never once raged at us or raised his hand to me.

I'm convinced that more emotional scars were created by my ACOA mother than by my alcoholic father and grandfather combined. It's no wonder I drank heavily as a teen. I mean, who do you want to be like the drunk or the mean lady? Both my parents were in the bars a lot. Scar wise I think Ma was actually looking for that connection she never had as the middle child to her own alcoholic father. Her emotional scars left her and her alcoholic partners emotionally unavailable to one another. (Most people in modern society recognize the scar where the daughter of an alcoholic finds herself an alcoholic to bond with.)

Up till her death, I don't think she'd ever been diagnosable as a substance dependent or alcoholic. The closest she ever came was probably the time her date came to our house late at night and told us that she was in the hospital. He said she hit a fire hydrant while following him to his house from the bar. The accident was literally 100 yards from her favorite bar in Towson called Velleggia's.

I clearly remember where it happened because years later I would skateboard past that hydrant. I would recall seeing her car smashed into it as we passed it on our way to the hospital. (Trauma, damage or scar?)

I remember going behind the curtain in the ER, seeing her drunk face and the bloodied bandage around her head like you would see in an old war movie. She expressed no concern for the experience of her children at that moment. I remember her drunk face seeking sympathy instead of providing reassurance. She did get a DWI and they were quite hard to get in the early 70s. By the Grace of God she didn't hurt anyone else. Other than that she never showed any real signs of addiction. I think we would've welcomed the excuse.

PACK YOUR SHIT

It should be obvious by now that there was very little stability or predictability in our lives. Stability and predictability are necessities for

44

healthy childhood development; without a sense of certainty, children turn into adults with a predisposition to anxiety and depressive disorders. That is of course after they spend their childhood being children with anxiety and behavioral disorders. (If you notice behavioral problems in your child please seek help for your entire family.)

Friday would often be the day that we would hear from our mother about where we were going to be sleeping that weekend. "I can't deal with you kids; pack your shit you're going to your father's." Other variations included; "Pack your shit you're going to Busha and Grand pop's house" or perhaps even "Pack your shit you're staying with a friend of mine." When we were taken to the house of people we had never met before she'd say, "You'll like her/them." (I remember once thinking as a child, Yeah because I hate you, anything would be better.)

One thing's for certain when we went somewhere else the people always had food and they were usually better caregivers. The fear of what could happen to her on one of these trips and her verbal disdain for us always left me in fear of total permanent abandonment. I would wonder if this was the place I'd be living forever or if they would send me to an orphanage when they got tired of me too. We were forced to face this instability and uncertainty for one reason and one reason only; so that she could party, bar hop and pursue rich men.

As mentioned above the sad truth is that these strangers often took better care of us than she did. I remember Ms. Lil's mother the most. She had a cool tree for me to climb in her front yard and she always made good old fashion food, not food from a box or bag. The house was a little freaky though. She was a doll maker and collector, so the house was full of baby dolls with scary eyes; thousands of scary eyes. She had those new dolls whose eyes opened and closed when they lay down and some had the eyes that followed you around the room. So what! The food was good and I had dealt with scary eyes most of my life.

When my "mother" announced that she was taking me to one of these strange places I would usually ask in my 7-9 year-old voice, "HOW LONG AM I GOING TO BE THERE." I usually asked this well

45

before I was even told where I was going. You had to ask because you never knew; it could be a night, a weekend or a month. She'd say pack for 2 days, 3 days and sometimes a week or two. That was life with Ma. Things could change at any minute without any notice. You could be having fun playing on the rug with your cars and then the rug would be pulled out from under you by a scream from the other room. "Pack a bag!!! I'm goin' away!!!"

I have to say that beyond the invisible emotional scars of abandonment, nothing bad ever happened when we went somewhere else. Since my sister was 4 ½ years older we didn't always go to the same place. It became obvious later in life that our father would have taken us every time (except when out to sea). Selfishly her resentment and spite towards him would limit that option. Sometimes it just wasn't his weekend but I believe she was purposefully trying to penalize us all; like she didn't want anyone to have a bond that she couldn't. (According to her own father she was always a very spiteful, bitter and resentful child; a condition she obviously never grew out of.)

THE SHORE SEEMED NORMAL

I started to spend a lot more time with my grandparents: I loved it there. They lived across the street from the bay and across a bay tributary from Martin Airport (now Lockheed Martin). This was the Vietnam era. While I didn't understand all the dynamics at play I was a little boy and what little boy doesn't like being 500 yards from the end of a runway watching big army planes take off and land all day.

Before my grandparents purchased that house they bought a little sliver of land on the water we called "The Shore." It was a waterfront property 35 feet wide and 300 feet long. We used it for Sunday get-togethers but mostly so my grandfather could do a little farming, boating, crabbing, fishing, and clamming. It was his dream to have a place for the family to get together and play in the water. It was also the place where I learned how to do all of the above. It was a great place to be a little boy. When I stayed with them we went there almost every day.

While every little boy wants to be like his dad it turns out that I'm a lot like my grandfather too. The older I get the more true this seems. He lived into his late 90 so that's good if you want to live a long time. Despite all the craziness in our lives, we did have some good old fashion family-type interactions at the shore; very wholesome experiences. If it wasn't for Grace periods like those I don't think I'd be who I am today.

Looking back I can still remember hearing my Busha yell; "Grand-pops home get his slippers." That meant he just pulled into the driveway from work. As I got his slippers I would think to myself, this must be what it's like for kids with two parents. "Here Mann, give Grandpop his beer" (my first bartending gig).

Those were the good times at my grandparents but there was one occasion in particular that wasn't so pleasant. While there wasn't any physical violence there (he never struck her) my grandfather would become very loud and mean to my grandmother when really drunk. He was a "heavy-drinker" then; what people often refer to now as a functional alcoholic. Back in those days if you paid your bills, kept your job, didn't get arrested or fool around on your spouse you weren't an alcoholic.

My grandmother was one of the warmest, nicest people to ever walk the Earth and everyone knew it. One night when I was there my grandfather yelled at her so harshly it made her cry. It was confusing because I had never seen them act like that before. I really had no idea they ever argued. That night she hid in her room leaving me outside it with him. I wasn't fearful as he never hit me or talked mean to me but I never saw her separate herself from company before, let alone a grandchild. When he passed out in his chair from all the beer I quietly called my mother. She asked to speak to my Busha but I told her she'd locked herself in the bedroom. Hearing this was so strange for my mother that she immediately drove down with my sister. She threatened to take my grandmother back to our apartment. I have to admit that I wasn't really sure if I was going with them or not; it seemed like it was going to be a girl thing. I actually remember thinking she was going to leave me there with him and that she would give Busha my bed.

Long story short: My grandfather quit drinking the next day. He never took another drink for the rest of his life; even after she passed. While he obviously had a lot of willpower I think that he knew he was facing the loss of the best woman on the planet so he quit. His strong faith aided him in his effort. By the time he died, he had around 30 years sober. He never went to AA or treatment or anything; he just quit. (I jokingly say he was the first drunk I ever sobered up. I was a budding social worker interventionist and didn't know it.)

THE INSTALLATION OF FEAR

"Pack you're shit you're going to an Orphanage, I've had it with you." This was a new twist on her old command, perhaps with an even more sinister spin. Nothing terrifies a child more than hearing that your supposed mother wants to throw you away.

Was I a bad child? No. Was I a little willful as a child when this was happening? Probably yes, perhaps like a lot of other little boys that had crazy mothers. Perhaps the real problem was that I was just a little too rational for her. Not smart-ass smart, just too rational; I used my brain because trying to live on emotions at our house would be an emotional death sentence.

By this time I knew how to "pack my shit" but now my mother was dating a Cop and I guess she figured that she could use his position to intimidate or manipulate me even more. She convinced me she could just get rid of me if she wanted to. "I can't take you anymore, I've had enough" she'd say. The threat was used more days than I can remember. It went on for years, by age 8 I'd learned how to walk on eggshells. I was so afraid of being sent off that I stopped asking for anything, even food less I become too much of a bother. I was even afraid to be sick less I be thought too much of a burden.

The "afraid to be sick" damage has left a long-lasting scar and has caused major health anxieties. I'm still afraid to be sick. It translates to me being a bit of a hypochondriac now; certainly a person with a health-based anxiety disorder. I feared that getting some type of illness could alter my life because I would be too much trouble to take care of. Since I was already aware that I wasn't worth having I learned how to turn off my feelings and my needs in order to avoid abandonment.

I know that some people reading this are just like me in that we all grew up in a generation with stories like Oliver Twist and post-depression era homelessness. When we were kids we all had a construct of what an orphanage was. I'm pretty sure most of us even thought that the kids in the orphanages all had English accents.

So when my mother got annoyed because her life was more complicated than she thought it should be she'd use this threat against me. Sometimes my sister would even play into her manipulation by telling me horror stories about kids in orphanages that had no food and had to beg on the street for whatever they could get; just like the movie.

E-1's threat usually started with the "I've had it with you, pack your shit you're going to....." When her options ran out as to where she could send me it became "You know what, forget this, when Officer Ron gets here I'm just going to have him take you to an orphanage to live." I would go hide in my room under the bed or in the closet for a while and sometimes the threats would stop. Other times she would come in the room and literally make me pack while I was crying. "Say goodbye to your sister, you won't be seeing her anymore." "VICKIE!!! Come here and say goodbye to your brother, get his toothbrush." I would start crying, please please please I don't want to go, I'll be good, let me stay. "TOO LATE!!! I warned you before." (The installation of shame.)

Sometimes I would cry for hours. She would then come into the room a few hours later with some excuse that she would give me one more chance. I got better at walking on eggshells being worried about every possible wrong move. (This kind of emotional abuse can push some kids to perfectionism and others to murder.)

Most anxiety disorders are the result of inside scars; I know mine are. Think about it. Where does a child go for emotional support when his own family members are outwardly plotting to get rid of him? If you ever want your child to lack trust in any of their lifetime of relationships just use the above examples.

I really hope you get my point here. The sickest part of these behaviors is that my own mother used my desire and thirst for a real mother as ammunition against me. A thirst for approval and value met with disapproval and disregard. (Is it damage? More than that, it's how you create a monster.)

While I felt it almost every minute of my childhood it took me half my life to realize that my mother was not emotionally available to me or anyone else for that matter. What this did was create a pattern of trying to love people that weren't emotionally available either. If they were truly available for me I probably wasn't interested or at least not for long. Real, unconditional love from a woman didn't fit my programming.

I believe trying to love someone that is emotionally unavailable is one of the most torturous of human emotional experiences, yet millions of us still try it every day. It leaves the bearer of the scar trying to bond with someone that is actually impossible to bond with. They're actually attracted to people that are almost impossible to truly connect with. A perverse reality is that even when you figure this out, you keep trying, hoping it will work. It's futile because you can't actually have what isn't available. It leaves a person seeking out people with the same type of damage then connecting to them in what is perceived of as a love bond. In reality, it's just a shared damage and sorrow bond. It results in couples where neither person can operate any differently than how they have. Despite being in a couple it manifests a form of loneliness created by emotional walls: The same loneliness that can be experienced in a stadium full of people. Perhaps the saddest outcome of all is that it sentences a person to a lifetime of failed relationships; believing no one is good enough, because you weren't.

CHAPTER FOUR

FAMILY VALUES

"MAKE ME A DRINK MANN"

The nickname "Mann" (sounds like "mann-er.") is how my family shortened my name. It was a shorter version of Manuel (Emmanuel). When it was used it was almost always spoken with a kind tone; even by my sister (in later adulthood).

As I referenced earlier my father was an alcoholic. He drank Old Grand Dad my entire life. He drank so much that I used to think it had his name on the bottle, at least the Dad part. As soon as he trusted me enough to hold the bottle without dropping it he taught me how to make him drinks and I loved doing it. I loved the power it gave me; the importance to him and even some status to others in the room. Everybody waited on their drinks and the party couldn't start without them; it couldn't start without me. There was even a milk crate for me to stand on behind the bar to make me feel more equal.

In hindsight, my early bartending years were a very stark way for me to literally see the progression of the disease of alcoholism firsthand. To make my father's drinks I was directed to take a small Highball glass and put two fingers up behind it while I poured the Old Grand Dad to the top of my fingers. I would then add ice and top it with water.

My reference to seeing the progression was not about how many drinks, they were constant. The progression came as my fingers grew so did the number of fingers used to make his drinks. By age 10 it was 3 fingers and by age 12 it was 4 fingers, then just metal tray ice cubes and no water. While be it dysfunctional, making these drinks for him felt exactly like getting my grandfather slippers after a day of hard work.

My bartending skills were held in high regard. It became a source of entertainment for the adults to watch how well the little kid was making drinks. As you can imagine the kid starving for attention and value always sucked in the accolades and validation. It made alcohol very important to me.

I didn't really like the taste of liquor but I was always allowed to sample it. I would stir it with my fingers and then lick them clean. (I can smell it and almost taste it right now as I write this.) As his disease progressed and as I aged into my early teens my father could drink as much as two $1/5^{ths}$ a day and most people wouldn't have a clue he was even drunk. I still like the smell of Old Grand Dad; it still reminds me of him.

WHERE'S THE ACTION AT?

It was the early 70s and my very popular father had lots of female friends. They only seemed to come over when my sister didn't, but her being there wouldn't stop them. I think it was odd for him because the girls weren't much older than she was.

When the girls did come over the parties were much better and my bartending skills were in even higher demand. When my father was around 48, he was seeing a very young girl named Pat (19). I only saw her two or three times over a 6 month period but I remember her name and a lot more.

My father had three row houses in Baltimore City combined into the previously mentioned rooming house. The backyards were all connected into one big oasis in the concrete jungle of East Baltimore. It literally looked like an oasis. There was a huge section of grass, trees and bamboo along the entire fence line, a pear tree, a pergola, a hammock, a round concrete table and chairs; even a handmade waterfall and a 15-foot stone fish pond with rocks we personally retrieved from a local reservoir. There were different color flood lights that adorned the entire pond and backyard. There was an outdoor sound system and a hard-lined gas grill: All very rare in the 70s. It was a very popular place to party. All the drunks, potheads and family members loved it but it was very exclusive and by his invite only.

Back to Pat! I remember Pat mostly because she came over one night when we were camping out in sleeping bags on the grass, under the pear tree, next to the bamboo. Pat came over after the bars closed and she was standing above us talking. My father said, "Mann, sit up I want you to see something. I want you to see what real legs look like, so you'll know."

He said, "Pat is a Grecian model, you know, for the statues." "Pat, pull down your pants" he requested. She blushed and he said it again. With an, "It's OK, your legs need to be seen," reassurance this time. Sitting on the grass my head came up to about her thighs. He pulled down her pants and seriously, at that age, all I saw were her white panties in my face. I remember Pat well and in case you are wondering yes, I remember her legs too; they were amazing, unusually muscular for the time. She looked just like he said, like one of those statues with no head, because honestly, I don't remember seeing her face just then.

I'm not sure if this would be classified as a scar or not but it was most certainly etched into my psyche. Not sure of what the opposite of a scar even is, bliss maybe, a formative moment? Regardless it was etched. If I'm being honest I'm not sure it didn't scar me because I never saw another set of legs like that with that the exception of a beautiful ballet dancer named Sharon whom I dated decades later. What I am sure of is that my father certainly imposed some unusually high standards on my choices for women's beauty. He was either trying to spare me his past mistakes or dooming me to a similar fate.

THE PIGPEN

The Pigpen was a place but it wasn't on a farm, not even close. The truth is it was a reference my father used for a local bar that we rarely went to together; at least not until I was around age 8 or 9. It was on Oldham Street between Fleet and Conklin. Its real name was the Play Pen. It wasn't really a strip club as we know them today, more of just a seedy bar that had 60s go-go dancers that probably turned tricks on the side. At the time Go-Go bars and Go-Go dancers were a part of the

American urban landscape. What I remember most about the place is that we were treated really well, almost like royalty. It was a far cry from being treated like paupers in a very white Cockeysville.

It's important to state that I wasn't really sure what my mother did in the bars because she never took me. She would never want people to know she had kids because most men would run in the other direction. I know she wasn't a dancer; because dancing was never her thing. Her modeling and good looks left her as more of a poser and trophy type. Regardless, bars were obviously a family stable. My father had a huge bar and party room in his basement too; a place that he and his band had actually played 20+ years earlier when it was a private club. It still had all the brass poles left over from its nightclub/speakeasy days. The stage was gone but for him, the memories remained of his glory days. But I digress.

The Pig Pen was the site of one of my most vivid "positive" rites of passage memories. At least it was a positive memory that most young boys would never forget. In reality, the Pig Pen could have been the birthplace of my own sexual evolution but nothing too untoward ever happened while I was there. What did happen however was etched into my brain. We had been there before and I always sat in the same place, with my back to the stage against a support column where I could only see one of the dancing girls on a stage in the corner. I always thought the girls kept their bikinis on when I wasn't looking but one day I turned around while my father was talking to a girl and holy crap Batman! There they were, right in the open, each rotating in a different direction. I turned back around real fast so as to not let anyone know I had looked. My father noticed what I had seen. He smiled and continued on in his conversation with one of the girls. Later my father seemed to make a point of introducing me to the one I saw naked. I won't tell you her name was Grace because you wouldn't believe me. I was pretty sure that I was required to have a crush on her for years after what I was allowed to see.

That night they put "Play" back in the "Pig Pen" for me. To be honest, I figured out later that my father called it the Pig Pen because he thought the girls there were what people now refer to as skanky or trashy, some were even opium addicted and he didn't approve. Personally, looking back, I thought that Go-Go bars were where all males saw their first naked girls. All I cared about was that I would have one hell of a story to tell back in Cockeysville. I was always looking for experiences to brag about as there were few things I got to do before the rich kids.

LEFT WITHOUT SUPERVISION

This may seem obvious but if a child is to truly feel valued and loved it's important that its parents are occasionally in the same room. Sadly for my sister and me, our mother's being there was of little consequence; the reality is her presence seemed to have the opposite effect. Supervision is important but parenting is vital to give meaning to experiences. As children, our behavior was only attended to or modified when it was an inconvenience to her. Most times we'd just be doing whatever we'd be doing whether she was there or not. Pretty sure we were the first real "free-range kids."

Some people reading this may be old enough to remember the days when a parent could tell their children to go outside and play. There were usually boundaries that changed and expanded with age but the limits had little to do with possible harm. Many were dictated by the parents' comfort level. More often than not our boundaries were usually set by our friend's limitations. Most of our playmates were limited by the sound of their parent's voices yelling for them to come in.

Not surprisingly, I didn't have anyone to teach me how to ride a bike. So my friend Eddy put me on a hill and pushed me; it worked. He would let me ride his old bike whenever I went over to his house. I can't remember who but one of my mother's various boyfriends just bought me a bike out of nowhere. I think he saw me running with a few kids on their bikes and felt sad for me.

I remember how all the other kids would have to go in when it got dark or when the building lights and street lights came on. Almost every night between the 3rd and 5th grade ended with us riding our bikes back to a friend's house and me watching them put their bikes away. My friend Sean always looked so envious that I got to stay out later; I'm pretty sure I gloated about it. I'd end up being that kid outside playing by himself after dark. I thought I was lucky that I didn't have to go in. I'd even laugh at my friends in their PJs staring out the sliding glass doors of their apartments. As fate would have it you get bored when all your friends have to go in. You get bored when there is no one left to play with or even kidnap you. After a few weeks, you get so bored that you just go in too. That is unless there was a Sapp kid available, that's when the real trouble started.

I may have felt lonely sometimes but you never let your friends know that or that you got bored without them. I would tell them I was out riding till 9 or 10 o'clock. I didn't want them to believe that having responsible parents was a better thing than staying out as late as you wanted.

Eventually, you internalize that it's because you're not as important, that no one really cares about you or what you're doing. You usually just go inside and hope your parental figure spends some time with you like the parents with the kids in the windows. I usually just got told to take off my play clothes before I sat on her couch.

It may seem sad and desperate but I remember that in order to get attention or time with my mother I would often just lay under her make-up table while she got ready to go out. I was actually convinced as a child that she had to go out at night the same way she had to go to work and how I had to go to school. If I was ever going to have a man in the house (food etc…) I would have to make sacrifices she'd tell me. Perhaps that was a natural form of denial I used to protect myself from realizing how insignificant I really was to her. Letting children think that way is neglect too. If you have similar shared experiences you've probably spent a lot of your life trying to love those emotionally unavailable people I referenced earlier.

PLAYING GAMES

I was around age 8 when my mother started dating a guy named Mort G. He was a professional tennis player and all-around Tennis pro. He managed an indoor racket club when he wasn't teaching in the school system. Somehow my mother convinced him to watch me during the summer months. That meant that I was going to learn how to play tennis for free. Not only would I be playing a lot of tennis but I would unknowingly be playing tennis with some of the best people in the country at the time.

Along with several other major cities in the 1970s Baltimore had a tennis team called The Baltimore Banners. Several of their top players practiced at the club. These were the people I played with the most when they weren't playing each other. Aside from Mort the player that taught me the most was a female named Audrey Morse. Many of the team members would work out at the Perring Racket Club with us, even Jimmy Connors. They were obviously great people to play with but I also had unlimited time on the ball machines and countless baskets of balls to serve to an empty regulation court. Professional tennis was my summer daycare center for years and I got damn good by the time I was 12 years old. It appeared as though my journey toward professional tennis was set in stone. As time passed I got better and better. I was really fast on the court and had great teachers. After 3 summers of it, I was an aspiring tennis player that had the skills to play with the best in the world. Mort was a great guy and very liked by the tennis community. He was a good man despite his choice of women. He went on to become one of the best table tennis players in the world.

Sadly my mother was just using him to social climb and improve her social circle. Mort stayed in our lives over the years and he was a good role model for me. He was a graceful port in the storm well into my teens. He tried to guide me in a positive direction; his Grace was vital.

CHAPTER FIVE

DAMAGED GOODS

A TRIP YOU'LL NEVER FORGET

I was in the 5th grade when my mother decided that she was running out of free sitters for me so she decided to contact the Big Brother League of Maryland. (Pretty sure Mr. Richards the social worker suggested it.) I'd like to think my mother was feeling guilty for neglecting me but she never displayed that capacity.

My mother explained to me that having a Big Brother would give me the chance to do all the things that kids with "real fathers" got to do. I believe her exact words were; "If only their fathers weren't bums like yours." Regardless of the how or why, it was sold to me as a way to have a normal life. She suggested it was a chance to do some of the things that my friends in the windows at night and the kids on TV got to do with their fathers. Like it would be for any needy child the idea was exciting to me. I was however afraid that this would be an excuse for her to not have to take me to see my father anymore. Knowing her it's possible it was just another form of revenge on him; a way of replacing him and making him more aware of his own deficits. I loved the idea of it but since my father was the one that loved me the most I felt like I was being disloyal by agreeing. Intuitively something felt wrong about it.

Once I bought into the idea she prompted me to get my father to sign the permission slip. I can only imagine the heartbreak he felt at being confronted by his own shortcomings; how could he deny me what he was unable or unwilling to do for me. I still recall his reactions when I would share about the things we did and the places we would go. It was usually followed by a long drink and reassurance that it was a good opportunity.

Interestingly my father did start trying harder, he even got his first car and we started doing a lot of the things that my Big Brother and I didn't do. We took trips to see the Pennsylvania Amish/Dutch, went fishing, camping and one of my favorites, shooting things. That's when I got my nickname, Butch, as in Butch Cassidy and the Sundance Kid. We usually did our shooting under some highway bridge in the city. We were supposedly helping the city get rid of the pigeon scourge.

Sadly there would be a great cost for my chance at having a life like other kids; perhaps the highest cost of all, my innocence. That extremely rare commodity was taken from me one night at the Kings Dominion amusement park near Richmond Virginia by that Big Brother, a man named Robert Holcomb (born around 1953).

I remember lying on my back asleep in the hotel bed and then feeling something odd and wet. It felt like I had spilled something in the bed or peed myself. I didn't move I just opened my eyes a little to see if I did pee only to see that my so-called "Big Brother" had my penis in his mouth. I was so afraid that I just froze and pretended I was still asleep. I wasn't sure if he was allowed to do that or not.

Since I was a virgin still at 11, I remember thinking that he might be making me gay. He stopped after a while; after I ejaculated in his mouth. I didn't know what that was either. I don't think I had even started masturbating yet so I was kind of freaked out by that feeling. He moved back over to the other bed, rolled over and went to sleep. I buried my head under the covers in terror like I was hiding from a monster in the room. After a few hours of hiding I fell asleep, afraid that I was now gay.

Obviously, all this still plagued me the following morning. I knew that what he had done to me was a gay act and I began to question if that meant I could not date girls now; had he somehow indoctrinated me into their club? What about all that "man" training my father gave me? I knew my father wanted me to be straight. Was it now too late to be straight?

I wasn't 100% sure it wasn't just a bad dream. I had had plenty of bad dreams by now. I was confused but I knew I was certainly not going to be telling anyone about what happened because I didn't want to be in the gay club. Denial protected me as I didn't really know for sure that it had actually happened. I remember thinking about and becoming quite sad about how I would never get to have a wife and kids. I thought that maybe this was just another sad thing that happens to poor kids; you know, because we don't matter. Maybe I wasn't supposed to breed.

The morning after the rape there was no change in Bob's behavior whatsoever; it was like nothing ever happened. He took me to the park and treated me to everything it had to offer. I stared at him most of the day waiting for a kind of sign. My only hope was that he thought I never woke up and therefore "never allowed it;" that way I wouldn't be a homo. I couldn't beat him up and I figured killing him would be hard to do. I knew my life had changed at that moment but not exactly how much. Like most of the people that were supposed to care for me, he didn't do it either; he was ignoring what he did and what happened along with my fears and feelings. I didn't matter once more.

I was 200 miles from home, the second furthest I had ever been in my life; the furthest I had ever been from a blood relative. What would happen if I screamed for help to some stranger in the hotel or on the street? Would he kill me in the woods? Denial set in and I began to pretend that it was all just a bad dream. I began to convince myself that it never even happened. I wasn't really sure but then I was left to process the dream itself and why I would have a dream like that. Did that mean I was gay?

My first awareness of men being with men was when a pervert at the YMCA was trying to talk to me while I was with my father and his friend. My father caught him so my father's friend Angelo went to talk to him as my father took me to the locker room. I think he was roughed up and told to never show his face again at the YMCA, he never did. After what happened to me I didn't want to be one of those guys either.

When you live with abuse for years it's more than just a story; it seems even more horrific now as I describe it in detail. That one single event caused more serious emotional and developmental damage than anything I have ever been through. That one event changed my emotional capacity for a lifetime. That scar is the deepest and seems to be the most resilient; fifty years later I still feel that damage, horror and loneliness now as I write this book. I've actually been quite shocked by how hard writing this book has been because of it. I feel like barfing now.

Have you ever woken up from a dream with your body physically reacting to the dream? It was like that but much worse; it was real, not a dream. As an 11-year-old I had heard of sex and even blowjobs, we even had perverts that drove around our apartment complexes with their penises out asking us little kids if we wanted to make a dollar. In fact, one day my cousin George actually got in the car and we all watched as they sat there. Suddenly George comes running down the street with a pair of pants yelling and laughing, "I GOT HIS WALLET!" We all got ice cream from the Good Humor ice cream man with the money. We never saw that guy again but there were plenty of others.

Back to the pervert pedophile Bob. It seems as though the oral rape I experienced emboldened the pervert Robert Holcomb to try it again. The next time it happened was at his parents' house when they were away. He was there watching their house and their dogs. It was in a part of Baltimore called Rolland Park, a place we called the really rich neighborhood. That neighborhood and house were only a quarter mile from the hospital I was in for my 3rd-grade anxiety that developed in Ms. Tate's class.

I remember Bob putting me to bed in what he called a special bed that had been in the family for decades. It was one of those beds that was really high up off the floor. He set himself up in the room down the hall so I thought I would be safe; he even shut the door when he left the room.

The same thing happened. I woke up feeling like I had peed myself but when I looked down the cover was literally bob-bing up and down like a ghost was under it. He couldn't see my face and I couldn't see his. I still closed my eyes and pretended to be asleep. I figured out that night that as soon as I ejaculated it would end, he would stop and he would disappear. I began to question if this was a trade-off a kid had to make to get to do things like ball games and hiking and stuff.

I remember going to Big Brother events and wondering if all those little boys had it happening to them too. (Sadly many probably did.) I remember seeing the "Bigs" standing around leering and giggling. I'm not sure how many times he raped me like that; it could have been like 6 or 7. I only really remember 3 times but think it could have been more. It's possible I didn't even wake up for all of them or I just blocked them out. (I'm a light sleeper now.)

The third time it happened we were camping at a YMCA site called Black Rock where I had also gone to learn to ride horses with my mother. I was zippered up in a sleeping bag thinking I was safe but when I woke up the same thing was happening. I ejaculated and he got off of me. (It's no wonder I associated the YMCA with perverts.) It didn't help my trauma triggers any when the YMCA song and The Village People group came out a few years later.

During those rapes I learned how to leave my body and sort of did it whenever the song triggered my PTSD. I also learned how to control my orgasms; to turn them on and off at my whim. I am certain that he never tried anything else besides once feeling him rub his junk on my foot while he was blowing me. I did want to kill him for that. I was really angry at all the people that made this perversion possible. (FYI, it's a bad thing when an 11-year-old is thinking about killing people. I'm certain now that this is an all too familiar emotional landscape, one that often prompts children to commit heinous acts.)

If the story isn't bad enough already my sister told me a few years ago that pervert Bob had actually come to my mother to confess that he had done some "inappropriate touching" and that he was ending his role as my Big Brother. According to my sister my mother's response was "Oh, he seems fine, I know he really liked going to the places you guys have gone together." (If your jaws are open right now it's OK to close them. Even knowing my mother my jaw did the same thing when my sister told me her exact words.) I thought it was a secret into my 20s.

Sadly this confession of his might have been a chance for me to get some help but my mother's lifestyle was obviously paramount. (Not getting children care is neglect.) While I openly discuss my abuse now I know that a lot of people who know me don't know these details about my life. Why? Because I wear my vulnerabilities, damage and scars on the inside where all real men wear them; where they can't be seen.

The pervert Robert "The Bobber" Holcomb did disappear shortly after that conversation with my mother. By disappear I mean he left the state to avoid prosecution or being murdered. The pedophile fled to Raleigh North Carolina. (Laws were different back then and these creeps were protected by state boundaries; many statutes still need to be changed).

Decades later I was working as the doorman at a popular music venue when Holcomb's first Little Brother and I reconnected. I remember him asking; "Did Bob do weird shit to you?" I remember replying "Yeah, that fucking fagot sexually abused me." He said, "Me too, I always felt guilty about not speaking out because I was afraid he would do it to you too." He then asked "Did it happen in that bed at his parents? I'm sorry about that." I said, "Dude, you were what 15?" He asked me if I ever heard from him again. I said yeah, after I got out of jail (we'll talk about that later) he called me and said he was sorry for what he had done years ago. He wanted to send me some money so I could go out and get some new clothes and stuff. (I had lost everything I owned when I was arrested because my mother threw everything in a dumpster. She threw away every good memory I ever had from yearbooks to pictures of my then-dead father.)

Sorry BOB!! That little appeasement didn't fucking cut it! It didn't fix anything! It just made me even more of a commodity that could be bought and paid for. (I apologize if the harsh language and graphic nature of this book offends you; you should probably stop reading it now.)

I did contact Bob when I was around 30. I was in Raleigh traveling with my girlfriend and her show at the time. I had been working on my child within stuff so I thought there would be some benefit to having him apologize in person. I got him on the phone and said I was in town. Predictably, pussy faced Bob freaked out. I guess he thought I had other plans for him. I think he worried about the "jail me" and not the innocent 11-year-old boy that he raped. I had no plan to do anything bad but who knows. I was a practicing Catholic at the time and forgiveness was important to me so I doubt I would have hurt him. I did get a little pissed when he pussed out. His ass apparently left town that night or went into hiding or something. When I called him back he said he had to run out of town for work. A cowardly lie! I learned later that he might have been working in a boys' group home even then.

I know you can sense the anger in my words, a change in tone for sure. That's because that's where the scars on my soul still reside. That tortured part of my heart can get quite scary. Why? Because that tortured part of me may have an inability to bond with partners (always women) in a healthy way that isn't just physical in nature. (For most abused people that limitation is a life sentence.) That part of me is dangerous because it was forced to learn how to shut off emotions and feelings. Abused kids also struggle to prioritize their own needs in a relationship. Further, people who can shut off their feelings are dangerous, maybe even more dangerous than people that have no feelings whatsoever. The hardest feeling to shut off is the most dangerous of all, anger.

For people that were sexually abused finding true love is extremely difficult because the physical always takes priority over any other human values. Neglected and abused people often fall in love with bodies or the high that another person wanting them might give them. The emotional high of being relevant or needed can block an individual's clarity. It blocks them from seeing the good and the bad. It can limit their ability to see how great of a partner they may have because the emotional extremes aren't there. These intense emotional extremes are often confused with the heightened feelings of being in love. (Abuse lasts a lifetime but I'm still working hard to see that it doesn't. Trying to remove the last remnants of that stain is another reason I wrote this book but being able to spare others some suffering is my hope. You are not alone.)

When someone makes you a "thing" and removes your personhood for their own personal sexual gratification your perspective on the world is tainted. When their sexual needs are put above your psyche's health or when there is a total disregard for how you will function for the rest of your days on Earth you can get a little bitter. FUCK YOU ROBERT HOLCOMB, (now 70ish) I HOPE THE FIRES OF HELL ARE BURNING BRIGHT FOR YOU. (If anyone ever needs me to testify against this asshole POS please contact me. Hopefully, he's dead and gone.) To the Big Brother League of Maryland, FUCK YOU TOO!! You exposed lots of us to these freaks so you are culpable. You failed me. God knows how many other little boys got trafficked in that pedophile scheme of yours.

Please be assured that the tone change you noticed was not poetically structured to make the book read better. It's the raw reality of how that scar presents itself to this day. It's a glimpse of what it looks like when trauma activates. (This reaction is subtle compared to what happens within many treated and untreated survivors. I'm actually quite healed now. The real problem with healing is the limbic system doesn't have a clock. It's structured to respond to threats for a lifetime. That makes it hard to erase the hurt stuff. Had I not been "Graced" by the people I have, I don't know what I might have done to get even.)

DEAL WITH IT!!

So what did I do as an 11-12 year-old trying to carry the burden of sexual abuse all by myself? Personally, I tried to find ways to avoid feeling it, ways to push it deep down where even I couldn't find it. Like many abused children I worried that because my body responded to physical manipulation that it somehow meant I must have allowed it. Not knowing that those bodily sense reactions were out of my control I feared being gay or altered by the experience; I accurately sensed I would never be normal because of it.

Prior to the abuse, I didn't know that there was such a thing as a bad touch. No one told us about that stuff. For that reason, children of our era believed that because someone touching us stimulated us that it must have meant we somehow participated. It's as if being stimulated was somehow a form of consent or approval. For a child whose mother never seemed that interested I figured that my only real value or usefulness in life must be in meeting the needs of others. In a very sick way, there is a sense that being "useful" for the sexual gratification of others at least gives you purpose. (Stain?!)

It is in that very first moment of sexual abuse that you become a thing, an object; you cease being a valuable individual in almost every other way. You learn that other people's needs and desires must be more important than your own. You "believe" your innocence is of little value; merely a commodity to be exchanged for some babysitting services or a baseball game. Sadly every one of those "normal memories" of ball games, hikes and amusement parks is tainted with the memory of the abuse I suffered. Just a few days ago someone posted a picture of Brooks Robinson; guess who I was with when I met him? That's what I remember, being raped.

In the years that followed (in my early teens), I began to think that I was meant to be a sexual being more than an intellectual being. In a possible attempt to overcompensate, I decided that I would become a sexual dynamo with the ladies; that I would become really good at giving them orgasms. By doing so I would prove that I was a real man. If I made them feel better than anyone else they would never leave me. The need to overcompensate seemed not only legitimate but essential. Don Juan was my new hero and Caligula the new standard. Svengali's feats would set the bar that I would attain, must attain. You are either everything to people or you are nothing to anyone. That was my experience. (All this at age 13; the fact that I knew who the above people were should speak volumes.)

In my early teens, I actually wanted to become a stripper for women, go figure. It wasn't like I hadn't ever danced in bars; I did that for years

67

and I did it for money too. Perhaps I'd be the best male dancer ever (one of the long-haired versions). Perhaps even an American Gigolo. These thoughts struck me years before the movie and dance groups were popularized. When they did evolve I saw it as validation, a sign even. Perhaps the industry interested me because I was seeing female strippers and GoGo dancers in the bars as young as age 5. Perhaps this potential was already inside me before the abuse, perhaps it was destiny. Perhaps my sexual energy drew in the abuse. STOP!! See what happened there in my young teen mind. IT MADE THE ABUSE MY FAULT. It even justified it in an attempt to understand it and regain control. (It was my sexual energy that was responsible.) Damage? Stain? All I thought was I wasn't going to be the victim, not wounded or hurt. Since no one had ever suggested a state of victimhood to me, I never entertained it.

This is another horrible ramification of sexual abuse on a child, another form of damage. Not only does it make the victim second guess their value to others for the rest of their lives it makes them culpable in it. It sets the shame stain on the soul for a lifetime yet to come.

In many ways, I was like most young males of the era. At times I didn't see the need to overcompensate sexually for the abuse because the scar was so deep I couldn't sense it. I decided that I was going to cope the same way that we little poor kids with the free lunches did; I was going to make this adversity into an asset. (I had already had more blowjobs than the other boys.) While some sexual innocence was certainly lost at the Pig Pen GoGo bar on Oldham Street the rest of it was all stolen at King's Dominion off of Route 95 in just a matter of seconds.

All that jukebox dancing I did as a kid made me a great dancer. Thanks to some good genetics and my father's singing abilities I could do that too. I felt like I needed to become rich and famous; that I had to in order to prove my worth; that was my training. I would show them all how valuable I really was and make them all want me more than they ever did. I would make them regret not treating me better. I would make them beg to be in my life.

My motivation to conquer the past was spurred on by all the emotional damage I had suffered. The abuse would remain a secret to assure that no one could use it against me; throw me away as tainted goods. I would take it to the grave. It would remain set deep within me with no hope of new insight or perspective from anyone. That darkness would never see the light of day. (Sadistically, sexual predators rely on this phenomenon of shame to keep their victims quiet.)

Sadly my dreams of being a rich stripper did not concern my mother at all. She was actually hoping that I would fulfill her lost dreams of stardom too. Not for me but for her, so that she could ride the wave and brag about it to her friends. A sick reality is that I got my first G-string from my mother. It was a Christmas gift before I turned 18. I didn't even realize that it was awkward and creepy until many years later when I shared the story with a female friend; a real mom.

When it came to singing and performing I used to think that I would be a great frontman one day. That I would write songs that healed people's hearts or at least just make them really horny. Either would be fine with me. I just wanted to matter and make people feel. I wanted to do exactly what Prince was already doing but with a more masculine presentation. I actually thought I was a better dancer because I was man-sized and expressed myself with a more masculine style of movement. (Prince was special but his damage got to him in the end.)

I believe all this focus on sex is 100% the result of being hyper-sexualized by the abuse at a young age. This is what happens to the young brain that is sexualized (damaged by sex) too early. Abused children that are attractive enough to evolve into sex objects do; their scars don't leave them any choice.

Damaged children like me think this is the way everyone thinks and feels. I assumed that everyone wanted to be a sex "object" but that most people just weren't cool enough, hot enough or talented enough to make that happen. (Similar beliefs are why some people are extremely driven to be famous; stardom is a must for them. Instead of exploding on people in the public square, they self-destruct right in front of our eyes on the news.)

I believed most people just didn't share their desires for fame out loud because they had too much shame. They were afraid of being ridiculed or spurned because of their dreams. Damaged people that can't live out these distorted drives just stuff their needs down even deeper inside, never to be satiated. I believe that the people who repress these drives are the people that commit mass shootings, heinous family murders or at a minimum become abusers too.

Thus my motivation to be famous wasn't really about fame at all. It was about needing to be wanted, desired, cherished and valued (a sick result of abuse and neglect). It was about relevancy and importance; about meaning everything or nothing. I know that had I not had this sex object option to exploit I would have eventually acted out and made people pay in order to get the emotional attention I needed.

The people we see in the news are really just trying to let people know how bad they are wounded. They see these over-the-top solutions as the only way to be seen or heard. We need to get them the Grace they need. We need to understand that their pain isn't only their problem. We need to let them know their pain is seen before they have to show us.

The need to have their pain recognized is why some of them become dangerously hurtful people; even stalkers and killers. Once they learn to shut off their feelings they become afraid to turn them back on out of fear of losing control. People that can't feel their own emotions can't empathize so they hurt people with no sense of internal conflict or guilt. People without any hope for relief just explode!

Some abused children eventually figure out that there are other ways to matter in people's lives and that getting attention doesn't always have to be through positive interactions. Once they start gaining attention through negative behaviors they become unruly. Seeking attention to meet their needs they become very dangerous people because they realize that they can matter just as much by hurting people. When you rob someone, carjack them, rape them, attack them, etc... you become very significant in their lives. It serves as a form of forced relevancy. (By sharing our Grace with people we make them relevant so they don't have to act out. You can call it validation but it's more than that to them; it's sustenance.)

PUT ON THE RED LIGHT

By this time my sister had already launched her career as a stripper working in Baltimore's Red Light District, known as The Block. I wasn't personally aware of this at the time. We had no awareness of our similar mindsets or distorted personal values. From what she has shared with me and from what I was to eventually learn or see for myself, she'd do all the things that one might expect while in that industry. The truth is that our mother taught her how to chase men and how to get men's money in exchange for sex and attention. Our mother was a model alright, a living role model for how to monetize oneself. As pathetic as it may sound at least my sister was getting paid upfront for her services; my mother was never that smart. When it came to my mother no one had to buy the cow because the milk was free. It's like she'd do the deed and then wait to be acknowledged by monetary reward. If the reward wasn't given then she would passive-aggressively exact her revenge. She either had poor business management skills or no imagination.

Does that sound bitter? It isn't meant to be. You see as I mentioned earlier, children that are neglected and abused learn how to turn their emotions off. She taught me not to have any feelings of my own toward her; to shut them down. It was too hazardous to connect my feelings to her actions. I now regard my views of her as quite detached, even clinical.

CHAPTER SIX
TAKING CONTROL

GOING TO POT

By the 6th grade, we had all heard about pot. It was the 70s and hippies were everywhere. My cousin David and another boy had found a bag of weed in the woods near one of the tree forts. The two of them had already smoked weed twice by the time I had learned about their having found it. Once I heard about them doing it I started making plans to try it myself. I was certain people like me had to do drugs. I was pretty sure that if you were cool you had to at least try them so that you could say you had. My long hair had already earned me the moniker "Little Hippy" so I thought using drugs was inevitable.

We were the generation just before the "Just No Generation." We were the "Just Say More Generation." We were the natural evolution of the 60s "Just Say Yes Generation." My friends and I had already been using that gateway drug called nicotine for years. We already knew how to get money for it, hide it, smoke it and cover up our breath; the only difference with pot was that we had to learn how to treat our red eyes. (That was only a problem for kids whose parents were paying attention.)

Two weeks after David's experiences with weed, he and I went to visit my father for the weekend. It was getting late, around 11 or so, and David and I were up and at um. Wanting to shut us down my father asked. "What do you all do up there in Cockeysville to have fun?" To my father, Cockeysville was way uptown where the money was and not a place he could ever imagine living. He was a Greek from Greek Town, a city boy, a place he had lived his entire life with the exception of his time in Korea and the Merchant Marines. While my father loved the countryside there weren't enough bars and liquor stores to meet his needs; not enough action. In some respects living in a place like Cockeysville was a little alien to him.

In response to my father's question David suddenly blurts out "GET HIGH!" All I thought was, NOOOO! Wrong answer!! I was sure my first ass beating from my father was on the way. Even though I hadn't smoked pot yet I knew I was going to so when my father looked at me and asked; "Do you get high?" I quickly said yes even though I hadn't; I figured I'd just get the ass beating out of the way now. (I was pragmatic like that.) My father stood up, turned, and walked over to his desk. I thought he was getting something from the desk to punish us with.

He opened the file cabinet where he kept his pistol and pulled out a HUGE bag of weed, almost a pound. David's eyes got big; he looked like a kid in a candy store, then toward me with adoration that my father was really cool (David never saw his father). All I could think was that my father was being bad all along. Being more of a 50s greaser type I thought he was better than all those hippies he always made fun of. I then thought, he does look like Johnny Cash and Cash had just gotten in trouble for marijuana possession. It all suddenly became very clear.

My father grabbed some rolling papers and sat down in his chair while I made him a drink. David leaned over the arm of the chair as if he was waiting for someone to give him a bowl of ice cream. My father proceeded to take his time rolling several joints. (Unbeknownst to me my sister and father had already been getting high together for some time, she was nearly 18.)

I had been stealing cigarettes and cigars from stores for years so I knew how to inhale. I thought; same thing, no big deal. My father was there and I always trusted him to look after me.

We all took a couple hits but I really didn't feel anything. I struggled to understand what the big deal was. I probably got more of an effect out of a cigarette back then. My father sent me to the bathroom hallway to space walk; he said it was cool when you were high. David later told me that when I was gone my father asked him if I had ever smoked before. David said he didn't know for sure but that I was always smoking cigarettes. My father already knew that because I had been caught doing it. My father smoked between 2-3 packs of Pall Mall unfiltered cigarettes a day but he had just started smoking Winston because smoking was now bad for you.

That night my father essentially taught me how to smoke pot. David and I would try to take a hit and pass it like on TV. This frustrated my father and he'd say, "Take your time, hit it a few times, there's no hurry, you're not going anywhere; we have plenty." He would later tell me that I could never do any other drugs: I was cool with that deal. I also remember him warning me not to smoke any of my cousin's pot. I figured out later that was because my cousin smoked flakes (PCP).

It was around that time that I began to learn more about my father's connection to organized crime. I was beginning to understand that all those Mediterranean men were not just his friends. The boarders in his rooming house always seemed like people that were in the country to work, not people visiting on vacation; I was getting the big picture.

My father's connections became even more clear in a stark warning not to hang around my cousin Manuel because he was about to be taught a life lesson for selling things in the neighborhood that he wasn't allowed to sell. The Greeks didn't even want a cut of it; they just disapproved of PCP outright. At that time PCP was "the crap the bikers made and sold" and they saw it as bikers making money off of their neighborhood's grief. My marijuana use with my father became a fairly regular thing. I still wasn't allowed to smoke cigarettes around him, they were bad for ya and God didn't make those.

If you have a sibling then you know about the often strange points of contention that develop. As suggested before my sister was always jealous of me and my value to our father. That was just the way it was back then. It was just a cultural thing between Greek/Middle-eastern fathers and their sons. It was also the early 70s and while women were fighting to be treated equally they still weren't. This was the same era that women stopped wearing their bras in protest. That never made sense to me because I always thought that it made them more of a "thing" to stare at; you know like the Go-Go girls. I was not aware that my objectification of people had already begun.

Long story short, my sister, father, two of his friends and I were sitting in his kitchen one night around 10pm. My father's friend brought over some Hawaiian weed so we all began to smoke. There we sat around the old 50s style kitchen table just like we were having cake together. When the joint went to my sister she refused to pass it to me, trying to pass it back to the person that gave it to her instead. My father commanded, "Pass it to him!" "No!" she said. He scolded her, threatened to not let her smoke and she passed it to me. Of course, she got the little brother HAHA!!! Then I blew the smoke in her face and she ran out of the room bitching.

Let's be clear, her resistance wasn't because she was concerned for my health it was just that she didn't start smoking with him until she was a few years older than I was at the time. I think she thought that this was their thing, a thing that I was excluded from. It's plain to see that family dysfunction occurs on many levels and family emotional dynamics transcend morality and legality.

It was around this time that many of the other kids from poor dysfunctional families in good ole Cockeysville also started smoking weed. The rich dysfunctional family kids joined us a little later. It seemed like one day we were all just kids outside playing then poof, we were all going outside to smoke and drink. In an instant we when from being the kids at Skateland to skate, to being the kids going there to smoke and have sex up on the hill behind it. We started putting our skate money together to buy beer from "The Village Inn" bar across the street.

I went to Skateland A LOT!!! I loved to skate; still do. I was really good at it, fast even. I remember drooling over the rich kid's expensive speed skates; skates that I didn't ever dream of owning. At that time you could buy a car for $200 and these skates were $200 and above. I also remember whipping the entire speed team's ass with my poor kid's rental skates. Speed teams would come from other areas to compete. They would always laugh at me as I lined up to race with my rental skates but they quieted down after I whipped their asses too. I almost never lost and as you might guess, I out-danced their butts when it came to dance skating. You can imagine the fun I had at the one-hour sock hops.

Skateland was an important place to me. You see one night Jenifer H. my girlfriend at the time let me take things to the next level, literally. She was the girl I skated couples with and made out with in the back when the lights went down. She had been letting me take her up on the hill near the end of the night for some 1st through 3rd base petting. Sometimes we would go out early for just that reason. It was on one of those splendid nights up on the hill that I lost my real virginity. That was my first real sexual encounter with a partner that I chose; my first mutual consent experience. It certainly felt more natural than what I had known thus far.

I was a big man that night as I came strutting down the hill with my arm awkwardly around her shoulders. Then I heard a boy yell; "We saw your ass sticking out of the grass man!" Now I was really cool, I didn't even need to tell the story, everyone knew it. Finally, a sexual experience that I could talk about: I even had witnesses that I was not only straight but even sexually advanced. (I felt truly straight for the first time.) While Jenifer laid there like a log, I'm pretty sure I wasn't her first.

It was around this time that I started asking for more money from my mother to babysit myself with. My new babysitter was Skateland and it was worth the $3 for her to get rid of me. I had a paper route for about a year that paid me $12 a week for delivering the evening paper. On top of that good ole Herk was still in the picture so I could get some good "skating (beer) money" from him too.

Herk had a friend named Lou Kousouris that owned a sub shop in Lutherville called Pebbles Pizza. He arranged to get me a job that I started at age 13. That's what Greeks do; they put you to work early. Pebbles Pizza put beer and weed money in my pocket. It also meant that I could buy weed by the ounce and sell it too.

GET YOUR GUNS

Skating wasn't my only out-of-school non-supervised activity. When parents aren't involved in a child's life the police tend to be. In our town, we had good ole Officer Speed. That's right; in a place full of attitude called Cockeysville, you have an officer named Speed (real last name). By most standards, I guess you could say he was a good cop. He certainly worked hard. Aside from all of the typical young boys being bad stuff, Officer Speed was my first real encounter with the Police. That is unless you count skateboarding at the shopping center or in almost empty swimming pools. (Yep, we invented that too, in 1973.)

Around age 12 my cousin David and I had both acquired BB guns. It was a rite of passage in those days. When not in the woods we would walk around the apartment complexes and neighborhoods with them in hand, like a little mob. The crazy thing is no one freaked out or called the cops because it was just kids with BB guns.

We became pretty good shots after a while, but like little pothead want-a-be-s often do, we got bored hunting birds and cans. I guess there is no real gentle way to say it than to simply say we started shooting out windows. Not in old buildings though, in people's apartments. "If the world doesn't care about me why would I care about it? I bet you notice me now!"

The first people we targeted were the people on our "shit list." You know the people that yelled at us kids for skateboarding, told on us for being out too late or outright called the cops. I guess we started the "snitches get plastic windows for a week" gang. We certainly shot out enough windows for the cops to hear all about it and go on the hunt for us. The scariest part was we'd do it at night when we could see them in their apartments but they couldn't see us outside. It sounds horrific in light of today's problems but it wasn't so traumatizing back then because it was just seen as vandalism. (Take note of how minor we viewed such an act. For people who live with extreme circumstances, extreme circumstances aren't extreme.)

As poor kids we had a lot of anger and jealousy for people that had more than we did. (You know, like moms and dads in the same house.) Some of them even ate dinner together at the same time every night. The pop of those sliding glass doors shattering definitely halted their Hallmark moments.

One day David and I were walking down the edge of the Longview golf course. That's the place where the wealthy people played and where we weren't allowed. It's the same place we passive-aggressively tore up the greens while jumping sand traps on our bikes. It wasn't like we'd ever be members or anything so what did we care, "eat the rich," right?

The John kids had recently leapfrogged over the Sapp's financial status because Ma had a richer boyfriend. Once they moved to Town and Country Apartments E-1 decided to go one step higher to the more luxurious Briarcliffe Apartments; our apartment was at the 17th hole.

David and I stayed near the fence line because the guy with the red golf cart and the rock salt shotgun might spot us; we needed a fast escape. (Yes he would shoot us and he did.) One night without warning David just decided to take out a window in an apartment. Good ole white trash David from the lesser apartment complex hated all the people in Briarcliffe except for us because he knew we weren't rich.

He made a comment, "Fuck these rich fuckers" then he aimed, took a shot and just when he did a man stood up in front of the window. The glass shattered as the man was struck right in the temple. We took off running and jumped through a hole in the fence near the playground next to our unit. It was now getting dark and we thought things had cooled down. Just then Officer Speed came walking around the corner of the building. I stood there with my gun hidden down the back of my leg. David was carrying his in both hands, right in front of Officer Speed without a care in the world, daring Speed to ask about it. (Remember, this was around 1975 and kids with BB guns were a part of Americana. It was just past "the wonder years" and Daisy BB guns were as common as 2 wheeled bicycles.)

Officer Speed said, "Can I see it?" David handed him his gun and Speed put the gun up on his shoulders and just started walking away without saying a word. David started yelling at him "GIVE ME MY GUN YOU PIG." Then David turns to me and says "Give me your gun I'll shoot that black mother fucker," Speed wasn't even looking back. I waved David off telling him to be quiet because I didn't want mine taken too. David chased after Speed. I hid my rifle in the house and then followed suit. "Tell your mom she can pick it up at the police station when she pays for the window; I'm Officer Speed." We cursed him out as he drove away with David throwing rocks at his car. (David did get his gun back. His mother Carol didn't take any crap from the cops either but you better believe she used her charm or who she knew to get it.)

About 2 weeks later I was on the grass behind our bottom-floor apartment shooting my gun at soda cans. Howie P who lived upstairs came out on his porch and displayed his new one-pump Daisy BB gun. Mine was a BB and pellet gun but his was one of those air guns that could hold 100 BB's.

I shouted to him "Those are weak." Out of nowhere he pointed his gun at me and shot me right in the thigh. I rubbed my leg, turned toward him and raised up my gun. He raised his gun again so I shot him right in the face with a pellet. Blood started squirting out. As he realized what happened he started screaming and ran into the house to his mother. Without blinking an eye I almost took out his. There was nothing his mother could do because she knew he was out on the porch with his own gun. It's all fun and games until somebody loses an eye right? No worries it was just a scratch, no stitches but as far as I know he still has a scar just under his eye on his cheekbone. If you know him you can check for me. In those days things like this didn't stop us from being friends.

CHAPTER SEVEN
MO-MENTUM!

MO-MONEY!

It didn't take long for me to realize that all these little rich kids had pockets full of daddy's allowance money. While I wanted that money I needed something else even more. Perhaps more than most people I needed to feel a part of something; I needed to feel relevant to somebody, anybody, anyhow.

Making friends is hard enough but without any training in relationships, it almost seemed impossible. "YOU DON'T MATTER EMMANUEL" had become the loudest noise in my head. I had been trying to get my mother to want me my entire life. Suddenly a switch flipped when I figured out that other people were actually easier to win over than she was. Don't get me wrong, I was OK being alone; I was bred for it. I loved solitude but at this age girls were obviously becoming more important. I no longer questioned my sexuality and neither did they. Turned out I was a pretty good kisser and I had a few other things going for me too.

Focused on their money I devised a plan to get it from them. Thanks to my Pebble's Pizza money I had capital so I started buying ounces of weed and selling a few Nickel and Dime bags here and there. In those days an ounce of weed averaged about $30-35 but you could also find Mexican Dirt weed for about $25 an ounce and even homegrown for $5-10. Most kids didn't know the difference but the Columbian weed meant more return customers because it was better.

Working at Pebbles taught me that if you have a good product people would travel pretty far to get it. Lou K. and I became very close as he taught me the Pizza business. Lou loved beer and the kitchen fridge always had a few cases of Bud in it. It quickly became routine for Lou to offer me a beer after a hard night's work in front of the Pizza oven. I was 13 and Lou treated this little Greek kid, with the Greek first name, just like family. Eventually, I didn't have to ask for a beer and he would usually retort with, "What you can't get one for someone else." Our Solo cups hid the beer from plain site as well as from the other employees.

Lou didn't believe in weed; he was old school. We weren't allowed to smoke weed at work because he didn't want us to be there high so we waited until he went home for the evening. WE PARTIED OUR ASSES OFF IN THAT PLACE!! It started with drinking as soon as he left then once he called us from home we would start smoking weed. We would stand on the toilet and blow the smoke into the fan. What the big cook fans didn't remove, the food smell overpowered.

I was eventually made the manager because Lou trusted me with the store; that made me feel important. At 13 years old I was managing one of the busiest sub shops in town. I had the keys before I turned 14. I was learning how to be the boss. I was learning to manage people and even how to have authority. Being the boss had its perks too, especially with the ladies. Jenifer might have been my first girlfriend but we didn't have monogamy rules back in the 70s. Besides that, she was my Skateland girlfriend because she lived too far out in the boonies. My work girlfriends weren't possessive either; probably because I got them high and I was a cool manager. They were all older than me too, by as much as 4 years.

I had this thing about smacking girls on their asses in those days and some actually liked it, a lot! I freakin loved going to work because the girls had great butts. I would make out with one when she came back into the kitchen then catch a different one coming out of the bathroom or while we were in there smoking. The culture was simple; we just made each other as horny as possible as often as possible. I don't really recall anything going past "3rd base" in the store but there were some really good rides home.

RESERVED SEATING

As mentioned earlier we were the poor kids in our schools. The Johns and the Sapps were two of the few families that didn't have a mom and dad in the same house. The lack of dads at home might be why we were all little badasses. Not the jock good at sports kind of badasses but the "those kids are crazy, you better watch out for them" type of badasses. I guess the truth is that we seemed more like bad kids than badasses to some but we knew that other kids didn't think like us. Our poor kid struggles made us tougher and that seemed to scare a lot of them. Maybe we were ornery or maybe we just had to be that way to survive.

Essentially what all this attitude and angst gained me was my own seat at the school's main office in Junior High. It wasn't assigned or anything but I was there most days. The seat just became mine because I was in it more often than anyone else. I was there so often that the other bad kids just stopped sitting in it. It was the chair next to the door so sometimes I could actually sneak out of the office and smoke a cigarette, then return without them noticing I even left. If the school staff didn't see me at least once a day they figured I was absent.

Since my office sentence was usually just to sit there until that class ended they never really knew if I was coming or going. I often acted like the school lawyer when some scared kid would be sent down there for the first time. I'd ask them "What are you in for kid" like I was in some old jailhouse movie. I would then tell them what to say and what would happen if they followed my advice. (That may have been my first school counselor gig. I certainly made a lot of friends through my pro bono work; even a few new customers.)

My intellect was always a good power struggle match for the teachers and even the principles (see family training). My management skills from Pebbles made me very confident and cocksure. In our house, you had to learn how to protect and defend yourself in emotional arguments and that's exactly what going to the office was all about.

Most people that work with teens will tell you that the moment you get into a power struggle with them you lose. I must have known that because I used it to my advantage. My Vice Principle Ms. Thomas certainly knew it. Her instructions to me were quite simple. If I had a problem with a teacher I could send myself to the office before it got out of hand. (I know right; that's giving a kid a lot of power.) I was given permission to get up and leave a class if I had a problem with the teacher. The other kids would always look so stunned but the teachers were usually relieved to see me go.

I figured out later that this was to spare the teacher not to aid me in any way other than my not getting kicked out of school. I removed myself so many times that I was later asked to just let the teacher know I was going to the office instead of just walking out. They had stopped suspending me because they knew it just meant a day off of school. Being suspended allowed me to carry more weed for sale without the threat of being searched. I would just stand across the street in the morning and after school to sell my pot.

In the office, you could hear, "Emmanuel John is on his way down." I know this because I sometimes made it there before the teacher called down. I did that on purpose, sometimes I even ran there because I knew it made them look bad when I got there first; like they weren't doing their job right or something. It also allowed me to set the narrative for the exchange. Usually, I just used that time to smoke a cigarette in the boy's room.

We all had smokeless bowls for weed back in those days and sometimes I would even catch a quick buzz if I thought I was going to be at the office for a long time. You could hit those smokeless bowls anywhere in the school. You just had to find a place to blow out your smoke or hold it until it disappeared. Once I went to a friend's classroom, laid down on the floor in the hall and blew the pot smoke under the closed door in the back of the class. It was hilarious if you were high. Especially when my friend acted like he was breathing it in.

It wasn't just female teachers I messed with. I remember one day Mr. Foster was mad at me because I didn't dress for gym. Reason? "I Forgot my gym shoes." You see it was the 70s and my 4-inch platforms shoes made it hard to run unless the cops were chasing me. (While my mother didn't care about much she made sure her kids looked fashionable. She wouldn't want to be embarrassed.) One day Mr. Foster shoulder-checked me telling me to get out of his way while saying "MOVE!!!" I told my father about it during the next weekend's visit as we smoked up.

My father gave me a special message to give to Mr. Foster. I waited until I knew all three of the gym teachers were in their office. I figured I'd just set them all straight at the same time. (You know, me being pragmatic and all.) Since they all hated me I got the "what do you want" look. I walked up to Mr. Foster, stood about 2 feet away from him, looked him straight in the eyes (he was a Barney Rubble type) and gave him the message. "My father told me to tell you that if you ever touch me again he's going to come up here, drag your ass out into the street and beat the shit out of you." It was really quiet for a moment as I waited to hear a response. There wasn't one so I just turned and strutted out the door in my 4-inch heels. I would not be taking gym class that day either. I did see the other teachers look away smirking at Mr. Foster, like he had that power struggle with the wrong kid.

It was around this time that my mother informed my sister that she and I would be moving to a two-bedroom a little closer to the city in a place called Towson, MD. This was her not-so-subtle way of saying that my sister wasn't invited. The new place was really close to my mother's favorite bar called Velleggia's (less distance to drive drunk). Somehow my mother asked for and got special permission from the board of education for me to finish out the 9th grade school year in Cockeysville. (I think they felt bad for her having to deal with a kid like me.) Sympathy is one thing that Borderlines are really good at attaining. Especially when they are as pretty as she was. I have to say, she owned those nerdy Principles and board members; she knew everyone in town.

As suggested earlier they knew I was selling drugs but they couldn't catch me. In Junior High School most of my sales were prearranged the previous day and people had to get it first thing in the morning or I would sell it to someone else.

Aside from the office visits I also got in a few big fights with the Jocks. One of my biggest fights was a complete school spectacle. It started out righteous enough. A jock named Mick thought he was better than everybody else so he'd just butt in the school lunch line. (Come on now, there are good rules in life.) I said, "Hey Dick, I mean Mick, wait in line." He came over to bully me like I was supposed to be afraid of him; I wasn't. (I was actually on the school Jr. Varsity football team with him earlier that year; mostly because I could still run fast. I don't know why the gym teachers thought I needed the discipline.) Mick and I started pushing each other and I did what real men of honor did in those days. I said, "Meet me after school mother fucker!"

I thought that it was going to be just Mick and I but the other kids who hated "Mick the school bully" told everyone. It got around the entire school. The bully was going to get his ass kicked by a freak. The school administration knew about it but did nothing to try to stop it. In fact, the gym teachers had heard about it and actually started pumping Mick up to kick my hippy ass. It was raining so the gym teachers actually encouraged him to put on his cleats and some other padded gear.

School ended that day and I went to meet him up at the corner where fights happened off of school property. The same place kids smoked before and after school. I was out there standing in the rain for quite a while. I was beginning to think he chickened out and went home on the bus. I asked if he got on his bus and one kid said "No, he's in the gym, a bunch of the jocks are down there getting ready to come up here and fight." I was beginning to think that I might be fighting more than just him. I had been in fights with groups of people before so that wasn't new just difficult.

I heard someone yell, they're coming and I thought who the hell is they? I looked down toward the school and 50 jocks came running out of the school by the office carrying this dude on their shoulders, cheering like they had just won the super bowl. I stood my ground, or what I could in my platform shoes. Mick and I were surrounded by about 100 kids. We started going at it and all I can remember was slipping around on the wet grass in those damn shoes. When I went down Mick was on top of me (because his cleats didn't slip). I kept trying to get up; I even kicked him in the balls which slowed him down. When I would get up I'd just slip back down again. Then, suddenly, one of the black jocks named Derrick (Mick's friend) grabbed him around the waist and pulled him away from me. The crowd parted and three of my favorite people, all "H" brothers" came to pick me up. They stood their ground against the jocks even pushing them back. The jocks all cleared out when they realized that there would not be a freak beat-down today and that the odds were a little better now because I had backup.

Randy busted in and said; "What's the problem? Robby started jumping around like what, what and Louin stood there with his hand on his crotch trying to look pretty for the ladies. Randy asked me if I was alright, I said fuck them jocks who were mostly gone by now. Then the H's gave me a ride home in their cool black Camaro.

Boundaries were set with that rescue and the message got around without me knowing it, that I had people in my corner. For most people, both black and white alike, their having helped me meant something. I know it meant a lot to me. (More mob fights followed and a few more rescues too. For years Robby would jokingly ask me if I ever got into fights with one person at a time.) Since the school couldn't catch me dealing they couldn't stop me. A short time after the big fight my mother was notified that I would have to transfer to Towsontown Jr. High if I wanted to stay in my current grade.

FRANCHISED

My drug business hadn't really paid off yet. Up to this point, it was mostly about status, control and keeping myself in personal supply. Giving me a new school just meant an entirely new customer base closer to my job at Pebbles. Now I had two Junior High schools; three if you counted Ridgley (in between). I did have some crossover sales with Dulaney Senior but as a family courtesy I left those for my sister who never really optimized it. I always got her overflow when she was out of product.

Towsontowne Junior High was a partying school. It was the "Ridgemont High" of the county. From sex to drugs to explosives in the drain pipes and toilets, to smoking in the boy's room and the gymnasium, it was true 70s Americana.

While attending Towsontowne my father gifted me with a small Berretta handgun. It was really small for the time and could be carried in your pants pocket without bulging any more than a big bag of weed. I was good at hiding stuff from the cops so it meant nothing for me to carry it to school. It was more of a conversation piece than anything else. I was already breaking one federal law by dealing and that was worse than a carry charge at the time. (Does an angry hurt kid in school with a gun sound familiar?) I didn't know all the kids in the new school but I would be competition for anyone else that was dealing. I thought it would be better to have it and not need it than to need it and not have it. I knew that from day one I would certainly be on someone else's turf.

Despite the new turf, there were never any problems with other dealers at Towsontowne; I even befriended a few. We all just had lots of fun together. People seemed happy to have more options. It was during this time that I really started moving a lot of hash. Since no one else was selling it it wasn't seen as competition. Crazy as it sounds the only real problem that I ever had there was with a very bossy fairly athletic lesbian chick. For the most part she never really bothered with me but she did test some of the other guys there. To be blunt, she liked to make males look like pussies. Since I grew up in a family full of angry bitches she would not be a problem for me.

There was however one day when a large group of us had just been released from detention. There were about 15 of us standing outside the front door to the school; most were waiting for rides. I was still the new kid and I was having fun with a bunch of new friends when she must have felt a little socially threatened by me. She was wrestling around with some other guy and he was not doing very well; probably because guys didn't manhandle girls in those days. She knew that and she would use that knowledge to push things even further. She attempted her little game with me thinking I wouldn't push back. She said; "Come on new guy you want to wrestle?" I said I don't fight chicks. She said, "What if I want to fight you?"

In about half a second I pulled that Berretta from my pocket without thinking about it, planted it on her forehead and just said, "BACK THE FUCK OFF, BITCH!" She backed off very quietly and we never had a problem again. In fact, she never ever spoke to me again, ever. Pretty sure that upped my standing with a lot of people that day. Everyone loved watching another bully get put straight (no pun intended).

TRUST

Along with the new school came my new nemesis Mr. Trust (another gym teacher). That dude watched me like the FBI watched Trump. Things suddenly changed one fateful day when I was getting high in the gymnasium with a friend. After taking a hit from a bowl, I stood up from behind the backstage door while simultaneously blowing out smoke. As I raised up my head to see where Mr. Trust was I saw him staring dead at me from across the gym floor. My first thought was damn it, that dude's a marathon runner and here I am again with these damn shoes. I knew he saw me blow out the smoke and he knew my face so I was caught.

Mr. Trust took me directly to the office. I was searched and of course, I was holding. There I sat in the principal's private office with my ½ ounce bag of weed on the table waiting to learn my fate. I'll never forget the 7th-grade girl that came into the office to get a permission slip signed. She was in there for a few minutes before she turned and saw the weed on the table. I stared at her waiting to see her reaction. Boom, her jaw hit her flat chest and she turned to look at me. It was probably the most weed she had ever seen in her life. I gave her the whatever eye roll look as I tried to figure out how to get my weed back. In 1978 that weed was worth more than some people made in a day's labor.

The weed was there because the Vice Principle Mr. Cunningham forced me to take the bag out of my pocket during the search. I threw it onto the table hoping that some of the weight would be lost to the floor as it spilled out (less weight meant less charges). I smirked watching him as he took a big manila folder and used it to scrape all the weed back into a pile and then into the bag; like he had done it before. It looked like he was cleaning my weed for me and I was high after all. I'm pretty sure he noticed it was really good weed because he looked at me quite inquisitively. (Might have been Sensimellia, I can't remember for sure.)

I was only a few months from age 15 when the bust occurred. I was expelled from the Baltimore County public school system and I didn't even bat an eye. I remember my mother calling the house from out of state, Vegas I think. I recall telling her matter of factly that I was kicked out of school. Her response was; then you're going to start working full-time (at 15). I thought that would be just great, like I said I loved my job at Pebbles and I was already working almost 40 hours. Less school meant more money to me and not having to wake up early every morning. My sales would not suffer and E-1 seemed to think it was a cheaper route for her. No more school clothes or books or even lunch money for that matter. I started working seven days a week.

HIGH SOCIETY!

My mother must have been working her magic spells well because she was asked to move in with her new mark. This meant another move but this time to one of the largest houses in town, in one of the richest neighborhoods. E-1 had landed the big big fish. This fish was named Ben and he owned the largest stereo store chain in the mid-Atlantic region at the time; probably one of the largest in the country in 1978. It was a precursor to Circuit City or Best Buy called Stereo Discounters. He had stores throughout the Mid-Atlantic region. Ben was a poor redneck from Virginia that made all his own money. He was so rich for the time that at one point he almost bought the then, Baltimore Colts. I remember the cost of the team was only $12 Million at the time and he had about $7Mil in net worth. I even once saw a cashier's check for $1,000,000 that was headed to a Swiss bank. I also remember turning to look to see where the closest door was; wondering if I could cash it?

While I might have lived in a huge house I really didn't benefit much. I was still 15 working 40-50 hours a week. I was just an aging-out step-kid with an alcoholic gangster father. Ben had control; he knew my mother would do anything he wanted for the promises offered over the rainbow. I wasn't even given a bedroom in the dressed-up part of the house. I was given the maid and butler's quarters on the 3rd floor.

Obviously my mother and Ben would travel a lot; that's what people with money do. Sometimes when they did travel one of his really hot daughters would come and stay at the house to keep an eye on me. It was a freaking mansion after all and I was a kid kicked out of school for drugs.

I've been trying not to focus on sex in this book but it was the 70s. There was one occasion in particular when I called to his daughter several times and she didn't respond. I went into her father's bedroom and all I saw was this hot naked 22-year-old touching herself while holding a Playboy magazine. That's the stuff dreams are made of for a young boy. She was a knock-out too. My mind instantly pondered if this was more of my sexual destiny unfolding? Did she want me to come in?

I didn't go into that room looking for sex. I called to her to see if the room was empty because there was a refrigerator in the master bathroom that held two pounds of the best Hawaiian Sensemilla you ever smelled in your life. That was Millionaire dope in the 70s and it was good. I eventually ended up smoking almost that entire two pounds, one bowl at a time, sometimes with his horny daughters. Some people might see a sexual encounter like this as a good thing but what if it was your 14-year-old daughter with a 22-year-old man. Don't get me wrong, I loved the idea of it at the time but it would still be me servicing some adult's sexual needs.

As you might guess life with good ole Uncle Ben didn't last that long because my sister unwittingly ruined it. She got herself in some kind of trouble they wouldn't tell me about and she ended up homeless. She was living with my cousin and I think she kicked her out of her house for being a strung-out stripper mess. Apparently, my mother convinced Ben to let her stay in the Maid's quarters at the top of the house with me. He knew that she was using real dope (heroin) at the time and obviously, he was smart enough to know how that would go. After all, the dude owned a VCR and stereo store and we all know what addicts do with those. Her being there lasted about a month or so. I think Ben tried to solicit her stripper friend or something. My sister, never wanting to miss a chance to take my mother down a few pegs, told her all about the offer.

After getting tired of it all Ben paid for an apartment for us all back in good old Cockeysville. Ma would only be there during the week. He was also smart enough to keep her working a job and honestly, she knew it gave her leverage when he would push too far. I have no idea if my mother was faithful to Ben but she wasn't that dumb. Pretty sure there was some creepy couple stuff going on with the two of them and her old friend Carol who by this point was engaged to Ben's best friend Bruce. Ben and Bruce had just opened a bar called the Alamo and that's where the 4 of them spent most of their time.

BOOM TOWN!

The move back to Cockeysville was a boom for business. It was also a chance for me to reenter the social circles there with a lot more experience and a larger network of suppliers. I was admitted back to school but because I was expelled I had to go back and finish the 9th grade. I already had the people in my grade as developing customers, but now I had the younger kids that seemed even more willing to spend their parent's money. I didn't realize it at the time but being older meant more influence over my classmates. I came back with the reputation of having been busted out of school. That rep actually gave me more social credibility in the party circles. It also let people know I had access to drugs.

No matter how much money I made dealing I always maintained a real job too. I don't know where that drive came from back then; perhaps my mother's gold-digging role modeling or the "never enough" scar she passed on to us. I certainly associated money with being OK and safe. I was also convinced that if you wanted to be wanted by women you needed to have it. Of course, money was also a remedy to being hungry. I was absolutely convinced that all rich people were happy. Regardless of my motivational origins, there certainly existed within me a fear-based emotional scar that prioritized wealth (a security scar I had no conscious awareness of back then).

RESISTANCE IS INEVITABLE

It was around this time that I started having to deal with a lot of the older jocks and rich bullies that didn't like my station in their social circle. They didn't like the fact that a poor kid had control over their coolness factor. They certainly didn't like having to come to me and ask nicely to get their needs met.

Their discontentment presented in many different forms but the most difficult were when they would try to rip me off, rob me or beat me up. Like most bullies they tried to extort me but that stopped when I started catching them walking to school alone. They didn't like having big rocks thrown at their heads.

Others tried to strong-arm me or burn me by not paying for the drugs they asked to buy. That didn't work either because they would always want more later and they didn't get "more later" until they paid what they owed. Then they started coming at me in large groups, trying to beat me up and/or steal my drugs. Did I mention how fast I could run yet?

Sometimes I would just be walking home from school and carloads of kids would suddenly come to a screeching halt and yell, "There he is, let's get him!" It happened so often that I actually became traumatized by the sound of cars skidding to a stop. (I still react to cars slowing down behind me while I'm walking.) A few others actually tried to come to my house but they never tried it twice. Home visits didn't happen often because everyone knew about my fondness for my nunchucks, bow & arrow and swords (I often practiced outback).

If you did rip me off or owed me money I'd just walk up to your house and ask your mother if you could come out and play (you know, like in the Warriors movie). Parents would yell, "Some kid named Emmanuel is here he wants you to come out and play." They weren't so brave when they were alone.

My rep for dealing grew quickly after the move back to Cockeysville. Graduating to Dulaney Senior was huge for business. My sister was long gone so the "High" School was all mine. Sure there were other dealers but their branding, marketing and people skills sucked.

To set the stage, imagine if you will a public school that actually had a smoking area for teachers and students. There were no cigarette age laws back then to speak of. There were no health education classes and Nancy had yet to start saying NO!!! It was really easy to make smoking weed look like you were smoking a cigarette. We were all pros at hiding our cigarette smoking and now it was actually ok to smoke at school. Think about it, kids that couldn't smoke at home were allowed to smoke at school. Brilliant right? Just another reason why we all thought that the entire education system was retarded as we sang "Teacher, leave those kids alone" from the latest Pink Floyd album.

My afterschool homework was a little different than yours. While you may have pulled out books and pencils I pulled out baggies and scales. After I counted my earnings for the day, my homework consisted of cutting up weed into nickel and dime bags. I eventually did away with the nickel bags as the business grew. It became dimes and half ounces; ounces were special orders and usually only to the two or three guys I had selling for me. I sold out every day at school so I didn't need to sell quantity. (Not selling ounces meant about 15% more profits.)

ECONOMICS CLASS

Let me explain the economics of late 70s pot dealing. A nickel was $5 but at that time that meant about 3.5 grams. A dime was $10 and amounted to 7 grams and a half ounce weighing 14 grams was $20. A $35 ounce was 30 grams (people got an extra 2 grams for buying bulk when I agreed to sell it that way). When I was done sorting out all the counts they'd be stashed up in the back of my sleeper sofa till morning. There was a really convenient ledge in there that could hold 3 pounds easily. I often forgot my books and gym shoes but I never forgot my weed and some bills to make change.

Since most of us wore pretty tight clothes in those days carrying the weed meant being inventive. Most days this meant 4-6 dimes in my front pants pockets, 2-3 dimes in each sock and 4 dimes in each of my breast shirt pockets. Then a few more counts in my coat that I knew I could distribute before entering the building. There was always a threat of cops training canine dogs during classes so I never left anything in my locker.

Winter was nice because Parka jackets could hold pounds of weed. I remember I used to carry an ounce or two in my hood as it hung down my back. On average I could make $150-250 before noon in 1978 dollars. By contrast my 40 hours at Pebbles would only gross me about $84 a week: I was more than doubling that while at school in a single morning, usually by lunchtime.

As crazy as all this sounds sometime I would need a ride back to my house before lunch to restock. All that cost me was catching someone a buzz. Selling a pound of weed a day was my goal. If I could knock out 1/3 to 1/2 of that before getting home after school it was a very successful day. One-half pound equals 8 ounces with 4 dimes each. Eight times 4 equals $320 by three o'clock. If I managed that then I could just chill and sell from the house. School was great but most of my dealing was actually done from home because most of my customers weren't the academic types. Let's not forget that I still had 3 schools to serve; 4 if the rednecks came down from Hereford and the PA line.

There's a unique feeling you get when you sell drugs to someone that can't find any. They actually respond like you're doing them a favor. Personally, you feel a satisfaction similar to feeding the starving masses. They appreciated you because they knew you took a risk to sell to them; people appreciated dealers for their service. They also knew that any wrongful act or misdeed could mean that you wouldn't sell to them in the future. It was actually quite an interesting relationship dynamic. There was never any doubt that being a dealer gave you the upper hand socially too. Buyer and seller are not equal relationships in the drug trade. The customer wasn't ever right and they didn't expect to be. There were no refunds or guarantees unless you were really into branding. Sadly for the adolescent dealers this dynamic doesn't allow for them to learn the balance of a healthy peer relationship because dealers leapfrog over normal social development. They miss out on the kinds of relationships that develop naturally within the typical give-and-take of an adolescent friendship. Power does corrupt. (Sadly I thrived on the imbalance; it made me feel wanted and accepted.)

SCARED TO DEATH

One night while working at Pebbles Pizza I got a call from one of the guys that moved weed for me. He wasn't the sharpest tool in the shed and he wasn't very good at selling either. Lou shouted for me and I picked up the phone. The dim wit on the phone (Billy P.) said "Man I'm so sorry to hear about your father." I said, "What are you talking about?" He said, "I heard your mother and my mother talking on the phone, they said your father died." Of course, I freaked out. I started crying and made my way into Lou's office. He knew I wouldn't be able to close the store that night so he took me home. I cried the whole way.

My father had been in the hospital but my mother and sister had convinced me not to see him in his dying days. They suggested that my father wouldn't know who I was and that he was so ill-looking that it might be better for me to remember him the way he was. In reality, I have to entertain the idea that my mother was still trying to stick it to my father by withholding me from him. As sick as it sounds my sister was probably trying to keep him to herself.

If you're an emotionally disturbed stoned teenage boy in denial about his father's dying then that all sounds like a great idea. When I got that call it hit me that it was too late to ever see him, I had lost my chance. Worried I would now be alone in this world hurt even more.

My father's being ill was not a secret. He had been dying a slow death from what now looks to have been metastasized lung cancer or lymphoma. (Aside from the weed and cigarettes his time around asbestos in the merchant Marines didn't help.) He had been in the hospital very ill for a while; I thought he was too cool to die.

As mentioned above all this now seems like my mother's last chance to really screw my father for ruining her life with 2 kids. She has never denied that keeping his pride and joy from him while he was dying was the final fuck you. While I may have been smart I was obviously emotionally troubled; I never went to see him. To be clear he was everything to me but I was manipulated by my family and my own fears to act otherwise.

Being convinced that seeing him dying would be too much for me I just hid in the drugs and the dealing. They said I should remember him for the man he was; that his not knowing me would crush me. So for the last months of his life, I didn't see him. While my drug business was growing my father was dying and boy did the Quaaludes help with that.

Returning from work I came through the apartment door and my mother was sitting there on the phone as usual. She knew my schedule and asked; "What are you doing home?" Lou had walked me to the door and then left. In hindsight, I really don't know if she knew I had been crying or not. I cried out; "What am I supposed to do keep working? You can't even call me and tell me my father's dead?" She said: "Your father's not dead Manuel." I was now more confused than ever. "Billy told me you told Sylvia that he died." "No, I didn't, I don't know what the hell he's talking about." Now I didn't know how to feel. (I'm going to go ahead and wager that you've never had that level of dysfunction in your world huh? If you have then we're kindred spirits for sure.)

You can be sure that F-ing dude got a talking to. Unfortunately that's the price you pay for having potheads in your life. My father hung on for another couple weeks. Now E-1 was telling me that his side of the family didn't want me to come down there. After his death, she said they didn't want me to come to the funeral because I didn't visit him. I never got to see him in the end. It was heartbreaking. It made me angry, really angry; a regret that still plagues me to this day.

Not seeing him was probably one of the biggest mistakes of my life. The denial associated with not having that closure with him left me seeing him in crowds for the next 20+ years. I started to believe that the people he knew had helped him get away or that he was in witness protection somewhere. Honestly, I still don't know for certain. Sure people tell me things that they saw but I didn't see those things. That's how well denial, pot, LSD, Quaaludes and booze work (especially together).

CHAPTER EIGHT
GOING THROUGH HELL

SAD AS HELL

As the weeks passed following my father's actual death I grew more and more angry. Not the "phases of grief" kind of angry, more like the "I could explode on someone," kind of angry. My time bomb was ticking faster and louder with each passing day.

People that feel hopeless can be dangerous to themselves and others. Add in some isolation or loneliness and there is no one left to process unreasonable thoughts with. I was feeling very hopeless and very alone. I really didn't care about anything or anyone. In reality, my feelings were merely a reflection of the way I thought the world felt about me. Fairness suggested that "If I don't matter, you don't matter either."

The drugs were good at shutting everything off inside. They helped me shut the doors to my soul; even the dangerous ones. My father had given me meaning by making me feel valued. I always felt as though he was my last hope, my safety net; then he was gone. I know now that the denial and the fear that kept me from seeing him before the big false scare was a defense mechanism. It's simple psychology. My family's suggestion that I not go see him solved my inner conflict and the drugs kept me distracted.

At that age, I couldn't grasp that the drugs had limited potential for making the pain go away. Like most substance users I thought they were magic. I didn't understand that if I continued to use them to self-medicate with that I would eventually need more of them or stronger forms of them to avoid the same pain.

My father's death was a huge blow. He was my guide through this fucked up world and it's fucked up people. (Sorry about the language but those are the best words.) My life experiences thus far convinced me that the world was a miserable place that was only getting worse.

It seemed like the only other good person in the world that cared about me besides my father was my Busha. My father had always told me that my maternal grandmother was an amazing woman that I could go to for love and support. Even with the family animosity he still saw her as a very loving person. Even during the worst of times, all the attacks on him and all the lows of his alcoholism he knew her heart was pure. My problem was that she couldn't understand or even comprehend the world I was living in at the time.

My father was good, not the pay your bills, be sober and support your children kind of good but in the way that always allowed you to believe that you were the most important person in the world to him. He didn't tell you this through money or role modeling he said it straight to your heart with complete candor. He did it from the day I could hear him talk until the last day I saw him. (I do have that.) He used to say to me "You're my favorite pony even if you never win a race."

His moniker for me as a teen was the "42-year-old midget." What that meant to me was that he saw me as an old soul in a kid's body. He made me feel smart. Even as a child he acknowledged and cultivated my intellect. He made me feel special and important. Despite his shortcomings, he was a blessing. Then he fucking left me in this world alone without a real warning that I could see or hear coming. I was furious. Things got very dark. Not the "I don't want to go outside and play or party" kind of dark. It was the "Hey God of the Universe, bring back the flood, I understand why you did it now" kind of dark. "Kill them all, they're all useless and beyond help," kind of dark. It's in moments like these that Grace is most vital. If Grace doesn't show up in these moments people that feel like I did commit things like mass shootings, bombings or driving cars through innocent crowds. I actually had thoughts about introducing something into the entire watershed.

Trust me when I tell you the darkness didn't stop there. My drinking got worse (the weed use was already maxed out,) the Quaalude use got worse, the being short with customers got worse and my attitude towards the cops became very negative. My desire and capacity for revenge on the people that hurt me grew stronger; it became second nature to spite them. I wanted people dead. Not a few of them, all of them, all of you. That's how bad I was hurting and how much I wanted people to hurt with me. (We see these hurt people every day and then act shocked when they act out.)

As early as age 16 I started making arrangements, literally drawing up detailed plans for a cabin in the woods far away from people. Far away from the people that hurt people, people. I can still see the landscape of the hills in my head, even the hill slope that I wanted to build on (I still want that today but for different reasons).

My chemical use was always a way for me to connect to the Universe and even to God at times. When I was dealing drugs the Gods (some of them Greek Gods) were with me, helping me succeed. I didn't care if they felt sorry for me and thereby gave me my drug business or if they were actually my servants. You see, sometimes when you eat a lot of LSD and you have a name like Emmanuel, the idea that you are more than human easily presents itself. I knew I wasn't like everyone else; I had different insights and awareness. I sometimes felt like Christ must have felt when he was left to hang on that cross without rescue. I felt forsaken.

It was like being an egomaniac with an inferiority complex. You shift from being everything to nothing in the blink of an eye. Not a slow bi-polar cycle this was quick, fractions of a second. Was I the son of God or just an immensely powerful spirit? Was I a nut case or blessed? Anyone that knew me in those days knew that there was something else going on inside of me; something spooky, otherworldly, almost psychic.

I can remember a time before my father died when I felt so happy that I actually felt chosen. I'm pretty sure there was even a time when I thought that the pervert who abused me was sent to pleasure me as a servant. (I know, it's getting really dark, right? Hold on.) Believing this I began to wield my sexual power over females. Not just to please them but to somehow metaphorically win my mother's affection by proxy. What I really needed was a female figure to want me around; one that wouldn't leave me or abandon me to the elements of the cruel world and its people.

It turned out that making my female sex partners really want me didn't help me feel worthy at all, only valuable at times. I even began feeling validated that I was Svengali reborn into the modern era of the 60s and 70s sexual revolution.

As you can see the role sex played in my daily life started increasing once my father was gone. I no longer had him to process these things with. I truly believed that my father would have stopped this distorted progression because he was a good man with a good moral compass; amazing considering what he grew up with.

My father spent many hours over many years instructing me on how to see the beauty in women, how to treat a woman and how to stimulate their innate value as people. He taught me that it was a real man's responsibility to make a woman feel really valuable and really relevant: That you had to be there for her through everything. He said that if you could do it they would never leave you and always come back to you. The truth is this is probably how he scored my mother. He had a gift but he was gone now and I'd either be king or nothing. Sometimes I think he wanted me to be better than he was because I had his shoulders to stand on; like making me a great person was his destiny or something.

Let's be very clear here. The girls in my world just gave themselves to me, offered themselves up like sacrificial lambs. Not just little girls my age but all of them. Some of these women were twice my age including my friends' mothers. My sister's friends who were almost all 4 to 10 years older than me would come into my room at night and slide under the covers with me. I never had to push people to be with me.

The dancing of my youth set a great mold for the years to come. I was a moderately attractive person, funny and intelligent, when I wasn't mad or hurt. An Ex used to tell me "God loves you so much" because he gave me gifts and a certain talent for pleasure.

To this day, I have never forced myself on a woman nor have I ever disposed of any of them once we both got what we wanted. My father set a value in me and it was good when I was good but after his death I just didn't care; I became less considerate. My sexual abuse history actually made me quite protective of women because I hated men; most women reportedly felt quite safe in my presence. I was a good person at heart but my heart was sad, injured and neglected. It was damaged and it needed some healing Grace, BAD! My true self was obscured by calamity.

The point of my giving you this background is to show you contrast. That as a young man, teenager, man child, I valued women. I was a very generous person, even when dealing. When my father was taken from me it was as if the Universe had reneged on its deal of "If you are a good person you get a good life." Be good and good things will happen for you. Suddenly that was all a sick lie, a cruel joke, a scam. The omnipotent God they spoke of took my father from me, there was no other explanation. If there was a God he was a dick!

KILLER WEED

It was around this time that the US government started spraying marijuana fields in Mexico and Northern Columbia with Paraquat. For those that don't know Paraquat is a toxic weed killer/herbicide. They used it to kill marijuana on Central American grow farms. It's still sold today but in the late 70s it was used to kill marijuana and to actually make the marijuana into a poison for anyone that smoked it. The US government believed if people got sick from it they would stop buying it. Most of us got quite ill smoking it and who knows what its long-term effects were. It's not like you knew which weed had it and which weed didn't. It's not like those growers weren't going to bag that stuff up and sell it to the Gringos anyway.

The real problem for me was that this government interference started to hurt the availability of my product. No one stopped using weed we just figured that most of it was on the Mexican weed and we thought we could tell the difference. It's simple economics that when a producer of a product stops distribution that strains the pipeline. The South and Central Americans weren't going to stop selling weed to Americans just because it was poisoned. Eventually, the Columbian and the Hawaiian supplies dried up too due to the strain on demand.

All I could feel in those days was betrayed; betrayed by everyone from my father, to the US government, to the South American cartels and especially by God. I remember even considering getting a pilot's license and starting to import my own product but that level of dealing is pretty high up the dealer food chain. I was still too young and I didn't speak Spanish.

GOD DAMN GOD

So I was an abandoned, scarred and wounded child with a broken relationship with God and the Universe. I felt forsaken and I was mad about it. I wanted the world to burn and God wasn't doing his job right. The belief that God himself had abandoned me once again actually made my Emmanuel delusions feel more real. Once again I too, like Christ, had been let down by my father.

I really wanted God to fix all the assholes in the world but what if he couldn't? Who could or would? Maybe God was too nice, too righteous, too loving and way too forgiving. Maybe He was just weak. That's when it got even darker yet!

I had learned how to talk to God but they really weren't prayers that I was saying. My conversations with God were more like a Christmas wish list to Santa. Please get me this and give me that. If you...

If God loved me he'd do the things I wanted right? I was behaving and being nice considering what I had been through. (For me that meant not hurting people or stealing and even being generous.) Isn't that love? Doing nice things for people? Love is an act, right? I was making people cum hard, that's love, right? It was to me. Love is certainly not letting people down when they need you the most. I never let my customers down. (I lived through all of this but reading the story now is quite scary. I know how bad this kid felt and what he was capable of.)

So essentially God wasn't enough. Was there anything left that could help me? Something that could do whatever it took? Was this Trinumerary for real? Did I have the sign of a Warlock on me? What about that devil guy, would he be willing to do things in exchange for reverence toward him?

When most people say they worship God or the devil they mean they make that thing their superior. I viewed myself as a powerful force in the Universe, just currently stuck in this human manifestation form which limited my energy and power. (I told you it would get dark.) I believed that I could vacate this world quite quickly if I wanted to and then the "forces that be" would have to deal with me on a level playing field.

Maybe you're getting curious so here's my conception of hell: One that still rings true today. When you die and someone on Earth or in human form hates you, you feel that hate and you can't undo the hurt so you suffer. If they want you to suffer after your death, you feel the burn, you're in hell. Hell is manifested upon you by their hate, hurt and anger. You're dead but you can see their hate and even feel their hurt but you can't shut it off. You're forced to experience it as long as they want you to; for as long as they do. You can't go back and change it, only know it and feel it forever!! Hell is in essence manifested by our negative actions and misdeeds upon others. At that time I believed that Heaven worked the same way, we see all the good we did and get to live with that too, for eternity; that's Heaven.

Hell is eternal and since you can't go back to fix it you spend eternity suffering for the hurt you caused. If you do a lot of bad things on Earth you will leave behind a lot of hurt that you'll feel forever. There is no fixing it once you die, it's too late. As long as someone you hurt is suffering you will feel that energy in the afterlife. If someone living wants you to feel that pain and they want for you to feel it then you feel it even more intensely. That's what makes forgiveness so priceless. Forgiveness is Grace, a grace that we can give one another any time we

105

want. It's an even greater gift when it's undeserved. It's so great it can even free people from hell.

Want to guess who I was mad at? OK, not who but one of the people? If you guessed dear old dad for leaving me here alone you nailed it. You see I always knew my mother wasn't going to help me so he was my only hope and I was sure he knew it. One of my biggest heartbreaks was that my father's side of the family didn't fight to see me. They didn't demand visitation or even call me to give me their condolences for the loss of my father. The truth is it felt like they didn't want me to be a part of their family anymore; that they had kicked out the little ½ white kid.

Suddenly every failing that my father had been accused of became real to me; I had somehow forgotten every good thing. My confusion began with, "Why have you left me here with her" (E1) and then it became, "Why have you left me here with them" (the entire world of assholes)? Then it became "I hope you rot in hell you son of a bitch and I hope you feel the burn for leaving me here. I want you to suffer for what you did to me; for bringing me here to this world in the first place."

Sadly I think he did feel it, what soul wouldn't. Suddenly I had learned how to hate in the world of the spirit. No one or nothing that got in my way would be spared my wraith. I remember praying for Armageddon; a real FTW approach. THAT'S ANGRY RIGHT???!!! I wanted everyone to suffer. My misery wanted company. (Sound familiar?)

I was so angry and so filled with hate that I used to come home from school, use whatever drugs I could find and just hate in a meditative lotus position for hours on end. Then I added candles and incense, then the black candles, black incense, Black Sabbath and Judas Priest music and anything I could learn about demonic power, even spells from books. I never considered myself a witch I was beyond that already. My father, my sister and I all had what used to be termed the mark of the devil. The witch world used to call it a trinumerary but most people in the medical field today call it a supernumerary. It is the presence of a tiny third nipple just below the left one. Legend says it's where the devil gets to feed. (I confess I have to giggle when I think of some of the people that might be reading this right now. I think you should keep reading and learn about the Grace part. Remember, the Saints are the sinners that kept trying.) The supernumerary nipple was once thought to be the sign of a witch or warlock. I just thought of it as validation. A witch named Emmanuel, think of the irony.

As fate would have it my sweet 16 and I broke up (Imagine that, smart girl). She later told me that she had essentially been date raped by a loser named Doug who was staying next door to her with another family. I had met him before and I took his action as a personal affront; as disrespect to both her and me. I didn't allow males to hurt females and he had the nerve to do this to a person I still cared about. I could have been at that very party that night but I had to work instead. (I had already supplied the guy that hosted the party and most of his friends.)

Suddenly I had a direct focal point for all my anger. If I could have found him I might have beat him to death. Of course, I also had people willing to help and some that I could pay but this was personal. I was so angry at this time that even the devil was coming up short when it came to meeting my needs. I saw the devil as lacking imagination and as much of a failure as God. I remember pointing down at the ground and saying to whatever was supposedly there; "Mother fucker you don't want me dead, if I die I'm coming the fuck down there and I'm taking the fuck over you loser son of a bitch." I would think; Damn it, can anybody do their job right? Does anyone do what they're supposed to do?" How angry and dark is that? You can bet your life I believed every word of it. I had no fear about the chicken shit devil taking me out. After all, he was the world's greatest loser.

So since no one else could do their job right it was on me. Doug disappeared and could not be found, no one knew where he was; I looked. I decided that since I couldn't find Doug that I would just start visualizing his death, in essence praying for him to die. I did this every morning and every day after school. Black Sabbath playing, black candles and black incense burning and me sitting in the lotus position in a dark room; high on whatever I could find, even tripping sometimes. I would visualize him just being torn apart from the inside out: Day after day after day.

It was 68 days later on a Friday when I had talked to my ex-girlfriend's next-door neighbor Billy (the guy Douglas stayed with sometimes). He matter-of-factly said, "Did you hear what happen to Douglas?" I said, "No what happened to that asshole?" almost forgetting all my hard work. He said, "He was robbing a house in the afternoon and the cop that lived there was home sleeping. He got shot 6 times, he's dead."

I admit that for a brief second, I got scared. Could there be this much power out there that no one was tapping into? Could I have this much power and ability? In the days of Uri Geller I had always dreamed of telekinesis but this might be even better than that. I took a breath and owned that shit! Even more scary than all of that was I then thought, let's test this stuff out, who's next? (There were a few.)

My negative attitude and mood continued to decline and I felt more emboldened than ever. If the men in this world were going to try to take my women from me then I was going to take theirs; whenever I wanted. I might even just eliminate anyone in my way. I stopped caring if they had boyfriends and just started calling all their little boyfriends "pussies with little dicks." I didn't care if they heard about it either. I was truly one angry son of a "BITCH" with a death wish. BRING IT!!! I wanted someone to take me out but it was like something otherworldly was protecting me.

I obviously had trust and other issues so Karen and I moved on from one another. I think she may have seen some of the darkness and she didn't seem to have the heart for it. A girl I had a crush on named Wendy kept going back to her "little dick boyfriend" (she never denied it). I started trying to charm Karen again, flirting with her on the phone and her new boyfriend found out. He was friends with Wendy's midget man so they conspired together to come to my house to beat me up. They were afraid to take me on alone so they came together.

One school night at about 10:00pm the jealous boys came over to our apartment and knocked on the bedroom store window. I didn't know what they wanted but since I didn't like either one of them I came outside; they weren't coming in. As usual, I was lit up on some weed, some booze and even a few Quaaludes. When I stepped outside into the dark night from the lit-up apartment all I saw was a big black dot. I was trying to compose myself while listening to their whining about their girlfriends when BAM!!! Something struck me in the face. When I gathered myself they were halfway to their car. They knew there would be some hell to pay, so they ran, like pussies.

I remember going back into the house, going into the bathroom to see where the blood was coming from. I started picking out pieces of my teeth from my mouth and like some demented psycho in a movie, I just started laughing. Not at my teeth, but at the fact that they were so threatened by me that they had to come together and sucker punch me. (Suddenly I mattered. My relevancy was more important than my teeth.) What they didn't know at the time was that this was actually going to make me points with the very girls they wanted me to stay away from. The truth is I was only interested in the one that I hadn't "had" yet. Pussy Joe disappeared shortly afterward; he ran away only to become a crackhead. The other one went on to spend the rest of his life learning how to fight. Since he wasn't the one that struck me we were able to eventually become civil towards one another. (The world kept spinning.)

DECKING THE HALLS

Most families have holiday traditions and just because you're matriarch is evil doesn't mean you hate Christmas. While sometimes twisted, even dysfunctional families have holiday traditions. Since dear old Evil-One wasn't interested in participating with her children my sister and I started making up our own family festivities. The John kids weren't going to give up on a beautiful holiday like Christmas just because Evil slept in the big bedroom. We just acted as if she was on another trip and did things our way.

When my father was still alive he started his own Christmas tradition by giving us Christmas on Thanksgiving. I think it started one year when he got us for Thanksgiving and not for Christmas. Everyone knew that he really disliked the commercialization of Christmas; especially if he had a good buzz. He used to say that Christmas (Xmas) wasn't a time for gifts it was about God, so he decided that we would start doing gifts on Thanksgiving instead. He thought it would teach us about gratitude. I remember him saying we can't do it on God's (he meant Jesus') actual birthday in January because E-1 would say he's just being a bum and late with the presents. (He had that right but she still found a way to criticize this choice too.)

More for appearance's sake than of spirit, E-1 made sure that some form of a tree was in place. She bought a fake tree as a backup in case none of her dates brought us a real one. My sister and I created our own special holiday tradition that lasted for about 3 or 4 years. My cousin's old standby Flakes (PCP) was still popular. (That's the same drug my cousin once sold that my father warned me about?) It smelt like pine needles when you smoked it so boom, it's a Christmassy drug.

Along with a little Cocaine (Snow) one of us would also find a "can" of flakes (it came in 30mm film can-ister). Since I had the South Baltimore connection I got the flakes and she got the Coke. We would snort and smoke while alternating putting things on the tree. I have no memory of E-1 participating in any tree decorating after age 13. She was always out celebrating with the people she really cared about or at some guy's parent's house. When she would forget to buy a real tree or when she couldn't talk some dude into buying one she'd just pull the fake tree out of the storage locker. In those days they didn't have the spray smell for the fake trees so the flakes really brought in that sensory experience. She would drop the tree box in the living room along with the boxes of bulbs and say; "Set it up if you want a tree." Then she'd head out for who knows how long.

GRACED

The flakes did actually help that fake tree seem real; I think it even moved sometimes in the non-existent wind. I remember at one point we started calling it the "Flake Christmas Tree." We would laugh and she would wonder what was so funny, thinking it was a snowflake reference.

Everyone knew about how dangerous flakes were but Robert T and I used them quite often. Robert had become one of my closest friends after he moved up from South Baltimore. (It wasn't like the rich kids were going to befriend the poor kid coming up from 1970s Federal Hill.)

There was one exchange that made me think that I did actually have a real friend in Robert. When you're a dealer people are more interested in what you can do for them than for who you are to them. It happened one day during the paraquat months when we were experiencing what was known as a dry spell. Sometimes this happened as the result of the growing season changes in South America but sometimes it could also just be the result of supply and demand issues. This particular spell was related to both.

It was early one morning, about 11:30am when Robert called and asked the party code line; "What are you UP to?" I said nothing, meaning nothing for the head, no drugs to use. I remember being a little stunned when he said, "That don't matter we can still hang out." It actually took me a minute to grasp the concept. At that point in my life (around age 16) most of my interactions with both family and peers had to do with chemicals or sex; some type of a quid-pro-quo exchange (like me with the Flakes and my sister with the Coke).

I hadn't "just ridden bicycles together" with anyone for years and that's basically what Robert was offering. In essence, he was saying that we could be bored together. Needless to say, my thirst for just this kind of acceptance and value had me quickly place Robert at the top of a short list of my favorite humans. The fact that he had Greek blood made it even more real for me.

Being friends with Robert meant his two Greek uncles Nicky and Cleppy E came along. They were about 10 years older and were much larger human beings. Having them around gave other competitors and rivals something to think about before they would try anything stupid. They were large dudes that were happy to sit around and party. They were also the above contact for those great inner-city flakes and an occasional bag of weed when things were super dry. They were also good customers. I'm pretty sure that Robert was there for one or two of the Flake Christmas Tree decorating ceremonies but that drug made memories really easy to forget. What I haven't forgotten was his friendship during those dark days. Grace comes in many forms.

CHAPTER NINE
SMOKE FILLED

THE HIGH WAY

In between the dealing, sex, hating, worshipping and getting stoned I was pretty creative. I liked singing but I also liked to draw and design things. Clueless to the neglect I had experienced the school administration believed that my creative side was why I acted out. They encouraged my art, cooking and interest in architecture. Being practical as I was, I took their advice and I used my skills to draw my own bong designs before I made them. I always liked drafting and architecture so why not put it to good use.

I would use the drawings I made to figure out the size of all the clear tubes I needed to get from the hardware store. I would go to the store with a list of tube sizes and the guy would cut up all my pieces for my bongs. Once I got them home all I had to do was drill a few holes, sand and glue them together. I thought it was funny watching the old hippy-hating curmudgeon unwittingly make my bongs for me. It was hilarious down on the inside.

One of my coolest designs was hung on my wall; I titled it "The E.J. Way." It was a combination of glass, plastic, metal and ceramic. Add the water and fire to the bowl and you had all the elements. As cool as it was the bong is fairly irrelevant to this story. What I ended up doing was unwittingly creating an alias for myself. A few people saw the picture on my bedroom wall and started calling me E.J. It was brilliant and worked as a great alias. It was an alias I needed. I lived in a very white neighborhood where most of the kids had rehashed Irish Catholic and German names like Ed, Charles, Kevin and William. The name Emmanuel was treated like an ethnic foreign name at the time; almost not American. It was almost exclusively used by Greeks at the time.

If I was trying to brand back in those days the name Emmanuel would have been great but I was a criminal drug dealer. My name was a problem so my new alias was very welcome (just like my grandfather's at the port). In no time at all everyone was calling me "E.J." I saw it as a sort of backward stab at the rich titan J.R. from the brand-new series Dallas. It fit because I was the man and I had a lot of money.

BUSINESS WAS BOOMING

It was around this time that the structure of my business started to take on a larger scale. I knew about the different levels of drug sellers and the differences between sellers and dealers. I was at the turning point where I would have to decide what type of dealer I wanted to be.

Unbeknownst to many there are 4 main types of drug sellers. The first and the lowest level of drug seller sells drugs to keep themselves in supply of the same drug that they like to use. It's a way of covering the costs of using and essentially getting free drugs in the process. They're usually small-time and don't really turn much of a profit. They just save a lot of money and rarely run out.

The next and almost parallel seller sells drugs for more than just personal supply. This level of drug seller has learned that there are certain social advantages to selling drugs. This seller sells for what some people now call cred. It's a small level of social power that often grows over time if they don't get caught or robbed because their profile has become too high. They usually develop a loyal following of 3-6 buyers with some random sales too.

There are also many sexual benefits to selling drugs. Many females (and now males) are willing to trade sex for drugs. Some females even like the attention of "their man" having the social cred so they'll intentionally date dealers (so they don't run out either). They also benefit from the lifestyle perks of money, party invites and social status.

The next level of drug sellers learns through trial and error to never sell what they use: Not if they want to make money that is. Their priority has shifted from partying to making cash. This seller/dealer learns that business and pleasure don't mix. They usually sell products to keep themselves in a lifestyle that includes most of the previous levels. This seller however is still a wanna-be drug dealer because they're usually still taking huge risks by exposing themselves to arrest. His/her customer base is considerably larger than the previous sellers. The more change of hand transactions there are the more chances of getting caught. (Snitches rarely get stitches they usually just get reduced charges and plea deals.) Often times this level dealer has a few run-ins with the cops because they know about his/her activity; even where s/he does their transactions. This is where I was at this time but I was beginning to wise up.

The top-level drug dealer is the real drug dealer. They're not in it for the fame, juice, cred, drugs, or sex. This dealer moves past all that by letting other people take all the risks; that's what they're paid for. This is the real status dealer that I was becoming. What happens is one of your "boys" lets it be known that he's selling your brand. (He has your permission to do that.) Since he's doing the deals your risk is lowered. (Cops knowing that it's your drugs is hearsay under the law.) Sometimes people know what he's selling because he travels around with you. He's often asked to do the deals while in the same room. He gets his credibility lent to him.

In some circles, your "boy" may wear a piece of jewelry or clothing that covertly states his allegiances. He knows and you know that he will never get caught scoring from you. He is always watching his own back, mostly to protect his back from you. Working for someone also gives him some protection from being robbed. What this does is let people know that there are actual standards for quality, count and availability. It is a budding organized criminal network. (Sometimes people would come to me and tell me when counts were dropping. That usually meant I had to give them something extra to make them happy; to support the brand. This usually happened because the lower-level guy was using too much of what he was selling.)

These so-called "boys/henchmen" are not allowed to rip people off with bad counts because it's not their brand they're hurting. You might think of it as a franchise with standards and products via a single supplier. Sometimes they have the money to start out and sometimes they don't. This requires people to front them the drugs on credit. This usually happens because you're tired of him coming to you with a lot of little deals; almost pestering you. This credit is where some people can get into a lot of trouble if they don't pay back the money for the fronted drugs in a timely manner. (This is often the reason why little rich kids come crying to their parents for money that they owe the drug man.)

The top-level dealer takes almost no risk because there is no chance that they're going to be busted making a public transaction or deal. Real dealers know everyone they're transacting with. The lower-level "dealers" (slingers is a more recent term) are aware of the consequences of talking too much. There is an attrition process whereby the weaker henchmen or soldiers fade away or are just outright fired, sometimes even beaten up and let go.

I fondly remember some incidences early on when I found it necessary to do my own enforcing. Scarily there was a part of me that enjoyed it; it was like hunting human prey. It always seemed like such a righteous empowering act to threaten someone you had done a favor for by setting them up in business. Most of them knew when they were wrong; their sudden absence was a sign they were screwing up.

STACKS

My drug earnings peaked when I was around 16. I was on pace to make about $250k in 1979 dollars. It was about a ¼ million when millionaires were few and far between. I was making 5 and even 10 times what the cops were making and they hated me for it. Not surprisingly it was in that same year that I found myself back in another Vice Principal's office but by this time I was just too good for them to catch.

The Vice Principal (Ms. Thomas) moved schools when I did. I used to jokingly say that since she was the only rational person they had on staff that they moved her to Dulaney High School to deal with me. Ms.

Thomas was a good lady with a lot of Grace. She worked hard to help me find a good path. She openly acknowledged my intellect. In fact, she was responsible for the IQ testing they did on me and for sharing the results with my "mother" and me. She started having me tested back in the 7th grade. I was tested in every grade from 7th to 10th. The lowest score I ever had was 136 and the highest (while actually being high) was 152. (I hid that nugget on the inside two but I'm not sure having that information helped me out any.) I already thought I was smarter than most people and now I had proof. My intellect was one of the few things I ever received validation for as a child.

I remember Ms. Thomas sitting me down one Spring day during the 10th grade as she tried to rationalize with me, sincerely trying to convince me to stop selling drugs. She used to tell me, "There is so much you can do with your life; you can become anything you want." I would think, not a poor kid like me, I was born into the wrong family. The rich folks would never let a guy like me in the door to wealth: They had already proven that.

It was still 1979 and I asked her; "Seriously Ms. Thomas, how much do you make a year, 22 thousand?" By the look on her face, I nailed it. I then said, "Do you realize that I can make that in a month if I want to, half in your school." It actually took her a minute to compose herself. I don't think she was ready for that number, or maybe just not for me to admit it (hearsay).

Sadly she didn't have a comeback. Believe it or not, in that moment, I was waiting and even hoping for a realistic option. I desperately wanted an adult to make sense for once. She did the best she could. She told me to think hard about what I was doing, and whom I was hurting. I never went back to grade school after the 10th grade. I saw no value in it. I wasn't going to make more money their way and at that time in my life money was all that mattered to me. That's the scar that forms in those moments of being poor and hungry while trying to steal food. Violating morals to eat teaches you that morals are kind of dumb. I watched my mother sacrifice us for money. How could money not be important to me? (That's why some scarred people become thieves.)

The following school year came around and I was planning on returning to school for the 11th grade but I got a letter instead of my school schedule in the mail. It said that I had not returned my books and would have to pay $12 for them. I could have paid the fine but I actually did return my books to the front office where the lady told me to set them on the counter; that she would check them in. Apparently, she didn't. This was the straw that broke the camel's back for me. The system was screwing up once again. I just couldn't trust it.

THE COPS KNEW TOO

As I write this I know that the people who I grew up with in Cockeysville will be smiling as I say that I sold a lot of my product through my bedroom window. There is a joke in the area that 40 years later the grass still isn't growing under the path to my old room. In fact, a small-time seller and budding musician moved into my old apartment years after I lived there. He would tell me about people always knocking on the window trying to buy weed. He actually started a small business there and would sell out just from walk-up sales alone. (I still think Paul owes me some commissions.)

While I was in that apartment my long and somewhat shocking relationship with the Baltimore County Police Department really took off. Cops notice traffic patterns with people and my window was very obvious. In those days lots of people had long hair and having long hair meant you partied. On rainy days the hippy lampshade floppy hats would come out and people became much harder to identify.

Their surveillance started with a single cop car stationed on the closest street to my house (Sorley Rd,) only about 225 feet from my bedroom window. All that really meant was that the people who wanted to buy some weed would have to come inside to make the deal. People would call me up on the phone and say, "I was going to come over but there was a cop by your house." (There were no cell phones then so they usually had to drive to a phone booth.) I would ask matter-of-factly, how many (cops)? When they said one, I would say it's cool but you'll have to stay for a bit. Their staying for a bit just meant they'd be getting me and my friends high off the weed they just bought from me. Along with my own creations I was known for having a really nice bong collection too. That became a great sales gimmick. The 32-inch toke master was a favorite for the people that couldn't hide one from their parents. I think it made the pot seem stronger too. Then there was the Capital Hill and then of course my own inventions and designs. (I may still have a career in that field. Any manufacturers that want to "capitalize" on bong sales with a special author's collection just give me a call.)

At one time I had about 14 bongs. Let that sink in; I was a 15-year-old kid living with an adult that allowed these things to sit out in the open. These bongs sat out on the table and the smoke was so thick that my mother would scream to open the window. She knew what was going on and she didn't even smoke. I think she thought that as long we weren't bothering her then she didn't care what we did. I remember her yelling; "If you're gonna be selling that shit in my house you're gonna start paying rent." So I paid her hush money and she did.

I know it sounds egotistical but some people just loved the opportunity to hang out with me and party in THE ROOM. (That is how people referred to it.) I will try to explain the impression The Room left but it's hard. It really was something special; functional art, an optical fantasy land. I had drawn out trees on the walls to enhance the Roger Dean style posters, reflective sunglass walls and ceilings, a huge American flag and contoured netting that molded out the corners creating amazing optical effects. There were strobe lights, black lights, candles and one of the best sound systems for miles around. In fact, you could hear my stereo from more than ¼ mile away. I promise you that unless you were in there you've never experienced anything like THE ROOM. (Any interior designers that want to start a special Emmanuel Designs line should…. Kidding, sort of.)

Most Friday and Saturday nights in the room were set aside for close friends and dealers that I supplied. It was all very organized. Eventually, it became a habit to discuss and plan these evenings on Mondays after realizing the amazing "high times" we had had there. The less we could remember the better it was. Our recall usually started with waking up on Sundays and piecing together the events of the weekend by phone. Sometimes it was a group effort because people often passed out/crashed on the floor.

One Halloween night we all got so high we lost Wormo's car. We had to borrow his father's to drive around 3 towns trying to figure out where we left it. It only took 4-5 hours but we had party supplies so it wasn't too bad. Wormo was afraid that his father would actually kill him. (Turned out years later Wormo was the actual killer of his baby's momma. He got caught and then hung himself in jail. Seems John's father had scarred him with the physical abuse that he carried forward to his partner. Most people don't outlive their scars. Many scars don't have time to heal; his didn't.)

BLINDED BY SCIENCE

Our weekend party nights looked something like this. We would gather at 7:00pm. We would all eat our first Quaalude then smoke the best weed we had for about a ½ hour, all while listening to trippy tunes. Around 8:00 we would eat a hit of Acid (LSD, green dragon was a favorite). Over the next 4 hours we'd smoke regular weed and drink some Jack Daniels, Southern Comfort, Rum or Blackberry brandy. (Black Berry Brandy was a trip when you were tripping, especially on cold nights. You could feel that warm stuff move throughout your entire body.) At Midnight when the Acid had passed its peak we'd take another Quaalude to ease the acid crash. I'm pretty sure that we are the generation that actually invented the term "better living through chemistry."

Oh yeah, the buzz kill fuzz. Since business was slower on the weekends the cops had other things to do. All I wanted to do on the weekend evenings was party and I didn't want to have to do math when I was high; I certainly wouldn't cut out counts high. I required customers to come early if they wanted anything; it worked well since most people wanted their weekend party supplies long before the weekend started.

When we were trippin or really high we got into the habit of doing what we used to call "spacewalks." After weeks of listening to the latest Rush, Yes, Pink Floyd, or Zeppelin albums we started venturing outside to take a trip while trippin. (That was a really funny thing to say back then, when you were tripping, as long as you didn't trip and fall.)

The LSD we used wasn't the crap that's out there today. I would get our acid from the chemist an hour after it was made. Most of the chemists wanted to trade it for pot or hash so we had a great arrangement. While there was still some Mr. Natural going around we did mostly blotter and some microdot. The Green Dragon blotter was the best, probably because it was fresh. (LSD has a short shelf life.)

We would often lick the edge and then rub it directly into our eyes. A trick we learned from the Chocolate Mescaline days. Twenty minutes after eating the acid we could set a Coke bottle (16oz glass) on the table, stare at it, then have a group hallucination when the bottle melted into the table. We were long past random face melting by this time, we wanted to control it; at least I did.

Spacewalking became a bigger thing as tripping became second nature. During the winter months, we would often go on spacewalks in the snow; that's where the Blackberry Brandy really came in handy. (Crunching snow under your feet is a crazy experience when you're on good LSD.)

During the summer pool hopping was the thing and it was easy to do because the area had about 10 different apartment complexes. As luck would have it our apartment was right across the street from our Club House. We figured out we could get in by climbing the roof and going in through a skylight. This allowed us to party for hours uninterrupted. We'd have fun playing "2 minutes in the closet" and "spin the bottle" or we'd just dry hump each other on the sofas. The sex often spilled over into the pool when we were skinny dipping or when the girls were showing off their pre-thong underwear.

That January I attained a new 98 Rock calendar so I decided to keep track of all the LSD trips we took that year. Want to guess? I personally tripped 47 times in that one year with a total of about 127 hits of LSD (I still have the calendar). I mostly tripped with other people but sometimes I did it alone; the alone times were spiritual in nature as I sought to gain more metaphysical powers. In those days psychologists said that 7 LSD trips meant you were clinically insane. (I'm not sure they told their test subjects that though.) I just figured the sanity ship had sailed the day I was born into a family of people wanting me dead, involved in organized crime or just plain didn't want me.

It wasn't just my sister that wanted me dead either. Later in my 30's my mother made it really clear to me that if abortion was legal at the time that I would've never been born. Not sure whether that would have been a good idea or not. It might have prevented my suffering but as I started experiencing both Grace and non-chemical Bliss later in life I became very happy that I wasn't murdered. (See how the scars pop out in life? Just when you think they're all healed up. Now I have to consider if the world would've been better off without me.)

Oh yeah, the Cops. Sadly many a pool party's buzz was interrupted by the "fuzz." This usually happened when someone having sex near a window or outside would see the cops and scream COPS!! We were so fast that they never caught us. I remember one night we were running across the pool yard and a cop yelled, "Get them they're coming around the other side, freeze." We all stopped running, looked at the cop on the other side of the fence at the opposite end of the pool and laughed. "Dude! We know you're alone," then like gazelles, we leaped over the 6-foot chain link fence without a care in the world. Still taunting the cop as we ran, flipping him the bird while grabbing our crotches in full 70s style.

Sure, they knew who we boys were but we knew and they knew we knew, that if they didn't catch us in there they wouldn't have a good case against us. Motion lights and security cameras weren't around then; so it was a catch them doing it or run them off scenario. They knew that nothing was really going to happen to us and they didn't want to do the paperwork.

I eventually stopped running from the cops unless I was trespassing or carrying drugs. We'd be outside partying, the cops would come and everyone else would run but I'd just stand there and wait. (I made my boys carry for me. I would actually stay to distract the cops.) The cops would come running up to me, sometimes they even ran past me. I'd just stand there and say, "Can I help you?"

By this point, my Pizza business people skills coupled with my Eddie Haskel con man tact made me quite the smart ass. A cop once stopped 6 inches from my face and asked me; "Why aren't you running?" I said, "Because I'm not doing anything wrong, I live here." He said, "Why did your friends run then?" I said, "They're very athletic!" We all laughed and,,, No OK, I was the only one laughing and it was on the inside too.

The law was definitely not an alien entity to my family. Years earlier my father instructed me how to manage the cops after I told him about running from them all the time. He asked me why I was running; he said it makes you look guilty. This strategy worked but it didn't stop the cops from becoming very resentful of the little smart-ass skinny punk kid. I have no idea if those cops ever looked into my father. Pretty sure my mother would have just hit on them if they had rank so....

One cop lived about 150 yards behind me in the same apartment complex. He wasn't just a cop he was the local Lieutenant. His stepdaughter "A" used to party with us a lot. He became very annoyed by me as you might imagine. He knew that she was getting high somewhere and I was essentially right next door. He began a crusade against me; a very aggressive campaign at that. This included the 24-hour surveillance of my house that I mentioned earlier. Now when someone would call and say they wanted to stop by but they saw cops, I would just ask "how many," because there were sometimes 2 or more. When they were three

I'd just tell them to call me back in a bit. We knew everything about the cops; how many were on duty, when they changed shifts, where and when they ate lunch etc... We also knew where some of them were having affairs and where they would pull over to sleep in their cars at night. Some people would throw rocks at those cars but I figured it was better to just let sleeping cops lie. We had all this data without cell phones or the internet. We may have invented social networking in order to stay out of jail.

I guess one might think I was a little passive-aggressive but it seemed more like cosmic synchronicity to me. As fate would have it about a month after the Lt. started crowding me with his stakeouts his daughter invited me over to their house to catch her a buzz while she was forced to babysit. After helping myself to some of his food I wandered back into his bedroom. I was searching the place for weapons in a gun case or on the walls when my eyes met hers. She had followed me into her parent's room so I asked. Can we have sex on their bed? She said, "Heck yeah, it's better than mine." She gave her little sister an ice cream and put her in front of the TV.

I have to admit that some of these serendipitous opportunities started to freak me out a little bit; made me start considering things like fate and predestination, even being chosen or special somehow. That's what happens when you eat a lot of LSD. Sometimes it just felt like there was some kind of powerful force on my side setting these things up for me. Since these events often seemed a little spiteful in nature I assumed that those dark energies I had tapped into were just working better than I thought. That or it was my dead father trying to make amends.

I was smart enough to know that it could just be all the LSD we took but still, it was like too fortunate or something; especially for me. When you've had a life like mine you never expected easy; feeling a sense of support was just outright freaky. Things went so well for a short time I actually began to consider that there might be a God out there helping me succeed; like he felt guilty about all His other mistakes. Back and forth it went. I felt kind of chosen at times but then jinxed at others. Trust me, being a traumatized kid named Emmanuel and eating LSD does all sorts of stuff to your head.

One day I was walking with two of my lower-level sellers to the store to get cigarettes when the Big Man Lt L. rolled up on us. (A second car had two of his henchmen.) They wanted information about some car break-ins but I obviously wasn't going to tell them anything. I knew who did what where in those days because I would trade weed for some of the stuff they stole. I liked watches and jewelry.

My failure to play his game made Lt L. mad because he knew I knew everything that happened in that part of town. He made some idol threats then as I walked away pissed off I said. "Hey Lieutenant L, I really like those lace sheets you have on your bed, "A" showed them to me. Real Cute! Nice bed too, good springs." He knew exactly what I meant and I think for a split second I made two friends with the other two cops as they couldn't stop smirking and looking away. I heard one say, "I see why you have it out for him now."

All in a day's work my friends, but yeah, scary considering I was just 16. As crazy as it might sound he kind of left me alone shortly after that. Probably so he didn't kill me or have his own daughter get caught up in a bust. I had no fear; I just chalked it up as a victory.

Perhaps it was the Quaaludes that gave me that confidence; they were GREAT for eliminating fear, that's what sedatives do. There was one last rush at me before the surveillance stopped. I'm pretty sure he was getting flack from his bosses for wasting resources on me and getting nowhere. Their failures left me feeling like a natural at this organized crime thing; like it was in my blood. They weren't finished quite yet.

BAD TRIP

I did have one really bad trip while dealing but it didn't have anything to do with LSD. It seems that being the only guy in town with product can make you popular with the wrong people. Not everyone is willing to observe protocol, especially other dealers that have been losing money to you.

I was walking home from the store one night when 4 black guys from the country that I knew by name pulled up in a conversion van. They called my name and inquired about buying some weed. I knew they weren't cops but I was a little uneasy about their tone. A dealer doesn't always have a choice to sell. If people know you have product and you decide not to sell to them they can just rob you. It's not like you can call the cops. If you're unarmed and they are armed then things get really dicey. This was one of those times.

I asked how much they wanted and they asked how much I had. BAD QUESTION! (I had an ounce cut up in dimes.) They strongly suggested I join them in the van to get out of plain sight. NOT SOMETHING YOU WANT TO DO! Once I entered they asked to see the counts. BAD REQUEST! I showed them the counts and then they said thanks. BAD MANNERS!

I tried to get my product back but they weren't going to comply. One of the guys reminded the others that I was friends with another family in the area and that they'd be mad about them taking my shit. Then they started driving me out towards the country. BAD NEWS! Things get even worse when people start talking about you like you're not there and in the past tense. They drove and drove further away from the populated areas and then down a few dirt roads. There was talk about what to do with me as we came to a stop near a steep hill. I was instructed to get out of the van. The dude with the gun seemed pretty certain of his next move and he stopped looking me in the eyes. BAD SIGN!

Then suddenly the guy with the gun said, "You're lucky you're friends with the _'s." They then got in the van, closed the door and drove off leaving me in some dark part of the woods I was not familiar with. All I could do was start walking in the direction the van came from. Miles and miles down dark country roads with no lights, just a full moon. I was a long-haired hippy dude walking down redneck roads before rednecks had hair. After walking a few miles in the dark and the Grace of a farmer willing to pick up a stranger hitchhiking I made it home 6 hours later. Being embarrassed I never told anyone but Randy who said he would try to get me my money. All he got was a, "We won't bother him again." That was good enough for me.

HASHING THINGS OUT

A couple weeks later Randy and I left school with our friend Ron who had a car (he lived in Summer Hill with his upper-middle-class family). At the time hash and hash oil were all the rage because they were the strongest forms of THC you could get. For hash, the preferred method of administration was smoke under glass. For those less familiar "smoke under glass" is when you take a telephone book and a sewing needle, you stick the needle through the top 50 pages of the book so that it faces up on the table. You take a large chuck of hash, stick it on the needle and light it. You then cover it with the glass from an old lantern and place another book on top of that. You let the smoke fill the glass until the glowing hash coal is almost snuffed out. You move the book, place your face on the top of the glass, lean in, tilt the glass and hoowoop! You get one huge intense hit from a very potent form of cannabis.

If that didn't light your fire then the hash oil technique was next level from that. In those days' coke bottles had metal caps. People would remove the plastic liner from the inside of the cap and then measure out hash oil (extract) for sale by weight. Some people referred to the count as a Cap or Lid (not to be confused with a lid of weed). You would use a pair of roach clips (forceps) or pliers to hold the cap then hold a lighter under it until it started smoking. Then you would just use a straw to take a hit as the smoke burned off. Hash oil was about 32-36% THC so it was strong, real strong.

Randy, Ron and I were getting lit up. Randy was less aggressive with drugs than Ron and I so he paused to take a walk out into the living room because he thought he heard a noise. He suddenly came rushing back into the room with a horrified look on his face. We thought he was goofing around and then he said. "I know you're not going to believe me but THE COPS ARE HERE!" My first thought was he meant in the apartment. I said loudly, IN THE HOUSE? He whispered no, out back. In a whisper he said, "I asked them what they wanted and they said they wanted to talk to you." (Pretty sure this is still the fastest way to lose a buzz known to man.)

While most of the cops knew Randy's family he was still a black kid in a known "white" home, during a school day, in a mostly white town, in 1979. I stood up, took a few breaths then walked out to the living room. I didn't see anything until I noticed that the curtains at the sliding glass door were now closed as if to block out light. I thought Randy was playing around (because we thought cops were funny). Then I saw the arm patch between the curtains. I walked toward the door without a care in the world as if everything was on the up and up. I knew my rights and I knew their limits. I certainly knew about probable cause and warrants but I wasn't sure they didn't have one.

I asked the 5 cops my usual annoying question. "Can I help you?" They didn't bother asking if I lived there because they all knew me. There was a knock on my front door so I asked them; "Is that you?" They radioed those cops to stand down. By "all" I mean ALL 8 OF THEM. I found that interesting but I didn't flinch. "We got a call about a possible break-in." Shaking my head I said no, thinking about Randy. Such a lame excuse I thought. They then said, "There was a guy that someone reported trying to get into your window." I just smirked at them because we all knew the deal. (Did I mention that this was Lieutenant L my friend's father?) We all knew that sometimes people would just come into the room through the window because my mother sometimes complained about too much traffic through the house dirtying up her rugs.

I have to confess I was REALLY HIGH and you know how quickly you can forget when you're really high. "Did you know there was a guy at your window?" "No, wait, when?" They said, "15 minutes ago," I said, "Wait, yeah, maybe." Now they were trying to trick me!

I said, "Yeah about ½ hour ago." They said "Who was that? I asked why? They said, "Because he ran and we had to chase him all the way to Still-pond" (2 miles away). I asked; "Did you catch him?" Worried he had the weed on him that I just sold him. They said, "No, tell him we want to talk to him." I said, "I think he knows that already." His name was Brian G and he could always run fast, his nickname was Monkey; he was a police escape artist. He was often our second-story roof guy because of his climbing skills; he also knew how to hide well. After our little chat the cops walked away in a little cop herd. I looked out the window later and saw what amounted to about 8 cop cars and about 13-15 cops in total.

It wasn't just a possible break-in call, that was every cop on duty in Northern Baltimore County, it was all planned. They were just waiting on an excuse to raid the house. They either didn't know we were in there or they thought we were doing a big deal in the middle of the day. Thankfully it was Monkey and thankfully he escaped with the evidence. Monkey told me about the chase and how he made one of the cops slip into the slimy creek; that he laughed so hard he almost couldn't keep running.

After they walked away I went to the bathroom to pee and in the middle of my forehead was a black mark the size of a quarter. It was the carbon from the bottom of the hash oil lid where it was burned. I'm not sure what the cops thought as they stood there looking at that dot; like we were either Hindu hippies or maybe even Hare Krishnas (common at the time). They knew what kind of stuff we really did but they never asked about it. It wasn't like we didn't have a smell to us. Maybe they thought I was a Hindu/Sikh on holiday; it was dead in the center like a third eye.

As they left we settled back into doing some more bong hits as we giggled about the boys in blue. We were jokingly pissed that we now had to restore the buzz the cops had ruined. I was puzzled that they never asked why we weren't in school, it was only about 1:30 pm and we were actually hooking classes. I think they may have just been blinded by their contempt and hatred for me; that or they were just dumb.

COME PARTY

Out of nowhere, I started being invited to a lot of the rich kid's parties. I really didn't care why I just wanted to make money and they had it. Long before the invites started us poor kids would just crash their parties. Sometimes they would start crap, other times they would just make fun of our socio-economic status. There was a certain brother and sister whose last name began with a "W" that had huge parties at their parent's house. They had so many parties that they actually got quite skilled at hosting them.

The invites started shortly after we had crashed a big party during the supply chain crisis. The party was going OK with the liquor but then I showed up with about a pound and a half of weed. It sold out in about 20 minutes. Those rich kids had cash but since most of them were snobs there would be no price break for quantity. They needed the weed so they started trying to get into my good graces; meaning they didn't try to rob me. The truth is I made them grovel a little; one by one they had to ask me to sell to them. It was amazing how fast my ass started getting kissed. Randy was with me and I can remember us both smiling and laughing as they were made to wait in a line and hope that we sold them some before we ran out. I gave Randy some counts telling him to make them kiss his "black ass." Most of them hated him because the girls liked him. This was the kind of fun that only disadvantaged kids ever get to have. I made an even bigger name for myself at that party because my weed and counts were good. Business exploded, they even started saying high to me in school; even the preppy girls were smiling my way now (I really liked that).

So it began. The rich kids started preparing for their parties by getting the liquor and inviting a couple dealers to hang out; we took care of the rest. (I never really sold hard drugs because there were too many complications. Risks with people OD-ing and dying aren't good for branding unless you're selling heroin, then they come running to you for more.)

I devised a great marketing technique by accident. I would walk into the middle of the largest group at a party sharing a single bong and dump a bunch of weed onto a table. I'd just say "Enjoy" and walk away. The kids hoping to be gifted a hit from the stuck-up kids loved it and they loved me for doing it. It always made me feel like Robinhood. Most of the competition in those days was too greedy to care about branding or customer loyalty. It was always feast or famine to them. Some of them would even have bent scales to show their customers what they weren't getting. Since I grew up with a sense that life was unfair I always made sure to make it fair for the people who usually got screwed. That's how you build a brand.

STONEHENGE OF THE NERDS

As business continued to grow and as my reputation for quality and reliability improved I started to be approached by other segments of the teen population. While the gay and lesbian crowds were growing in number nothing was as lucrative as the Nerd market. That's because the nerds were always getting ripped off by all the other dealers. They never got the same counts and always just took whatever they could get from whoever would sell it to them. That usually happened because they were always last in line and because most of the school sales were preorders from the day before. The other dealers would only sell them the counts that they had used for personal throughout the day. Some dealers even kept "beat-up counts" in a special pocket.

I remember this one nerd very clearly; I can see what he was wearing and even his face to this day. His initials were JH. JH approached me in this very meek-mannered way and he asked, "Would you sell me some pot?" I knew his face from homeroom; my answer was quite simple, "How much you want?" He said, "I got $20." (Remember minimum wage at this time was about $2.15 so $20 bucks was more than ¼ of a week's paycheck for a 40-hour employee.) We were out back at the student smoking area so I took out one of the half ounces and showed it to him. He said I only have 20 bucks, I said that's a ½ ounce 14 grams,

20 bucks, you want it? He stared at me like it was a trick. Since he had never been offered a full count to buy in his life he didn't really know what one even looked like. He said, "Dude that is so awesome thank you so much." (Yep! Drug buyers thank the sellers.)

I did a bit of a double-take and just figured I made his day. He said Bobby never gives me a deal like that. I said then stop buying from Bobby. He asked; "Can I come back to you, will you sell to me?" I gave him a stern look and said yeah, but keep your mouth shut. He said no problem, thanks man and walked away like he was cool now.

Not three hours later guess who I see walking back towards me with high eyes? Yep, JH! He said, that stuff was great, JP wants me to buy him some, can I sell him mine and get some more from you. I just looked at him like he was angling me "How much?" He said, "I'll take another $20 if you got it." Boom!!! Nerd market cornered.

JH actually became quite a big dealer for me. I told him to keep his mouth shut and not to tell any of them where he was getting it from and that I would deal only with him. I warned him that if one of those nerds came up to me and asked me then I'd stop selling to him. There were months when JH would buy pounds from me with never a break for quantity. That means as much as $1000 a month in a time when a minimum wage worker would have to work almost 500 hours to make that kind of money (3 months' worth of minimum wage wages). Little JH was doing pretty good work for me and not bad for himself. It seems that sometimes being nice does pay off, literally (pretty sure he was ripping off the nerds too).

I have to say that there was never a single issue with JH or his group of friends. The only people that ever had a problem with it were the rip-off dealers who got mad at me for spoiling them (their actual words). I ran into JH in a nightclub about 10 years after we left school. He was excited to see me and asked me in the exact same code we used as teens, "So, what are you up to?" Code for, have anything to sell. He said it like he was ready to start right back up where we had left off. I was shocked that the customer loyalty was still there. (FYI, he was still a total nerd; some things never change.)

FOR THE LOVE OF... QUAALUDES!

Everyone that I've ever asked about their Quaalude use still has fond memories of the effect. Those of us that grew up in a family that manufactured anxiety disorders miss them like a departed lover. Sure, I had a lot of love for alcohol over different periods of my life but Quaaludes were the girl I was hot for, my real love, my first true love, the one that got away.

It turned out the Quaaludes or Ludes as we called them weren't just a drug to get high on; they were actually a legitimate medication for anxiety issues and sleep problems related to stress. We viewed them as freeze dried alcohol that didn't make you piss. It seemed you could even fight better when you were on them; I know I "usually" could.

Mixed into the previous year with all the LSD was a lot of Ludes. They sold for $3.50 a pill. One could get you high for the night but 2 would make it a great evening. When the bounty was plentiful 3 to 4 would be about the same as drinking a little more than a 1/5 of alcohol: Sometimes it only took one to cause a good black-out. That's how we lost Wormo's car except that night was Halloween and we probably smoked 4 of them and each ate about 8. (As I write this it's astounding to think of how utterly stoned we were and how we must have looked; how close we were to death and how no one did anything to stop it!)

Quaaludes were so powerful that you really couldn't sell drugs when you were on them and I didn't. I did however make a few promises during blackouts that resulted in people showing up at my house when I didn't know what day it was. As I mentioned earlier my entire group of friends would get together the day after we partied to try to recall where we actually went and who we saw the night before.

Unlike the party kids I used the Ludes to shut down the feelings associated with the childhood abuse and neglect. I used them to treat the damaged parts. Pretty sure I wasn't the only one but I don't think any of my close friends had been neglected or sexually abused. In all likelihood, some of the girls were molested but no one talked about it, ever! I think there was a lot more physical abuse of children in those days and Wormo was a sad example.

DEALER'S EMOTIONAL STASH

You might think that a person who sold drugs and never really got caught for it would walk away from the trade feeling pretty lucky. Surprisingly this wasn't the case. You see there is unknown to most, a series of invisible scars that mark the young drug dealer, sometimes for life. Dealers aren't innocent victims by any stretch. They ultimately decide to take the risk to be dealers so the damage they endure is usually of their own making. Very few dealers know about the risks they take emotionally but there are consequences. The emotional damage they face is not only related to their loss of innocence but to their abnormal social development as well.

If power really does corrupt and absolute power does so absolutely then those "mean old drug dealers" certainly take a hit. Most people don't realize that these young entrepreneurs miss many of the major milestones of normal childhood development. Drugs harm in many ways and some of those ways are usually only understood when it's too late. Some people may think they deserve what they get but many are still children by most standards.

One of the most devastating forms of long-term damage isn't really noticed until later in life but it does start affecting them early on. You see, being a drug dealer leaves you without social peers with the exception of other drug dealers. Those relationships are so complicated by competitiveness that they rarely have any real friends at all. Real friendships require balance and trust.

Drug dealing leaves a child with a distorted sense of their own emotional worth. Much like the sexually abused their value becomes about what they have to offer people and not about who they are as people. Dealing also diminishes the value of everyone around them to mere customers, hangers-on or employees. Everything and everyone becomes a commodity to be used, bought and sold. People put up with your shit because they want something from you and not because they like who you are. (It's a lot like being very attractive.)

Since people befriend and sleep with dealers because of what they have to offer they end up with a very distorted and maligned sense of worth and value. Personally, I never learned how to be a fellow with other teens. Instead, the abuse I experienced along with the dealing taught me how to use people just like they used me. Everything gets measured and everything becomes transactional. Additionally, the secret of my sexual abuse provided the cement to build the walls that no one could get inside of. The dealing was the rebar that made those walls strong enough to hold back almost any feeling, good or bad. Intimacy became almost non-existent.

My relationship dynamics became even more confusing because some of the people around me continued to let me lead them long after I stopped dealing. There were quite a few sycophants that seemed emotionally bonded to me. At the time I didn't really respect their motivations because aside from my drugs, quick wit and physical attributes I was a dick and they acted like I wasn't. I was angry and they were weak. Survivors of emotional abuse are trained to be either the victim or the perpetrator. It's safer to be the emotional perpetrator than a possible victim; dominate or be dominated, those are their only options.

The anger I already had inside was ratcheted up a notch as I took on a leadership role. It started seething in me and my socially-imposed superiority allowed me to dismiss my conscience when needed (dangerous). I knew that I was going to be too old to deal safely as I neared 18. Being a legal adult meant I could do real-time in jail if I got caught. It was around this time that my self-medicating became a priority and you can't deal successfully if you need to stay really stoned.

The Quaaludes had been drying up for some time. Many people in the country were suggesting that the rise in drug-related deaths were specific to methaqualone; a drug that Ronald Reagan and Congress worked to outlaw both the manufacture and use of. The illegal labs were still making them but the prices were going through the roof as the chemicals to produce them became more restricted. The bootlegs were good but they became harder to come by; a replacement was needed.

So what does an addicted person do when their freeze-dried alcohol runs out and the closest possible replacement valium is just too unpredictable and even more deadly? They find a new favorite. This is why the supply war on drugs and even guns will always fail. It fails because demand is the real problem. Not demand for a specific drug but the demand to escape reality. Want to guess what an aspiring sedative hypnotic fan does when their emotional problems are getting harder to ignore. They seek their second favorite lover. They do the legal drug!

The real problem with using alcohol as a medication is that it has a really short half-life and it alters functioning a lot. If you want to use alcohol to feel OK you have to constantly consume it. That becomes hard to do when you're not yet of age and can't access the alcohol you need. Most kids just find another illicit drug that they can get without being carded. This is why so many kids huff or use things like pills and heroin; they're easier to get. People never go backward in chemical strength only forward to more of the same or stronger substances. Alcohol is one of the hardest drugs there is. It kills more people than any other. Addiction is still the only disease that kills people that don't have it via accidents, robberies & burglaries gone wrong and loss of self-control. The people that love addicts actually kill themselves when their zeal to care for people that don't care enough about themselves goes unchecked.

CHAPTER TEN
DOUBLE-BIND

GET OUT!

Just before I turned 16 my mother devised a new way to absolve herself of the responsibilities of motherhood. Whenever she felt cornered emotionally or when her guilt became too cumbersome she would throw her favorite trump card. It was quite possibly the worse threat that any neglected sexually abused child with abandonment issues could ever hear; "GET THE FUCK OUT!!!"

When the dealing later decreased so did the extortion money that she demanded in order for me to deal out of her house. Like the other males in her life when I didn't have any money I was of little use. It was during these times that the scream evictions were most likely.

In the 70s it wasn't illegal to kick your children out onto the street. I know that some of you may even think that a kid like me deserved it. That still doesn't take away the damage that the threat leaves on the psyche of an emotionally developing teen, well-behaved or not. That kind of added damage makes immature minds dangerous because in their minds they have nothing to lose; add the invincibility and impulsiveness of youth and BOOM! (Every time she did this the little kid that was threatened with the orphanage felt it: It triggered that trauma.)

In those days you could literally just send your kids packing. If you lived in that era you remember the epidemic of street children and runaways. Many of them were kicked out or were essentially refugees from dysfunctional homes that hurt too much to live in.

Like others, I had a vision of a kid running away from home with a stick on his shoulder and a bandana tied to the end with a few personal belongings or food in it. Unlike them, I never had to run away because my mother was always taking off. All I had to do was wait her out and it was free time. I recall my sister bickering with her one night and shouting; "Don't you have somewhere else to be? Why are you even here?" Evil-One yelled back, "Get the fuck out! I mean it, Get the fuck out!!! I'm calling the cops."

Sometimes the locks would just be changed when you got home from school or work. Sometimes you could get in before she got them changed which meant she had to wait until the next time you left the house. She did this so often that she actually kept spare door locks in the trunk of her car. She changed them so many times we just kept the old keys. Most times we'd just let each other in then she'd bitch about us letting our sibling in the house. It happened so often that I honestly have trouble remembering the first time; they just blended in with the orphanage threats.

Essentially she just stopped the "I'll have you put away" threats and just began telling me to leave. There was never any warning whatsoever just, "Get the fuck out of my house" (or anyone one of her other top 10 screams). It would come out of nowhere. She screamed our names so much my sister legally changed her name because of the trauma that was being activated by anyone that would say Vickie too loud (It's Ashly now).

What do you do when you're a stoned kid and someone tells you they don't want you? Well, you don't try to stay after years of rejection. When you're from my family you say "Fuck you you fucking bitch." Then you go get some clothes and all of your product and walk out the door. (Obviously, there's no longer a reason to be mannerly.)

In hindsight, she didn't really start kicking me out until after my father died; mostly because she didn't want him to have me. I'm sure she kicked me out weeks after his death. You know, when the support stopped. (It hurt even more because suddenly he wasn't an option.) I took my product, my sleeping bag and a small bong and I hit the bricks. There was a place under the power lines near the Masonic Home where we had been having field parties almost every night. I just figured hell, I'm here every night anyway I'll just make this my home. It ended up being a great time because dozens of people joined me. There were always at least 2 or 3 people that would last the whole night. Sometimes we even helped our little girlfriends climb out of their second-floor apartment windows to join us.

Since we were born in the 60s, we all knew how to "hippy in the woods." The sun would wake us up in the morning and we would help the girls get back into their houses before their parents knew. Sometimes they just snuck in the front door while their parents were still sleeping. Every girl in town knew how to make their bed look like someone was in it; at least the cool ones did.

The colder rainy days were a lot less fun; rain meant finding shelter. Sometimes you climbed into one of those windows and slept under a friend's bed. This was nice because they could sneak food to their rooms; the bathroom breaks however took some effort. No matter where I slept I often went home and broke into my mother's house to take showers, change and sometimes eat her leftovers while she was at work. I would even hang out in my room until around 4 when I thought she might be coming home. I could also just wait until she went out to come back. Sometimes I could sleep under my own bed or in my own closet.

In the shadow of all this sadness and abandonment Grace reappeared in the form of invites to stay with friends' families (I almost wrote people, but they were friends). Most of the time parents were mortified to learn that a child was being put on the street. (Since the law didn't protect children like it should have, a child's only redress would be in the courts. The police would actually remove a teen if they were called and I knew that they would gladly remove me.)

There were several very odd experiences for me during this time. I like to call them acts of love; they were certainly acts of Grace. This love and Grace presented as offers to stay with other families long-term. The first family was the Jameson family via Sue and Debbie's mother. Marge was one of the first adults to really validate my own mother's shortcomings for me. She knew more about her because she also knew my sister. (Godspeed Marge you had a great heart and you Graced me more than you knew.)

All I was trying to do at that time was stay alive and not be cold. Before they took me in I was sleeping where ever I could. In a town with about 10 apartment complexes, there were always options. I had learned how to break into apartments when I was in the 3rd grade so that was useful for accessing the empty units. I was so good at it that when I was a kid the neighbors would actually come to our apartment when they locked themselves out. They would ask my mother if I could climb their balcony and unlock their doors for them; they usually tipped me for doing it. They knew I could do it because as kids we'd climb up to the third-floor balconies and jump off them into the big bushes practicing to be stuntmen. (I'm laughing inside visualizing a 9-year-old flying past a second-floor window.) It started as just a way to get out back quicker; instead of walking all the way around the 3 buildings. But I digress.

The apartments offered other options in addition to breaking into an empty unit and sleeping on the hardwood floors. There were also storage rooms with lockers. With a few boxes and pieces of wood placed in the right arrangement, they could become like little apartments that you could even put a padlock on. You just had to keep real quiet so people doing laundry didn't hear you or smell you smoking.

One morning I was leaving one of Town and Country's laundry rooms when I saw Sue and Debbie Jane leaving for school. I liked the Town and Country laundry rooms because they were small and for just a dime you could get the dryer to run for about 20 min. Put in a dime, open the door, put your finger on the door button and you could heat up the small area and your clothes too if needed.

I ran into Sue and Debbie one morning while leaving a building near their house. They were shocked to see me because I was not a morning person. I remember them telling me that it wasn't OK to be sleeping in the laundry rooms. They asked if I was hungry, took me in the house and Ms. Jameson (Marge) fed me while Sue drove Debbie to school. I stayed with them for a few months until by chance I ran into my mother at the shopping center. I remember her sternly asking me "Where the hell have you been." I remember snapping back at her "What the hell do you care? You threw me out remember?" She actually said, "I'm still your mother Manuel, you need to let me know where you are." I remember being a little dumbfounded that she could say something so stupid but then I just remembered who I was talking to.

For many people, there comes a time when they're confronted with the reality that their parents are nowhere near as smart as they told us they were. This came very early for me. While she never did drugs that I know of it was like she was a burn-out. I gradually started realizing that she may have just been a "dinghy blonde." It didn't heal any of the hurt that she'd inflicted but it did sort of depersonalize it a little. Sadly that just made it God's fault for putting me with her.

Not knowing when you would be kicked out created a lifelong fear/trauma of always waiting for someone to pull the rug out from under you when things were good; also known as an anxiety disorder. For some reason, her evictions seemed to happen the most when I was feeling unusually safe and secure. It was totally unpredictable. We could have the biggest family argument and nothing would happen. Then there were days when I went to school or work just to come home late at night to find my key didn't fit the lock.

BIG BEN'S WAREHOUSE

There was one advantage to having a rich almost ex step dad that owned a chain of stereo stores. That advantage being that he could not only get you a discount on a good stereo but he could also invent a job for you. This was my first and only taste of nepotism. Despite selling a lot of drugs I knew that you had to work to survive; I never considered dealing a job even though it made me 20 times the money.

The job that "Stereo Discounters Ben" actually created for me was running the warehouse in Timonium. (By running I mean loading and unloading stereos from trucks and doing COD orders.) Stereo Discounters became a famous place for music lovers in the area. It held an annual Air Guitar contest that was known around the entire Mid-Atlantic region. Thanks to all the practice sessions in "The Room" I could really air-rock it out but I was excluded because I worked there. I did get to be a judge and that didn't hurt my social status any.

The Air Guitar Contest was exactly what it sounds like with the winner getting a huge stereo package. It was a fun job to have in the late 70s. The company also had a department called "Music Sound" that sold band equipment. This meant meeting lots of musicians as they came through the warehouse to pick up their equipment. By this time I had already learned to play the hippy acoustic guitar but the cool kids were all playing electric instruments now.

I started that job just before I turned 16. Like any kid, I was waiting for my 16th birthday and the chance to get my license and even a car one day. I had been hitchhiking around the area since I was 11 or 12 but I always fantasized about that 16-year-old rite of passage into adulthood that all the little rich kids around me were beginning to experience.

HAPPY WHATEVER DAY

I woke up a little early on the morning of my 16th birthday in anticipation of what I might experience on this momentous occasion in a child's life (I must have been high). E-1 was already gone. I looked around the house for a card or a note or something but there was nothing. My sister walked past me but not a word about the special day; it wasn't really expected. Dejected I walked back into my room and did what any 16-year-old red-blooded American boy would do on his birthday: I grabbed the half bottle of Jack Daniels off my dresser and took a big drink in sorrow and anger. Then I grabbed my 32 inch Tokemaster bong and some of the free weed that was sitting in the deseeding tray on top of the TV and began to celebrate. Damn it, I would Happy Birthday myself if I had to; maybe even get pissed enough to do a hate prayer.

No one really hid booze at our house except for my sister; she had locks on everything from a deadbolt on her bedroom door to a padlock on her closet. Pretty sure my mother was always in there snooping around whenever she didn't come home (I found out later that she was trying to prove my sister was prostituting). Vicky was 20 at the time and she paid rent so I never paid any attention to what she did. Security didn't matter to me because I was always home. Since I never bought a lock for my door my mother was very aware of everything in my room from scales to baggies to bongs to booze.

Since it was my 16th birthday I made a point of being around the house when my mother came home that day. It was a typical Spring day in Maryland, a great day to be outside. Still hoping to be valued by her I waited around to see what she had gotten her only son; her baby. She was great at promising stuff, so I looked forward to even a good promise, like I was going to get my license soon. I was in my room when I heard her setting things down in the kitchen. I put on my good kid face and went out to see what she got me for the biggest birthday in my life thus far. It wasn't about stuff at all, I had money. It was about wanting to be tricked into believing that she actually cared. (A "scar-script" I would later adapt with romantic partners.)

I walked out and she said; what are you doing here. (I actually considered for a second whether or not I was supposed to be kicked out.) I said; nothing watching cartoons. No questions about if I went to school that day or not. (I was going for the profits in those days but often going late or leaving early.) She asked if I ate and I said no thinking maybe a birthday dinner at Ponderosa Steak House was in the offering; but no. She said, "I'm going out to eat so make yourself something." It wasn't like she ever made "us" anything; it was more like we got to eat with her once a month. As you might imagine I was a little stunned that there was no mention of the day. I knew this was a big day for any kid, I saw it on TV. Was there going to be a surprise or a card with money maybe? Maybe an emotional thought that counted; you know like you matter enough to get a card for.

Like I said I had some money but that really wasn't the point. The acknowledgment of this important day to a mother and child seemed right, but there was nothing. I remember reflexively walking back out to the kitchen a little later, just before she left for the night. I asked if I could have 5 bucks to get something to eat? "What am I made out of money, find something in the refrigerator, you got your own money, I have to go."

"YOU CAN'T EVEN GIVE ME FIVE DOLLARS FOR MY DAMN BIRTHDAY?" Her response was; "Today's not your birthday" and she laughed in my face. I just looked at her dumbfounded once again. I said May the 16th ever heard of it? She giggled and said, "Oh is that today. Oh, I'm sorry Mann I completely forgot" (well that's affirming). I just stared at her as she squirmed trying to figure out how to save face. "Oh, I have something for you that I made you. Wait here." (That she made? What in the heck could that be?) Walking back from her bedroom she handed me a black piece of material. It was a scarf that she must have crocheted the previous winter when she was friends with false alarm Billy's mother. "I'll get you a card later." (You know that thing dogs do with their head when they hear a strange sound? That was me.)

So I got a really nice scarf instead of a car for my 16th birthday, just in time for late Spring. All I could think was wow, no car kid here's a scarf for your cold walks next winter. I just walked away shaking my head. In her defense, there was 10 bucks hidden in the scarf. I guessed the rich boyfriend was sitting this one out too. She ran out that door as fast as her legs would take her and she didn't come home until well after the bars closed. When she did get home I got one of those drunken, "Are you still up? We'll do something soon, I PROMISE." I said; I just want my license, can we do that. I have to check with work she said. How about Saturday I asked, you know, for my birthday, "I can't I'm going to the Poconos with Ben." I almost made a joke about lending her my scarf but I was feeling too irrelevant to joke around and I wasn't giving up the scarf, she'd lose it.

It took almost a month to get my license but I do still have that scarf that she probably made for some dude that didn't like it. I've lost it about 3 times over the years but it comes back to me like an old traumatic "mommery." Forty-four years now I've had it; not sure if it's a scar or a testament to what I lived through. I wanted my license because I had friends' and customers' cars to drive. People loved letting me drive their cars while they smoked my weed.

I was repeatedly late hitchhiking to work so Ben told her to let me use the company car to get back and forth. (At the time we actually had a new 1979 Grand Prix parked at the house. It was a Stereo Discounter company car my mother used when her Dodge Dart Swinger was in the shop.) She hated me having it but I took full advantage of the boss's order. I had my own keys for it and she was always out. I drove that car so stoned and so fast while full of kids that I often had to hold one hand over one eye just to see straight. By the Grace of God, I didn't kill anyone or even wreck the car. I guess all those speed racer cartoons actually paid off; of course I wasn't Speed, that was a cop's name. I was his troubled brother Racer X.

YOU'VE BEEN SERVED

Court papers aren't the only way to get served. You also get served when you buy liquor. Like most kids from a party town, I longed for and dreamed of the day when I could buy my drugs at the liquor store. For many young people it's an important transition into adulthood; especially for the emotional wrecks and the budding alcoholics.

The drinking age for beer and wine was only 18 when I was young. Getting liquor was never really a problem but being able to buy it at the store would mean that I had become a man. It would mean that I was more like my father. (For many poor young kids without access to a car, getting served is just as monumental as getting your driver's license.)

In those days licenses didn't have pictures on them. If it had the right gender, hair color and height then all you needed was an old worn-out look on your face. Sure you had to remember an address but that was easy enough unless you were really high. If you ever tried to buy liquor under age you're surely aware of the expression "shot-down." That's what it's called when the liquor store clerk says no right after you said you didn't have an ID. Most times being shot-down meant they just laughed at you and said, nice try kid. If you never tried it it's quite a blow to the adolescent ego. On par with "Go away kid, ya bother me." It made you feel childlike but you always knew that one day they would have to hand over the goods.

Obviously, some people were better than others at looking older. Some store owners and bartenders were willing to take the chance because they just wanted to make some cash. Some looked to see who else was watching and others had the cops in their back pockets.

Of course, we also knew how to hustle liquor. That's when you stand outside and ask someone going into the store to get it for you. Back in the day, no one got arrested for doing something like that. All you really needed was a local drunk that would do it for some free liquor and the apartments were full of those. You could also steal it from your parents or from the store itself. Billy R was great at that. I never understood what they thought he was going in there for. He never bought anything with the exception of a Coke to go with the 1/5 of Jack he had under his coat.

Around that time I had heard a rumor that the Corner Stable (a bar) was serving a lot of underage people and that the bartender was actually pretty cool. The Stable was a small place that rarely had more than 15 to 20 people in it; it was always full of smoke and very dark which helped you look older. Sundays were really slow but you didn't want it too slow because then they would try to talk to you more and stare at you longer. An advantage of them being slow was that they needed the sales. (Yes I did actually consider all these variables at 16; that's what you do when you're ruled by an anxiety disorder. I was always trying to figure things out. Children from difficult homes are great at reading the room; they have to be. That "room reading" reflex is what causes many people to develop social anxiety disorders.)

Liquor stores weren't open on Sundays because of the blue laws so you had to buy it from a bar that sold carryout, like the Stable. I had already gotten served there for carryout a few times and they never asked for ID.

146

In hindsight, I'm pretty sure I was longing for the days of old when my father and I would spend hours together in a very similar atmosphere. So one Sunday when I was feeling a little lonelier and cockier than usual I thought I would just go for it. It seemed like being able to drink in a bar was somehow continuing the family tradition; I'm certain being in those places made him feel closer. I was a little worried that if I did get carded that I might not be able to get carryout anymore, but I missed my father.

Selling carry out to minors was less risky for the bar than letting kids hang out and drink. I certainly didn't want some cop coming in and spotting me because obviously they all knew me. The cops were all dying for me to become an adult so they knew I wasn't.

As a distraction, I arranged to go with my friend Vickie H (16). She had been going there on a regular basis with some older guy she was dating (probably like 20 or something). She was one of those taller hippy-chick types that looked older. Since she was already getting served at different liquor stores we decided to throw caution to the wind and try it. We planned to sit by the back door near the bathrooms; I figured I could just slip out if the cops came in.

If you wanted to get served you usually just looked to see who was working before you tried. After we checked we went in and sat down. The bartender said high to Vickie and gave me a double take. Vickie ordered two Buds and we got the beers. People said that placing the money on the bar before the drinks got there meant they didn't legally take the money from any specific person; hence not actually served. My father always put a 20 on the bar and said let it ride so that's what I did. He told me you get better service because all they focus on is their pending tip. The night went well. We had a good time pretending to be adult drunks. I was a little uncomfortable because the bartender kept staring at me funny. (Abused kids have special stare detectors.) No questions but she did look my way and smile a lot. She was an old chick, like 35, I was intrigued.

If you have children you know what a kid does if they get away with something, they do it again and again and again. After weeks of going there by myself, I grew more curious about why she hadn't asked for my ID. I was beginning to think that she really wanted me and I was quite generous in that department. (Yeah, I was a cute kid but because of the abuse and neglect, sex was all I ever thought older people wanted me for.)

I was sitting there several Sunday nights later around 11:30 when my curiosity got the best of me. (Is it odd that a 16-year-old was sitting at a bar drinking weekly?) The bartender and I were both feeling pretty good giggling back and forth. I kept letting her catch me checking out her ass as she walked the bar. Being both booze and flirt drunk I decided to put all the cards on the table, to roll the dice and ask why she never carded me. I had heard a lot about undercover cadets trying to bust bars in those days so I asked; "How do you know I'm not a cop?" She started laughing so hard she almost couldn't stand up straight. I was miffed. OK, I had long hair but that was easy enough for a cadet to get. "Come on why haven't you carded me?" She stopped laughing and said, "You don't remember me?" I knew I'd remember her if we ever did it. I said, From here?" She said; "I was pretty sure you weren't a cop." I asked how and she said; "Well, first off because I bought pot from you through your bedroom window with my friend one night and second because I've seen you selling it in here." (I forgot that I did a few sales in their bathroom without staying or trying to get served.) We laughed hard, flirted even more and then I gave her a bag of weed as a tip.

This started a relationship that lasted until long after I was 18. Back when I was still 16 she started coming to my house to buy weed regularly, she actually lived right behind me, above the cop I mentioned earlier. I remember how odd it was sleeping with her when her daughter was almost my age. Pretty sure she was committing statutory rape but she was also serving minors and smoking weed so…

Susan (the bartender) was really nice (I think that was her name). By nice I mean she never really freaked out when she found out I (at 16) had sex with her 14-year-old daughter too. She just told me I had to pick one of them but that I couldn't sleep with both of them at the same time. I picked her and her daughter just came to my house to get even with her over family crap. I felt really wanted at their house. Svengali was indeed on the rise but it wasn't that romantic of a notion because it was about attention for me, not sex. I was just a loved starved kid trying to fill up the "hole in the soul" and hide my scars the best I could.

Another one of my teenage bars was a place called the Storeroom. Once you got in the door you could drink all night. Getting in the door was about them knowing your face and how busy they were. Rumor had it that if you went up there enough times and even if you got shot down, they would eventually just start letting you in because you now looked familiar. Everyone knew the bouncer Jimbo and he was the only guy you had to get past. I loved the Storeroom because it was the first bar that I both drank and danced in since being with my father.

The neighborhood misfits had a great time there from 1979-81. We were there almost every Thursday night for the special Swamp Water Night. A drink made with some odd Green Chartreuse French liqueur made by the Carthusian Monks in the 1700s. Everyone believed it got you higher than alcohol.

18 AND I LIKE IT

After more than a year of dancing my ass off at the Store Room a very special night arrived. It was the eve of my 18th birthday. By this time I was not only getting served for beer but hard liquor too. They were even paying me out for wins on the poker machines. Why wouldn't they, it was free money and they knew they would get it all right back. Happy drunks spend money and they're bigger tippers.

I was drinking a Cuba Libre (Rum and Coke) and I was watching the clock for midnight to arrive. I wasn't certain if Jimbo knew my real age or not. I was staring at the clock when Jimbo walked by and asked me what I was waiting for. I said "Well," took a sip, "in about 10 seconds," took another sip, "I'll be," killed off the drink, "18!" Without batting an eye for referencing my age or drink type he said Happy Birthday and walked away. I stood there waiting for the shocked face that I never got.

As the weeks progressed I started drinking and dancing with two thirty-somethings that were both married to deployed soldiers. I thought us hooking up was my idea but looking back I may have been outsmarted. It was my first but by no means last married woman. I never saw fooling around as a sin or wrong on my part because I wasn't the one who was married. I wasn't involved in that contract; so not my problem. (Sadly as I'm writing this book I'm not sure of their names; Ramona and Sharon I think. I remember their faces and even their bodies but their names are fuzzy.) There may be an emotional message in the prior statement about what was important and what wasn't. I hope you're able to comprehend the point here. It's bodies, not people that the sexually abused are looking for. It's how we relate, physically. Just another sad scar for the sexually abused. When you become an object so does everyone else. Forever! (That scar doesn't seem to fade much.)

The next morning was my birthday. When I awoke (OK came to) it was full on 18th birthday party mode. I was hanging out with a girl named Ginger. Ginger was a lot like me; she hit it hard for a girl. She was always prepared to party. When we picked her up she whipped out a baggy with about 30 pre-rolled joints in it. Billy R said, "Yeah, you're coming with us."

It was a special day in Maryland and Baltimore. Not just because of me though. It was the 106th running of the Preakness Stakes and the infield awaited us along with everyone we knew that partied. Historically the infield was always the poor people's party zone. We did eventually let the rich people in but we kept them in tents like circus animals.

After a day of Black Eyed Susans, horses, beer and weed it was time for part two. The RUSH concert for the album Moving Pictures. Rush concerts required LSD; otherwise it would be a waste of the ticket. Unknowingly it would be the last LSD trip I would ever take. It was the best dream birthday party scenario of all time. Probably the best birthday I've ever had but that's not saying much; no one got hurt or arrested. We did almost lose another car in the Capital Center parking lot though.

CHAPTER ELEVEN
NEXT LEVEL

A MOVING EXPERIENCE

Just as my pure party self-medicating mode was kicking in, my mother decided that she would be moving to Pikesville, MD. It was about 25 miles away, on the other side of town. She said that she was only getting a one-bedroom and that I would have to find my own place to live. Just hearing that triggered my feelings of abandonment

To this day I have a deep-seated fear of losing my home. It obviously began many years earlier with the orphanage threats and being kicked out without notice or deed. It was a particular trauma that E1 seemed to purposely keep reinforcing. The power seemed to make her feel relevant when she didn't.

If you haven't felt abandoned to the level that it causes you to have abandonment issues, it feels a lot like getting really bad news out of nowhere, without warning. It's worse than your dog just got hit by a car and it's dead. It's the feeling of having the rug pulled out from under you when you weren't looking. It's a feeling that never goes away and can surprise you like a panic attack when you least expect it. Sometimes it gets activated just by hearing someone tell you no. I believe it to be the foundation of at least one of my anxiety disorders; certainly key to my need for sedatives.

I'm not sure why her plan changed but suddenly out of nowhere, my mother said that I could live with her but that I would have to stop dealing. I was cutting way back on that anyway because of my age. She also implied that there would be no drug use or parties in the house, neither of which I cared about at this point. I was mostly focused on alcohol now that I was legal. Pretty sure she just wanted help with the rent. I had a habit of tricking myself into thinking she actually cared and

I let it happen again. She was a user that always had an angle that served her; no one else ever mattered. I wanted to think she was being nice but I'm pretty sure she ended up having to get a two-bedroom because that was all they had in the complex. Her telling me I could live with her may have merely been a way to cut off my sister's options and reduce her own guilt. Not sure if she ever really had that much insight though. She probably just considered me a lesser of two evils and knew that my sister would try to work her way into that spare bedroom if it was empty.

COMING OF AGE

My income dropped when the dealing stopped but I still wanted stuff. I never considered myself a thief but as the "Yuppie" wealth disparity of the 80s grew my entire generation started to think that society owed us something. It seemed we would have to take what they wouldn't give us. I wasn't robbing banks or anything yet: I still had my Robinhood sensibilities so I just wanted to steal from the rich and give to poor old me.

The major thefts of our generation were left to car break-ins and crimes of opportunity. Stealing wasn't really my skill set either; I just paid people to steal the stuff I wanted stolen. For the most part, I was just along for the ride with other people that had gotten really good at it. I was more of a strategic-minded person who looked at landscapes, surrounding, access and egress; I liked the planning part. I also had this ridiculously good memory that I still have today (the same memory that allows me to write this book). I could remember where a car, van or truck was parked for years on end; probably because I was often walking and had time to take things in.

The summers before and after my 18th birthday were filled with helping friends siphon gas for their cars. One Friday night a car full of us partiers just decided that we should all go down to Ocean City, MD (150 miles away). That meant we would have to start by siphoning gas from a fleet of U-haul trucks that we knew were accessible. It only took about ¾ of a tank to get us down to the beach. We weren't penniless but the little money we did have was used for booze, buzzes, food and smokes.

It was during one of our earlier trips that Billy and I decided to get our first piercings. In those days a guy getting his ears pierced was quite the statement since it was mostly only gay men and hippies that did it. Gay people did it in their right ear. So if you had your right ear done it was code that you were gay or open to those types of relationships. Obviously, there were a lot of stupid people that didn't know the meaning of which ear was which so by getting either ear done you ran the risk of being harassed. We got them anyway. The straight males that did it were making a statement by getting their left ears done. The statement was that I am only straight and don't go both ways so don't even ask. In those days AC-DC was not only a band or electrical current; it was also your sexual polarity.

You have to remember this was the decade after the season of love and some of us just didn't swing that way. There wouldn't be any crossing of swords with a friendly girl in the middle either. Having been a victim of sexual abuse I made these boundaries very clear to everyone. On the upside, the chicks thought the earrings were cool. It seems that when you are a bad-boy it's easy to keep the bad-boy image rockin and some females just love the forbidden fruit. (Many females didn't have pierced ears at the time.)

As mentioned people didn't always know which ear was which so you had to be pretty emphatic about how you responded to the girly jokes. Overall having it just meant that you were comfortable with your sexuality and that you were absolutely sure about your preferences.

Regardless of the codes involved there were also people, mostly insecure jocks, that wanted to start fights and even try to pick on people that had their ears pierced (they were the homophobes). My earring spoke directly to those bullies and conformists with a loud "Fuck you! Say something! I dare you!" I never got in a fight over it but I heard a lot of "dude looks like a lady" jokes years before Aerosmith released the song. (The 60s guys invented that.)

The earring issue wasn't that big of a deal because you could also get beat up and have people want to fight you just because you were a "damn hippy." All of us long hairs could hear the banjos of Deliverance in the woods or on the Eastern shore of Maryland for that matter. There was a lot of hatred in those days but color had nothing to with it. Like now hatred was just there in some people's hearts, just looking for an excuse to present itself. All we really cared about was being able to put some real hoops in our ears. (Yep, you got it; we re-invented that to if you don't count the pirates with their clip-ons.)

GETTING HARD

As life and reality began to harden our hearts, our drugs became harder too. The realities of the world seeped in as what was left of our innocence trickled out. No matter what gateway drug you used growing up be it cigarettes, caffeine, weed, or alcohol, they all peter-out in their effectiveness. No matter what you use to self-medicate with you will either have to eventually use more of it or find something stronger. That is addiction science; it's called tolerance.

There will always be a level of curiosity related to substance use because some people just love the adventure of it. There's also a peer pressure factor that comes into play but the fact remains that if you keep using any substance regularly it will always take more later in order to have the same effect. If everyone is doing it then you're a nobody if you don't. If you use a chemical to cope with life, then you eventually can't cope without it.

By the late 70s, we had all done our share of cocaine up our noses (the hard way). Personally I never really saw the value in Cocaine because it was too damn expensive. The return on investment just wasn't there when things like alcohol and Quaaludes were so cheap. Even Crystal Meth had a better ROI (the crystal meth of the 70s is not the same drug people know of today).

Like most people with anxiety disorders, I was a sedative guy. The drug culture of the day meant certain unique social events (like

Christmas) did require scoring specific drugs. Once Richard Pryor set himself on fire the interest in cocaine use seemed to start heating up for all of us in the "just say more generation."

Like most drug-using communities we had a friend named Doc. (Some people know where this is going already.) Doc is a nickname that people were often given if they always had needles or if they knew how to use them well. (That moniker was also sometimes given to people that scored lots of pills.) In those days people just shared needles because no one had ever heard of AIDS or Hepatitis; drug illnesses were only seen in homeless dope fiends and Gays (GRID). In fact, people were still becoming blood brothers by opening cuts and mixing the blood together; sharing a needle became a very similar bond of kinship (sadly it still is).

When people like Doc showed up on the scene shooting drugs became a magic option to get more of a drug into the system faster and more efficiently. Doc's mother was a diabetic so he had permanent access to spikes/pins/works. In those days you didn't need a prescription to get a bag of needles from the pharmacy. You just told the pharmacists that you were getting needles for your diabetic mom or grandmother. If you didn't look like a drug addict they never thought twice. You could also just steal them from a local diabetic that probably wouldn't even notice.

I barely recall the date of my first needle poke. Pretty sure that I was already really high on something else when I did it. I'm pretty damn sure that I held my arm as Doc shot me up with cocaine. I know he owed me money from some credit I had given him in the past. I do remember where we were and that I did it a couple times that night. It still wasn't really something I cared that much for and my father had always warned me against it: I felt like I was violating the deal we made when he first got me high. Sadly when I was mad at him it was a way to get even with him; a way to make him see what abandoning me did to me.

THE PARTY

A couple weeks after we started needling each other and a decade or so before Wormo hung himself in jail, the time came for the big move to Pikesville. It was during this time that my dysfunctional love affair with alcohol began to deepen. I often referred to my connection to alcohol as a true dependency. Not a chemical dependency per se but an emotional dependency. By this time street drugs were becoming a little inconsistent for me. You could get good Ludes, bad Ludes, good Acid, bad Acid, good Hash bad Hash, good Weed and weak Weed but alcohol's quality was government regulated by scientists and I liked that. You always knew what you were getting with alcohol and it was much more accessible to me thanks to the 18-year-old legal drinking age. I became emotionally dependent on alcohol doing what it was supposed to do. Somewhere along the line, I realized that alcohol was in fact more dependable than most people.

As previously mentioned, one of the problems with dealing is that it separated you from the crowd. It put you in a different social strata and economic class. It created an entirely new set of haves and have-nots; one where I could be on top. Dealing was actually a very fickle experience; sometimes extremely lonely and other times full of emotional and social highs. If you wanted to have people want you around it was awesome. If you wanted to be wanted for who you were then it was impractical.

All I accomplished by dealing was to discover another way to monetize myself; another way to transactional-ize myself to others and further my sense of objectification. The abuse had set the stage for being a sexual commodity. Dealing built on that by giving me a way to make your head feel good too. They both made me important to you because of how I could make you feel. Not for who I was but for what I could do for you (E-1 taught me to focus on other people's needs).

As moving to Pikesville neared Wormo decided to give me a moving out of Cockeysville party. (It was like my moving to Pikesville was another state, albeit 25 miles away.) Maybe it was just an excuse for a big ass party or maybe an actual act of love and gratitude from a close friend. Once he got permission from his father he started announcing it to folks two weeks in advance. At the time this meant personal face-to-face invitations because there was no such thing as the internet, text or email; no such thing as home computers or printers.

The night of the party ended up being the same day as the move. Little did Wormo and I know that we were the moving company my mother hired; payment would be in alcohol and she agreed to have it for us before the move which she did. It consisted of a 1/5 of: Jack, Southern Comfort, Vodka, Two Fingers Tequila and a case of 16oz Budweisers. John (Wormo) and I prearranged the Quaaludes and the Sinsemilla while Ron brought the celebratory Coke.

We busted our butts that day moving all her crap. We ran a little late and we arrived at his father's house just before sunset. John's father agreed to let us use their house so he was there keeping things in order until we arrived. His father eventually left to go to his favorite bar so there was nothing stopping us from having the best party Cockeysville ever knew (no jocks or preps invited).

There were lots of people out front when we arrived. I took a seat on the bar with all the above bottles of booze surrounding me, along with several two-liter bottles of soda for chasers. Everyone that came in had to take a drink with me. The longer I sat there the more bottles there were. It was like Jesus with the loaves and fish; the booze just seemed to be increasing as it flowed.

The party was a very emotional event for me because I was leaving my town. It seemed pretty emotional for a lot of other people too as we rehashed all the old partying and growing-up experiences we had had together. It was a celebration of the life we all had before coming of age.

I was drunk as hell and I had eaten a bunch of Quaaludes (3 or 4). Ron and I got into one of those hugging drunk bro convos. He took me into the bathroom to share some coke. (Because that's where you use social drugs; in the bathroom away from all the people.) Ron suggested that we become blood brothers stating I was like a brother to him. We were certainly trippin buddies; we had probably tripped together about 40 or more times.

Ron took the razor blade that he was cutting the cocaine with and put a slight cut on his wrist area. We would shake hands and let our blood run together just like the Native Americans. I was very high and since Ron did such a good job on his arm I asked him to cut my wrist for me (that's trust). As Ron sliced my arm I reacted by pulling my arm away quickly. YEP!!! Huge gash, I could see my muscles exposed. I looked down and said, "SHIT!! I think I need a Band-Aid" but I needed more than that. I wrapped my wrist in a towel. Wormo and I left his house full of people with Randy in charge. Randy lived nearby so there was this sort of eminent domain thing going on on top of Sherwood Hill; the house would be safe.

Wormo's wasted ass drove me to the hospital. This was quite a feat as Wormo could barely walk and chew gum at the same time on a good day. He was 6 ft 7in and he got so bad when he was high that he would usually just give me the keys to his car whenever he saw me. Yes, it was the same 67 Malibu that we lost.

When we got to the ER they sewed up my arm. Once they realized our stupid story was true and that I wasn't trying to kill myself, they discharged me. That wound took 6 external and 3 internal stitches to close. (It's still there, more than 2 inches long on my wrist, as I type today.) You might say there was some of that Grace working that night too; you need extra Grace when you do stupid stuff. It's still a scar but it's a happy scar now.

Once I got sewed up we headed back to the house for more partying. (Now I really needed to numb myself.) The party was still going pretty strong at 1:00am when we arrived. The joke would become that my scar would make that party unforgettable and that I would always remember my friends Ron, Wormo and Randy. You can bet I do.

LET'S SHOOT UP THE BEACH

Let me put all the above events together so they make more sense. People can get pretty worked up about heavy drug use, especially about LSD but there is a bond of shared experience that using together creates between the people involved. The bond gets even stronger if years of time pass and those relationships are continually built upon. The bond actually sets into the psyche much like a survival bond. There is also a bond that is specifically related to puberty and probably another related to getting arrested with someone; sometimes even just eluding the law together. Many of the bonds we formed continued until the deaths of some of the cast of characters that I have mentioned. Some of these relationships still continue to this day on social media without much connection beyond those prior shared experiences. Sadly many have died along the way and some have just disappeared. (There were about 12 guys that partied in The Room on a regular basis. Nine of them were dead by age 25.) You can't party that hard and not lose people along the way. If you think you won't then you're not in denial, you're just plain stupid. (You can't take Grace for granted.)

Doc and I however were never really close because you couldn't trust people like Doc. Like most dope fiends Doc was as crooked as they come and if you let him talk long enough he could convince you that what he was doing wasn't really dishonest. There are some thieves that have no conscience or honor.

This is where friendship, trips to the beach, stealing and drugs all come together. My last experience with Doc started when Billy and I were out partying one Friday night. The group consisted of 3 guys and two girls. This is the group I referenced earlier that decided to go down to the beach to party for the weekend.

Thanks to that memory of mine I had been eyeing up some easy gas-siphoning targets near my new house in Pikesville; just in case my rides home needed gas for their car. I recalled a church van just behind the apartments for the gas and I wanted to grab some shorts since it was on the way. While we were stealing the gas someone noticed that the door to the church van was open. BINGO!! Since there was a bunch of camera equipment ripe for the taking we now had some sellable goods. We could easily sell the stuff on the boardwalk in the vacation town of OC and then have even more money to party with.

Sleeping in the car in OC was hard in those days because the hotels wanted to rent rooms. The cops that worked the summers there were from all around the state and some even came from Baltimore City (they were always a bit more aggressive). Thanks to all the hippies and people getting raped, the city of OC was really cracking down on people sleeping in or having sex in cars. In reality, a lot of people were OD-ing in the cars too. Dead bodies in hot cars during the summer are a bad mix.

Like every poor hippy kid at a beach during the 60s and 70s, we'd try to sleep out on the beach itself but people were also getting run over by the beach sweepers so most of us just slept under the boardwalk "to be safe." Lots of rapes happened there too but it was impossible for the police to check 27 city blocks of boardwalk without us seeing them coming. As long as you didn't blow a lot of smoke up through the boards, laugh too loud or make sex noises you were fine. The sand was obviously easy to sleep on; even easier when you were stoned. It was always nicer if you could steal a few beach towels or blankets that were hanging out to dry.

The first morning Doc and I got up early to search the area for food or drugs. We found a guy selling some coke but we didn't have the money we needed. Doc offered him some camera equipment which he was very interested in. There were no cell phones to take pictures with and very few options for instant photos so people still relied on cameras with film. We traded some church camera stuff for coke. Of course, Doc wanted to shoot it up so we went back to the car, snorted a couple lines then decided to mainline the rest because according to Doc there really wasn't enough to share with everyone. (Coke makes people selfless like that.)

There we sat in a hot black car on a summer's day at noon. Doc would shoot me then I would hold him off as he shot himself up. I was in the passenger seat so I turned sideways to give Doc my skinny right arm. Doc loved my arms because my veins would pop like a cut bodybuilder (I wasn't).

I turned toward Doc and looked back over my shoulder to see an old man and woman in their 70s staring into the car window. Wanna guess what I did? I yelled at them. "What the fuck are you looking at?! Jesus Christ a person can't even get high without some stupid fucking people putting their nose in someone else's business. FUCK OFF!!"

I have always hated seeing my own blood so I was already a little jacked before I got the drugs in me. If you know anything about shooting coke you let your blood enter the needle before you inject the coke; it helps you determine that you're in the vein. That's how needles often get viruses like AIDS/HIV and HEP in them (more Grace that I never caught anything from Doc).

The old couple scurried up the street in shock, their faces distorted after experiencing the reality of urban drug abuse for the first time in their lives. Neither Doc nor I had considered at the time that we were doing this with the police station right around the corner less than 100 yards from where we sat.

After we composed ourselves we were feeling pretty good chemically. We were now ready to walk the boards looking for girls. We had planned to share the Coke with everyone else but oops!!! Sometimes that happens. Doc quickly contrived a story that when we got back to the car to get the camera equipment it was gone. It was on the front seat of the car so it must have been stolen. He suggested that someone must have left the car door unlocked. Like I said, he was a good dope fiend; being able to make someone else feel guilty is a great distraction technique that addicts just love.

Surprisingly that was one of the first and only times in my life that I had done something like that to my friends. It might have been a sign of the progression of addiction but we just chalked it up to them sleeping in too late; you know, the early bird gets the Coke. The rest of the trip was pretty uneventful, meaning that no one got busted, wounded, or dead. We sold the rest of the camera stuff on the boards telling people we needed gas to get home (we might have invented that too). We used that money to get high and drunk, then we siphoned some gas from another U-haul fleet to get home the next day.

WHEN THE DRUGS RUN OUT OF SPIRIT

As the drug dealing faded from view, my love for booze grew; all while my doubts that anything supernatural existed in the Universe were being confirmed. As time passed I developed into what I later termed a "devout atheist."

Most non-believers are pretty lax in their doubt of God but not me. I actually started reading the bible to find the holes in the stories. I became a lay Bible scholar but not to support the belief structure, to pick it apart. I used the differences in the Gospels and their inconsistencies to argue against credibility. I would find counterarguments within the texts and use them against people who hadn't resolved them yet; I was good at it too. I often used my own personal wounds and experience to question believers directly. I ranted against God's obvious apathy regarding suffering and/or his lack of power to stop it. I knew I didn't have to disprove God, I just needed to create doubt and Lord knows I had plenty of that. Good or evil didn't matter; nothing was sacred.

During the late 70s and early 80s, the born-again Christian phenomenon was growing faster than crabgrass in Maryland. It wasn't like they kept to themselves. In those days they would proselytize to anyone that wouldn't shut them down. The Born Again Christians were no less aggressive than the Hare Krishnas at the airport. You could be out eating in a restaurant or at a sporting event and they would interrupt you asking if they could talk to you about Jesus. There wasn't an Internet, spam or junk mail in those days so they just spammed you to your face. It's not an exaggeration to say that as many as 4 or 5 people would knock on your door in any given week.

Their numbers only provided me with practice. I got so good at destroying people's arguments for God that people would call me over whenever someone started preaching. I played it like a video game; it was a sport for me. My trump card was that most of the proselytizers never experienced the things I had so I would just ask them why? The old standby "Why are children sexually abused or born with illnesses, why aren't they being protected" always left them reeling.

Most people are familiar with a phrase I used earlier; "Hurt People Hurt People." Well, perhaps we could also say that "Abused People Abuse People" and "Wounded People Wound People;" my goal was all of the above. If it was possible I was going to show you my scars and use them as proof that your loving God was a delusion. I know now that my misery wanted lots of company. I didn't want to just challenge you either; I wanted to give you scars. I wanted to leave you with questions to consider that would leave a mark on your psyche for life.

It got so ugly that when I would see street preachers and proselytizers in different areas around the city I would go up and start innocently asking them questions. Looking like a young Jesus and being named Emmanuel really freaked them out. I used the Socratic Method to trick them into intellectual corners of their own making. It went like this: "Can I ask you a question," and "If that is so then you must believe this or that," "Then if you believe that how can you believe this?" "Is God all loving? Is he ego-driven? If not, then why would He care if I believed in him or not?" "Why would I go to hell for doubting him when he was the creator that made it possible for me to doubt him? Why can't I just wait until the day of my death to turn to him?" It went on and on and on and on.

Our move to Pikesville didn't help these doubts of mine in the slightest. You see Pikesville, Maryland has one of the largest Jewish populations in the country. I now had a group of people that didn't believe that Jesus was anything more than a nice Jewish guy. I could now make the Christians prove to me that Jesus was the savior and then make them try to discredit the Jews. I'd just wait for them to become hateful so

I could then call them out for not being Christ-like; reminding them Christ was a Jew. "Are you saying that Jews don't love God?" Then I'd argue that Jews were more disciplined and were making more sacrifices than they were. I would suggest that they take a ride over to Pikesville on Saturday to see all the Orthodox people without electricity or cars. I could even use the two different Sabbaths against them both. Personally, I saw the Jews as a lesser evil than the "Born Agains" because at least they minded their own business. If I'm being honest I didn't trust the Jews any more than the Christians. They had too many secrets and they didn't want me either. (I had no idea of my own Jewish heritage at that time.)

This is what happens when children don't get adequate care and nurturing: Their misery wants company. (Sound familiar? Ever see that on the news?) The longer it takes for people to get the love and attention they need the more hardened they become. The less they feel good, the less they want to feel. The less they feel the less they care. This is how people become dangerous, even dangerously antisocial. They have no empathy because they haven't experienced it at a level that can actually heal.

ALMOST SKATED

Wanting to party meant places like Skateland would cramp our style so some of us began to skate outside in public spaces. Brian's family was full of skaters so he hooked me up with my first real pair of skates. I mounted skateboard wheels on them which allowed me to skate on nearly any terrain there was, even grass. The two of us started skating outside almost nightly.

Brian and I skated everywhere but since Brian was living with his sister in Druid Hill we skated in the city a lot. We were much more of a terror on skates than people ever were on skateboards. We liked skating fast but the pedestrians on the sidewalks got in the way. We solved that by skating in the street. We'd go from 29th and Druid Park Drive over to St. Paul's, then take that all the way down to the harbor (about 80 blocks round trip). We would often stop at the Mercy Hospital parking garage, take the elevator to the top floor, catch a buzz overlooking the city, then speed skate down to almost the bottom. Then we'd take the elevator back to the top to do it again and again. It was a great lot because it was all downhill, with no flat spots and all one way. We would then take our buzz and adrenaline rushes down to Harbor Place to dance-skate while dodging people at top speed. Some cops would kick us off but that was usually only on the holidays. (The signs all said, "No Skate Boarding.")

One 4th of July we got kicked off the Harbor Place pavement by some patrol men at one end so we just went to the other end and started again. We noticed 4 of the top police brass walking from our spot to where the other cops were. For some odd reason, the brass didn't bitch about us skating. So what do two angry young men do that hate control freak cops? They skate about 20 feet behind the brass as they walk and make faces at the peon cops as they pass by.

It was shortly after that event at the Harbor that Brian was ticketed for being "a moving vehicle in a pedestrian zone." He went to court and was fined for skating on the sidewalk. In all fairness we never really just skated, we flew down those sidewalks. We would scare the shit out of people but we never hit anyone. We certainly did shock people that didn't see us coming up from behind, wooossssh!!! To our credit, no one ever landed in the harbor or on their ass.

A few months after his above ticket Brian was then busted again by Baltimore City's finest but this time it was for being "a Pedestrian in a traffic zone." Of course, Brian was going to fight this charge too but as luck would have it Brian got the same judge as the earlier case.

As mentioned in the first case he was found guilty, paid a fine and told to stay off the sidewalks. In this case, he was found guilty and told to then stay out of the street. Brian was no shrinking violet when it came to the law so he countered the judge and said; "So what then, it's illegal to roller skate in Baltimore City?" The judge asked him what he was talking about. Brian reminded him of his earlier ruling. The judge then changed the verdict stating that he did not have the authority to outlaw roller skating in the downtown area of Baltimore City. He stated his first ruling would stand so it thus became legal to roller skate on the roadways in Baltimore City. Maybe he just wanted smart-ass Brian dead but as far as I know that precedence still stands to this day. (So we did sort of invent that.) Once we were no longer outlaws we started inviting females to come along for the adventure. It was a great way to exercise, flirt, party and see the city.

DIDN'T SKATE

Despite all the fun we had skating, skating did lead to my first actual arrest as an adult. It happened when I was back in good ole Cockeysville with Brian, skating around the pool hall. Right behind it was a place called Max's radiator shop. We all used to party behind it because they left at like six o'clock. We never really bothered anyone and it was off the main path. While we did leave hundreds of bottles and cans there the owner never complained.

One Saturday night we were all back there partying and Johnny Law came flying in; everyone but me went scurrying out. I didn't have a beer in my hand so I just kept skating around. The rookie cop asked for my ID (he didn't know me). I gave it to him and he sat in his car to "check" me for warrants. He was in his car so I just skated around it backwards.

The cop was taking a really long time and every time I circled his car I would see my beer sitting where I left it near the rail to the basement. So on one of my laps around I just swooped down and picked it up. I bent down behind his car and drank it. Just as I did his door opened, I slung the beer backhand into the woods; he never saw it. I swallowed the beer, he looked at me funny and said "Here's your ID you can go. We're getting reports about break-ins so you might not want to hang out around here, tell your friends." I said, "Break-ins by people on skates?" He shook his head and said we don't know.

All the runners eventually met back up at the pool hall. Brian and I got another couple quarts of beer. I set my beer on the roof, then sat in his car to remove my skates. Just as I did two cop cars came flying into

166

the lot. I jumped up and threw it into the bushes; too late! The cop jumped out of his car and yelled at me for drinking in public. He then went to get the bottle I had tossed into the bushes.

When you hear; "Turn around and face the car," the first thing you think is, am I just being harassed or am I being arrested. This time felt different. I knew I was going to jail because the cop stopped running his mouth. My name going across the radio earlier must have activated their resentments. When he was putting the cuffs on me all I thought was, only a poor kid in the county could get charged for this shit. I asked the cop, "Really? You're busting me for drinking a legal beer." "I should write you up for littering too." Priceless I thought, after all the stuff I had done legal booze is getting me arrested for the first time as an adult. It just seemed so petty.

The only person that seemed to still be hanging around was Randy. Brian had disappeared when they told him to get out of there; I'm sure he had pot in the car so I understood that. Since Randy occasionally worked at the pool hall he tried talking the cop out of arresting me but it was too late. As the cop car drove off Randy asked me by mouthing the words "Do you have anything on you?" I shook my head no and he waved bye-bye as the car drove off. I tried to get my cuffed hands high enough to wave but couldn't. (You know that trick where you bring your hands around in front of you while you're cuffed? Yeah, don't do that because then they go on real tight, tight enough to leave marks for days.)

I was an adult now and I didn't need a phone call for this charge so I just waited until morning to see the commissioner. Unbeknownst to me Brian and Kimberley had come down to the station to try to get me out; after he cleaned out his car of course. There was nothing they could do but it was nice to know someone had tried. I just took advantage of the acoustics and sang some old Beatles tunes along with some ASS-HOLE COP melodies. When I saw the commissioner I was given a court date and released on my own recognizance. I later went to court and was given probation before judgment. While spending time in an adult jail is a street cred rite of passage, it still doesn't look good on a resume.

THE OTHER FAMILY BUSINESS

Shortly after our move to Pikesville, I attained another Pizza gig at an Italian Restaurant named Giuseppe's. It was managed by a guy that was half Greek and half Italian named Steve. After he heard my name and watched me make a pizza I was hired on the spot.

Steve wasn't tall but he was huge. He was 5'7" on a good day but he had a 57-inch chest and 27-inch arms. He held a local record for the bench press at the time of 540 pounds. He had a picture of himself with Lou Ferrigno on the wall from when the Hulk was all the rage. Steve was about 10 years older than me but we became fast friends. Steve loved nightclubs more than I did but he hated going alone. He had cash that I didn't and a car too. He spoke broken English but he loved starting shit with guys that thought they were tough. We went to every club in town but Christopher's in Cockeysville was one of his favorites. It had recently changed over from Ordell Braase's Flaming Pit. The bar had a smaller sub-section called NUMBERS that had these old-timey phones on every table with a map of all the other table numbers. People sat at a table and called other tables to flirt with one another. It was our first form of social media dating. The Christopher's side of the club usually had 70s dance bands.

When things were slow around town or on the weeknights when I had off I would go to Numbers by myself. I started drinking there a lot and started making some older barfly friends. There were some women there but it was mostly a nice dark place where you could get good and drunk while talking smack. I met a nice old man there that used to drink his ass off. Every once in a while his sons would come in and hang out for a beer or two. The old man lived near me so he started giving me a ride home when he saw me hitch-hiking down the street from the bar. It got to the point where I could check the bar after a night of partying somewhere else to see if he was there. If he was I could hang till he left in order to catch a ride. Everybody was really cool, they just liked to sit around chat and drink pitchers of beer together. It was odd though, either they would all be there or none of them would be.

One night I was sitting there with this dude Sammy and he asked me what I did for a living. I said I worked with the muscle head he saw me with at a place called Giuseppe's restaurant in Randallstown. He said, "Oh, that's over there on the other side of town where the old man stays." I said, "Yeah he gave me a ride home a few times. What do you do for work?" He said, "I'm a pitcher." I thought he was making a joke about all the pitchers he drank. I said, "Pitcher, what the hell is that?" He said really slowly and clearly; "I pitch for the Orioles." I said, "Get the fuck out of here!" He pointed to the old man and said ask Cal. I said, Cal? He said "Cal Ripken the old man that drives you home, he's a coach. That over there is Dennis Martinez and Rick Dempsey the catcher." I said, "Oh shit you're all famous I've seen all you guys play, no shit." He said yeah that's why we hide in here. I said, "Your secret is safe with me." But was it?

The next week Steve and I went there together so he could meet them all again, this time with a better attitude of fondness and reverence. Steve had a hard time doing that with other men. It was sort of like a Napoleon complex or something.

Occasionally when Steve and I were hanging out together he would see some wanna-be bodybuilder acting like a tough guy and tell me in his thick Italian accent. "Go there, tell him I say fuck you." The first time I was reluctant because these dudes were way bigger than I was; basically the biggest guys in the club. Steve would say, "No worry, he no do nothin, he pussy." So I'd walk over to some big dude in a club and Steve would watch me deliver his message. "My friend told me to come over here and tell you FUCK YOU" (usually while in front of all his friends). The typical response was "Fuck your friend, who's your friend?" I'd point, Steve would stand up and flex a little, then the guy would say something like "I don't even know him, dude." Then all the target's friends would get to see him puss out. (It was a great way for me to get revenge on those Jocks from High School.)

It was a sport for us and after a while, I started getting a sadistic kick out of it as well as the drinks Steve would buy for me for doing it. Occasionally Steve would go walk by the guy just to give him a chance to say something. He'd walk by, stop, turn, stare at them without saying anything, smile and keep walking. They never did anything with the exception of one of the smarter meatheads that tried to make Steve his friend.

KING ME!

During our club nights, Steve got to see me dance with the ladies quite a bit. Steve knew nearly every Greek, Turkish, Middle-Eastern and Italian restaurant owner in the area. Steve's wife (yes, he had a wife and 2 kids) grew up with the band Molly Hatchet in Florida so they also knew a fair amount of people in the music industry too. They were quite the pair.

One of Steve's friends owned a small club on the west side of town called King Farouk's. One night he took me there to meet the owners. While we were there Steve suggested, ok nearly forced me to compete in a dance contest that I handily won. It was a male solo dance freestyle contest/audition designed to find talent for the new Ladies' Night strip shows. Some of the guys were muscular but that wasn't really the goal of the shows back then: It was about male dancing. I was one of the youngest people in the entire bar that night but no one seemed to notice but me. I had long hair down to my cute ass and it was the 80s so that was my thing. What everyone did notice was that this new industry would be a gold mine for everyone involved. One thing was for sure, it filled the clubs with "big spender females." (Males usually weren't allowed in the clubs on those nights unless they worked there, owned the place or were friends with the owners.)

So I found yet another method for objectifying myself and monetizing my value to others. (Coincidence?) Sadly this was even worse than dealing for me because it was sexual in nature. The way I looked, the way I dressed and the way I moved became more hyper-sexualized as I aged. So much so that I eventually became unable to shut the sexual energy off. What I lacked in looks I made up for with provocative eye contact and seductive retort.

Farouk's and another little place on the east side of town in Middle River near my grandparents were the only two places hosting male shows for females at the time. Chippendales was just getting started out west; the stage was being set for men to dance for women all around the country. Stripping for me was a possible post-dealing avenue of revenue but the music industry was calling my name too.

To say there was a hunger for male reviews at the time would be greatly understating the case; it was a huge groundswell. The women's liberation movement had grown throughout the 60s and 70s and the act of tipping and objectifying men seemed nothing more than fair. Thankfully for me, my mother didn't like spending her money on men so we never crossed paths (that I know of). My mother obviously knew of my talents but the last thing she was looking for at this time was another Greek to hang around with.

Farouk's was a Mediterranean male playhouse and a room full of straight white women with cash was a modern-day form of Caligula for us. They started having ladies' night every week but I only went there a few times. I loved the art of dancing and I didn't think stripping was real dancing. While I wanted to be a gigolo the stripping wasn't that much fun and some of those women could actually hurt you in those days.

My scars left me wanting control over who could touch me; it was essential. That and I became very aware of certain creepy looks some of the older women gave me; it took me back to the abuse. Maybe you know the look I'm talking about. When someone looks right through you but doesn't actually see you. That look is all it takes for those of us that have been abused to be triggered. You become hypersensitive to the energy of people undressing you with their eyes. The awareness of it becomes almost impossible to shut off. It triggers your damage and sense of impending doom. It can create some scary emotional reactions too.

Unlike female dancers with male customers, this was all about old ladies grabbing things; not about old ladies spending money for side dances or nights out. Not only would they grab but they would grab hard, like they were trying to keep parts of you. Their being much older triggered my wounds even more.

What stripping did do for me was open me up to the idea of finding a rich woman or sugar momma. That was after all what my mother had been modeling for me my entire life. Beyond the cultural norm of a man being the provider and paying the bills at the time I'm not sure why she ever started monetizing herself. There was never a history of sexual abuse in her childhood and her first encounter was with my father. It's possible she was just trying to imitate the early Hollywood bombshells of the time by gold-digging and landing wealthy men.

The bottom line for me was that I wanted to self-medicate so I slowly let the stripper idea fade as I leaned more toward professional dancing again. It wasn't easy being attracted to the good girls that were afraid of me while the bad girls were attracted to and very demanding of me. It would be decades before I would ever approach a girl in a club before she approached me. They always had to start the ball rolling. That's how you avoid rejection but it means you meet the crazy girls.

SHUT UP AND DANCE

Dancing drunk wasn't easy; especially if you danced like I did; the truth is it could be outright dangerous thanks to the types of music I liked. While there were some great R&B sounds going around, Hip hop wasn't really seated yet. I danced to rock music a lot and as you probably know without a steady back beat the changes in tempo can be tricky. Looking back I'm not really sure if all those years of LSD use paid off or not but I did have a very good imagination and I was very creative on the floor. Once I added a heavy dose of sexuality and a few stripper moves, people started to remember me. I was getting noticed and not just by the ladies. Almost every night some straight guy would come up to me and ask me how I learned to dance. They'd tell stories about how their life might be if they could dance like me. They'd often suggest that I must do really well with the ladies; some would even ask if they could hang out with me and learn a move or two. Others, including local musicians, would often ask for personal instruction. A few frontmen of popular bands asked if I'd coach them so I'd go to their shows and tell them what worked and what didn't as well as how to engage with the crowd more. I really enjoyed it; I got to meet a lot of people, some quite famous now.

A very odd thing started happening for me as the female population began to be more and more empowered. Back in the 80s we called it "freakin on someone," and then "grinding." Females just started coming up and dancing with me and on me; attractive females, almost exclusively attractive females. Sometimes it was hard not to look shocked by their interest; mostly because when I was in school these same types of girls treated us long-hairs as untouchables.

My love for dancing in the limelight grew rapidly. I was beginning to gain some recognition around town. People would ask, "You're that guy that dances right?" Their attention was an aphrodisiac for that lonely child within.

Sadly though, even the positive attention couldn't really be fully enjoyed. Trying to survive my past meant not letting uninvited people touch me in a sexual way. My impromptu dance partners wouldn't just put their hands on me, they'd also put my hands on them. These females were literally putting their butts right on my crotch, then rubbing themselves up and down my body. Unfortunately for me, the first feelings were fear and anger (thanks Bob); then quickly followed by a sense of being wanted and desired. Being noticed by both women and men filled the empty chasm in my soul that the abandonment had hollowed out. It was great while the music was playing but when the lights came up at the end of the night I needed more.

I was a fairly good-looking guy but I wasn't all that, especially back then. I was thin but muscular (a dancer's body) with really good hair and a nice ass. I knew that my dancing is what interested people, not who I was inside. I never really considered their freaking on me as dancing but

I wasn't going to stop it. Before I could get used to one girl I would be sandwiched between two, often with one on each hip. The truth is I wasn't really sure if it was fun or not until I started noticing the crowds watching me. I was getting hooked on attention and didn't know it; good times for a budding codependent.

I then began to think that since everybody wanted to join me or be me that I must actually be rising above the average guy. It was all or nothing though, no in between. Suddenly those girls that shunned me as a freak in high school seemed oblivious to their own change in attitude. I even confronted a couple of my old high school cheerleaders about it one night and their simple response was, "We were stupid then."

Perhaps one of the reasons I got so many dance partners is because my actual dance partner was often with me to get things warmed up. When you dance you end up with friends that love to dance too. You end up going to the clubs to work out, not to meet people. The crowds actually become invisible as your desire to improve on your artistic expression increases. In those days ignoring people actually seemed to make them desire me even more. Sometimes I felt that dancing helped me leave my body; a skill I had learned years earlier during the abuse. Anything of a sexual nature seemed to help me escape "dumb people." Bridging dancing and sexuality together allowed me to leave the room spiritually, sometimes even harkening me back to the days in front of the jukebox with my father watching. (One night, I even got to dance with and for, this girl named Joan while her song, "I love Rock-n-Roll" played at Hammer's. Another older chick! I was 18 not 17. Joan, I'm still up for whatever, call me!)

My dance partner Kimberly and I became a well-known duo in the clubs in those days. I drank, she drove and we went anywhere we heard there was a dance floor. R&B was a staple but Hip Hop and later techno started having a larger role as the disco music faded from the DJ's playlists. Most clubs in those days focused on one music scene at a time so if you liked various forms of music you had to travel. Since Kimberly was still under the drinking age we sometimes had to go to places that would take her fake ID or just not card a pretty girl. Sometimes they just remembered our dancing and gave us free cover. (The smart club owners did it because they knew that customers liked a show and that we got people dancing.)

Eventually Kimberly and I rose to the level of competing on an episode of Dance Fever at a local nightclub. We came in second to the new trend of Irish Dancing. We lost to a mother and son that surely had us beat on the old wholesome scale, as well as the old "makes you feel all warm and fuzzy" vibe.

Following that show I was dancing solo when a man approached me. I always questioned the motive of males so I was a little stand-offish but I was in my element so I felt confident. He identified himself as a creative producer at Merv Griffin Productions (the same people that managed Dance Fever). He asked if I would audition for him. Half out of breath I said, "Yeah, sure, when?" He said, "Right now, what do you want to hear?" I said, "Whatever you got." He said, "No, pick something so you can show me your stuff." He had a record in his hand so I said, "What do you have there?" "He said it doesn't have to be this." I looked down and he had the Prince Purple Rain LP and I said, "That's perfect," he said, "What track?" I said, "Any track." He said, "No, you pick one." I said, "Darlin Nikki." He said "Are you sure" with a smile. I said "OH YEAH!!! I'm sure!"

The dance floor had several tiers, brass rails and a set of steps. I used them all. Honestly, I loved Prince but I still thought I had him beat because of my physical form; he was certainly better with his spins (they're hard drunk). We shared the splits but I had a better high kick; probably his shoes and the fact that I didn't have to sing or play a guitar.

The audition rocked as I danced seductively looking to my friend Kimberly standing at the edge of the dance floor. I knew I was killing it because I knew that smile she had when she was impressed by and proud of her partner. When the song ended the entire club thunderously applauded; I felt like I had arrived. Right then my whole life made sense;

the dancing in bars with my alcoholic father, the hyper-sexuality from the sexual abuse and even the emotionally unavailable mother.

Sweating my butt off, I walked over to the producer now standing at the edge of the dance floor. He continued to clap with his hands high in the air with a big smile. It then seemed obvious to me that he was just a straight guy that loved talent and artistic expression. He said, "That was perfect!" We're starting a new show in a few months (he didn't know the name for sure). I want you to be on our first show doing exactly what you just did. He said, "Let's get some contact information; thank you for doing this for me."

I don't really think I ever danced for attention, I just loved dancing. I liked the attention but sometimes it actually distracted me from my dancing. Dancing for me was a meditative state that would often take me away from the crowd and closer to the vibration of the Universe. It was certainly spiritual for me and it still is today. When I was dancing I could feel my father watching over me in those bars as a child. That night I questioned if my life was about to change. If I was about to fulfill both my mother's and father's lost dreams of fame and fortune?

CHAPTER TWELVE
THE MOM-ORIES REMAIN

GUNG HO

Despite how well things were looking it wasn't long after moving to Pikesville that E-1's emotional problems surfaced once again. It seems she could talk herself into a deep depressive state by hosting her own self-pity parties. The theme song was a classic and it went something like this; "If it wasn't for these damn kids ruining my life I would be a famous model married to a rich man." Money and Greeks had her both idolizing and hating Jackie O.

In the great gold-digging scheme of things, she was actually doing fairly well for herself. Her problem wasn't finding the gold it was not being able to hold out or behave long enough to tie the knot with the rich mark. By this time Ben and Herk had both tired of her Borderline Personality Disorder as well as her deep-seated anger at the world of men in general. With the exception of an occasional old-school booty call, they seemed to be over her. Since they had money they just moved on to younger models or even some professionals my sister's age. I think that made her hate my sister even more. So what did E-1 do when she hit the skids of her own reality? She kicked the dog and since she didn't have a dog or my sister at the time, she emotionally kicked me.

It was a Friday night. I'd just worked a double at Giuseppe's. I was unknowingly coming home to yet another abandonment trauma trigger. Coming home meant trying to hitchhike down a dark vacant liberty road when everyone else was heading in the opposite direction out of the city. Sometimes cars would actually turn around thinking I didn't see them. My head was always on a swivel; it had to be because at the time rednecks still hated long-hairs. The reality was that most of the cars heading the other way were angry drunk rednecks that didn't get lucky at the bars in town. If I saw them turn around I wouldn't put out my thumb as they passed me the second time; I was always ready to run. If it wasn't a redneck that turned around it was usually some pervert. If I was really desperate for a ride I would put up with the pervs gawking at my crotch long enough to get where I was headed. (This is where being angry helps and why some people stay that way. They could see it in my eyes. I was about to snap on someone so they didn't even ask for what they wanted. They just drove me where I wanted to go. All I needed was a "Don't even say it" look on my face.)

I drank my ass off at Giuseppe's. By this time I was doing every job in the building. I did an occasional pizza or late night sub but I mostly waited tables and tended bar. I would lean down behind the bar like I was getting something out from under it, then reach up and grab a bottle and use the auto shot pourer to take a shot straight into my mouth. One for them, one for me; since no one inventoried liquor in those days it was literally all I could drink.

If I didn't get picked up hitching there was a "no-colors" biker bar called the Pikeswood Inn 1 mile down the street. If I didn't get a ride by the bar I got a beer, or 20. I would get so drunk at the Pikeswood that I usually ended up puking in the parking lot. I puked a lot, almost every time I drank there. I used to think that you had to drink hard until you puked then you could just drink slowly after that. It was like filling the alcohol tank until it overflowed. My brain didn't hurt when it was that drunk.

I would usually leave the bar and start hitching home about a ½-hour before closing so I could hitchhike the people leaving. While I met a few chicks doing it, that strategy didn't always work for the Pikeswood because everyone was drunk off-their-ass. Drunk drivers are often distracted so they rarely even saw me. I had to be careful they didn't run me over.

If I walked another ¼ mile down the road I could actually catch a bus that turned around to head back to the city. I eventually figured out that I could just hitchhike at the bus stop. You could get sympathy (and perv) rides from people thinking the bus was taking too long. Sometimes I would actually step away from the street when the bus came because the bus still meant another 2-mile walk when I got off it.

I arrived home that Friday night with a pretty good buzz on. I remember walking into the building and up the stairs with a bit of a stagger; just like dear old dad. I put my key in the lock but it didn't fit. Having not lived there long I wasn't 100% sure I was even in the right building so I went outside to double-check the number.

After I confirmed it was the right building I went back up to try the key again, making sure I had the right floor this time. After another failed attempt I sat on the floor in confusion. I double-checked my keys and looked under the mat thinking maybe she had to change the locks because she got locked out or something. Under the mat was an envelope that I thought might contain a new key but it didn't. There was a handwritten note along with $14. It was short and sweet. "You don't live here anymore don't bother knocking I went to the beach."

I knew I was screwed because these apartments had good locks and thick metal doors. We lived on the 3rd floor and these units were almost un-scalable; even harder under the influence. It was late and I was worn out tired drunk. The maintenance office would be closed until morning. I considered just lying to them and telling them I lost the key but I figured she may have had to pay them to change the locks. I knew that I had to be back at work the next day so I figured that heading back to good ole Cockeysville would not be a good plan. I just slept in the hallway. I went back to work the next day in the same clothes. Steve noticed and invited me to sleep on his sofa for a few nights.

There was a party in Summer Hill at Billy F's house that next weekend. I wanted to go because he lived right next door to my old flame Karen. Looking back it seems that whenever I was threatened with abandonment I would have this innate drive to rekindle some old love from the past. Pretty sure I just wanted to be wanted by someone that knew me.

I didn't rekindle any old love that night; she wasn't even there for some reason. While there I made contact with a good friend Denise Hanna and her brother who used to live across the street from the party. Back in the day when Karen and I were going steady, we'd all head to the Hanna's house after school to smoke weed and watch General Hospital; we had all become pretty close during those days.

The Hannas learned of my homeless status during the party. They invited me to come home and sleep at their house that night. They had moved from Summer Hill and they now lived about 100 yards from the Pebbles Pizza location. Their house was on my way to Giuseppe's so that worked great for me.

That night I stayed in Pat's room. Pat was one of her many older brothers. When I woke up the next morning the family was in the kitchen making breakfast. They looked like one of those TV families; a little freakish, like some Norman Rockwell scene or something, with lots of food on the table.

They fed me and started asking me about where I was going to stay; I didn't know. Despite being embarrassed I told them the truth. I'm pretty sure they could see the hurt and rejection on my face. Without blinking an eye Ms. Hanna says; "You'll stay here until you can find a good place to live. A place where you won't have someone kicking you out all the time." I almost cried but I didn't want all these guys to see that so I sat up straight in disbelief and tried to assure them I wouldn't need to stay too long. Ms. Hanna reached her arm across the table held my wrist and said, "It's OK, you'll stay here until you find a good place." Ms. Hanna was a real class act, a real lady, a lady with an innate Grace and warmth. In that moment her Grace probably saved at least one life.

I stayed with the Hannas for about 2 months. I barely knew Pat but he shared his room with me without question. The whole family made me feel extremely welcome. I never tried to join in on the Dungeons and Dragons games but I was happy to sit there and drink beer while they played. You could just tell there was love in that house; certainly a reflection of Ms. Hanna's warm heart.

As mentioned the Grace of the Hanna family probably saved my life, maybe even someone else's. I was angry and hurt back then but I wouldn't show it. I was good at keeping those scars hidden on the inside where only I felt them. Thanks to my father and Busha I was capable of really good manners when I needed to have them. My survival training from my family's dysfunction allowed me to adapt to my surroundings in both the good times and the bad. I couldn't forget people that harmed me but I've also never forgotten the people that helped me.

While staying at the Hanna's house I began to reconsider earlier thoughts about joining the military. When I dropped out of school I was 16 and I wanted to join the service back then. I didn't want to join the service to help my country though; I wanted to join the service to kill men legally and for a good cause. That's how mad at people (men) I really was.

I started contacting recruiters. I began the process to enter the Army or Navy. Wormo had joined the Air Force by this time but the Fly Boys seemed kind of soft and the Jarheads weren't exactly considered the intellectual set at the time. I needed to get some of my old health documents and papers so I called my mother one day to have her send them to me.

As soon as I said "It's your son I need my birth certificate and medical records," she started screaming at me. "Where the hell have you been? Why haven't you called me?" It was the same thing all over again, it was all about her. I said, "You kicked me out remember, why would I call you?" Again she rehashed an old line from our past. "I'm still your mother Manuel." I said "Is that what you call it? Can I just have the damn papers?"

She changed the subject and asked what I needed the papers for. I said, "Because I'm joining the army." She said, "Don't you need my permission?" I just laughed and asked when I could get them. She made a deal to meet me with the papers saying she wanted to see me. She asked me if I was dancing and wanted to know how I was making money. I said I'm still working at Giuseppi's. "Where are you living?" I said with a really nice family in Lutherville (A wealthier area than we could afford). "What family?" "Does it matter?" "No, I guess not." (I didn't want her starting trouble for anyone.)

So I let her buy me lunch one day and she started trying to make some deal with her own conscience. She said, "If you are serious about joining the service we can talk about you coming 'home' until you do." It turned out that her Jewish boyfriend was now staying there and that he was the one with the family loyalty conscience, not her. His name was Sandy; he owned a small glass company. He was her first non-wealthy boyfriend since the cop and good ole Uncle Jim in the first grade. As it turns out the new biker-looking Jewish boyfriend was teaching her some basic human values.

I eventually came back to the house and stayed for several months while my paperwork was processed to enter the Reserves. I couldn't go regular Army because I didn't have a GED or a High School diploma. The goal was to get through basic training and then transfer to full-time service. I was sworn in that December 4th (1981).

PACKING MY SHIT

It was a cold morning on February 25, 1982, when my mother waved goodbye as the recruiter and I left the house for BWI airport. I was on my way to Fort Leonard Wood Missouri or as I like to call it; my first rehab. I'd never been in a large plane before, only a small one piloted by some guy my mother knew. I was heading to Missouri for both Basic Training and A.I.T. (Advanced Individual Training). My Military Occupational Specialty was "62 Bravo" (Construction Equipment Repair/Diesel Mechanic).

I tried to prepare for my US ARMY rehab by cutting down on my alcohol use, but less and none are quite a ways apart. I started eating more and drinking less but I hadn't stopped altogether. I even started jogging and doing pushups but the haircut would have to wait. I had no idea when I would see my lover alcohol again. I knew there were other ways to catch a buzz if I needed to. Things like Nyquil (with the shot glass lid) could work but I wasn't sure if I could get that either. I wasn't shaking yet in the mornings but I was worried about not being able to get to sleep at night and having to wake up really early. When it came to enlisting I didn't feel like I had a choice; I really didn't see any other way to remedy my life problems. I knew the Army would always provide me shelter albeit sometimes in a tent but even that was more than I usually had.

The current conflicts were in South America with the Contra Rebels; it was becoming more volatile every day so the jungle looked like it might be my destination. I loved being in the woods. I pondered how I might sneak off and disappear into that jungle one day, maybe even find the pot growers. That was if someone didn't do me the favor of taking me out first.

There is a pretty good chance that my lifetime of risk-taking was rooted in the desire to have my struggle ended. There were times when it made me quite fearless and even scary to some people. The service was just a way to commit suicide without the cosmic ramifications. I viewed it as a federalized righteous twist on suicide by cop.

The trip on the plane wasn't bad; the stewardess was hot just like in the magazines. What I really liked about her was the wonderful little bottles of booze she was selling. My first thought was, that's a small bottle and my second was, how many can I get. I probably had about 4 on the plane and then I had another 4 that I put in my pockets to sneak into Fort Leonard Wood. I was 18 and she didn't ask for any ID for the hard liquor.

There was a brief moment when I looked out the window of the DC 9 and saw the wings flapping up and down in the wind as the snow was blowing over them. All I could see in my head was the old Twilight Zone episode where the demon ape thing appeared out on the wings. I just shut my eyes and downed another miniature.

The bus ride from the airport in St Louis to the fort took almost 3 hours so we wouldn't be getting there until around 1:00am. I drank one of the miniatures from the plane. Someone on the bus said the army did searches for contraband so I drank the other 3 bottles within the first 2 hours.

The fear of being alone left me fairly quickly as the bus pulled up to the reception station (where we'd be processed like sheep). We were funneled into a huge WWII barracks for the night. There were about 60 racks (bunks) in a large room with a 4-stall bathroom at each end.

Almost everybody still had hair with the exception of a few rednecks that probably never did. While some guys were acting tough a few of the more sheltered boys were still in their clothes crying under the covers.

This whole process was a major head rush for a "last buzz-having" budding antisocial empath like myself. Feelings were being felt everywhere in the room and I was trying hard not to tune into other people's emotions. The empathic skills that once helped me survive and even thrive in the drug business were suddenly going to have to be controlled or turned off without alcohol. All the emotions felt by the people around me were becoming a little overwhelming; I wasn't comfortable with honest emotions. I couldn't reactively turn them off in anger because I didn't know these people and some of them seemed damaged like me.

I was in a strange new world. I knew that without the booze or some drugs, these sensitivities and feelings of mine would have to be endured by pure will. I began to use some of the breathing exercises that I had read about and practiced in my conjuring days. It started to seem like some of my old hateful thoughts and attitudes may be necessary to survive the possible future ahead of me. I had lots of rage inside of me but now I was going to have to become a real killer, even though deep in my heart that wasn't my father's son. I began to consider that I might be quite successful at killing if I could adopt the right mindset. I pondered how the little Damien devil kid in the Omen movie rose up through the military ranks; maybe that was my path too. (Have you noticed that I was raised by the television).

The next morning we were woken up by shouting and yelling. We were beginning to learn the pre-basic basics of the US Army. I understood the need for rules but I was beginning to think these people hadn't really thought a lot of their methods through. The notion that I could help with my management skills was very short-lived.

Did I mention that I had hair down to my ass? There were some people in the chow halls that already had their new haircuts but not my platoon. Some of them tried to make me feel bad about the hair but the little poor kid in the free lunch line came out once again. I decided to spin that energy around and do what my father taught me; if you got it, flaunt it! I mean, after all, we all knew it was getting cut. People had suggested I get it cut before I left to avoid the hippy harassment but I figured that since it would be years before I might have it again I was just going to enjoy it for as long as I could. Why not let all these clowns know just how cool I was when I was on the street. So I just strutted my stuff, flipping my hair, hoping it might help me find some drugs or at least the druggy people.

FEELING DRAB

The first thing you get on your first day in, is a new outfit. The Army had just introduced the new Jungle Camo while the plain "Olive Drabs" were being phased out. Next came the dreaded haircuts. We were rushed over to the barber so we could wait in line. We remained in the "at ease" position until directed to take another step forward.

I figured out what they were doing. They were forcing compliance; they were dehumanizing us, conditioning us to be robots, eager to leap at their command. I understood it just fine, they were hardening us, even trying to make us mad. I didn't care because I knew they couldn't break me and I was already mad. I would just observe, adapt and overcome their little head games. In all honesty, I was distracted by the detox process I was going through; wondering if my hands would ever stop shaking.

So we stood there waiting in another long line. Hurry up and wait they called it. Made no sense but then again they weren't exactly the intellectual set. I had to accept that I would be ruled and managed by morons. Death could not come soon enough.

It took about an hour for the 60 guys in front of me to make it through the haircut line. (I thought, that's a head a minute; $4x60=$240 an hour. Somebody was making money and yes we had to pay for it.) I entered the shop expecting to hear some hair jokes but no one seemed to care. So I took a seat in the chair that would change who I was for years to come (notice who I am, was how I looked). The barber said hi, not oh boy we got ourselves one of them long hairs. I said, "Do me a favor, he said "A little off the top?" I giggled and said, "No, enjoy this because I'm gonna hate it." He said, "I'll try but it's just another head young man."

He started my transformation by taking out the part in the middle of my head first, then a strip down each side of that. I was looking in the mirror at myself with just long hair on the sides and nothing on the top. It was a reverse mullet Mohawk thing. I said, "Holy shit don't stop now" prompting the Sergeant in the room to shout "Language!" I went from pretty hippy to a Turkish-looking terrorist in about 30 seconds. Then I felt a breeze as I put on my hat and headed out the door.

I was already quite a different person from the one that had first stepped foot on Fort Leonard Wood. No drugs or booze, no hair, no cussing, no broads and not in control of anything. It was about as drastic of a change experience a human could go through in 48 hours.

We were barely there a week when people started trying to go AWOL. Two kids had taken off in the middle of the night and no one knew where they were. Lost in the woods some presumed. We heard about the search effort so the idea of leaving became quite dashed. We were 100 miles from a major city and surrounded by what most of us thought were the Ozark Mountains.

Psyched or scared we were all anxious to get to our final company assignment and begin Basic Training. There seemed to be some sort of a status thing about how close you were to being a soldier. They called us pukes and recruits because we hadn't finished Basic yet. They made it really clear we weren't soldiers until we did. I saw the mind game they were playing but I still fell for it. I now wanted to see if I was as tough as I thought I was; if I was as much of a badass as I thought I could be.

MY NEW DADDY

It was about 8:00pm on a Winter Sunday evening; half the guys were in their racks. It was dark and cold and I was about to meet my new best friend. Our introduction started with yelling at the opposite end of the old WWII barracks. I was far enough away, not yet being accosted by the verbal onslaught. We heard "Drop your cocks and grab your socks," so we did. When the voice got to us we "packed our shit" and were rushed outside to formation. There stood a dark-complected Hispanic guy about 5' 6, built like a tank, quickly pacing back and forth, yelling louder than I ever heard anyone yell in my life (and that's saying something). "GET ON THAT TRUCK!!! LET'S GO LET'S GO!!!! You fucking pukes MOVE MOVE MOVE!!!!." I could actually see the veins popping out of his neck. The so-called truck was what they called a cattle car. It looked exactly like the trucks they took cattle to slaughter in. It was the trailer end of a semi with a few small windows at the top: It reminded me of the Nazi train cars they used to move the Jews to the death camps.

"Get in that damn truck! MOVE! MOVE! MOVE! Come on ladies! Take a seat put that duffle bag on your lap and your face in that bag. What are you looking at Private, are you gay, do you want me or something? I don't swing that way private!" Oh shit, he was heading our way.

"Where are you from private, Texas? There are only two things in Texas, Queers and Steers and I don't see no horns little missy. Are you queer looking at me like that?" I giggled, "What are you smirking about private? Did I tell you to smile? You don't have permission to be happy. Put your face in that duffle bag and don't look at me again." Another guy looked up. "Drop and give me 40 son! Let me tell you pukes something. I divorced my wife. I shot my dog and I flushed my goldfish down the toilet. I have no responsibilities, you are my only responsibility and it's my responsibility to KICK YOUR ASS! I'm gonna make soldiers out of you so you aren't the first guy to die in combat just trying to make me look bad! Anyone want to leave, leave now cause you ain't gonna make it in my platoon. I'm gonna make men out of you if it kills you!"

I thought, what the hell did I get myself into now? I might have to kill this mother fucker is all I could think. Then I realized this mother fucker would be hard to kill. I immediately began plotting my backup escape plan. Not because I really wanted out but because it somehow reduced my anxiety to think I could leave. Sadly, in some perverse way, I had now found another place that I could be kicked out of if I didn't meet a certain standard. There would be no charm offense here. My sexuality wasn't going to work on this dude. I thought at least the playing field was level; money or where you came from didn't seem to matter here unless you were from Texas.

The next day we learned our company name and company motto. We were, wait for it, THE DELTA DEMONS. Was this another sign? Was the dark side reaching out to me? Was it just withdrawal? Too much LSD?

The demon word was cool but Delta was Greek. In mathematics/physics, the delta triangle represents a change in value. I knew change was hard and I had a lot to learn if I was going to master this system. Did I mention push-ups yet? Probably about 2000 in the first 24 hours, 40 at a time. The term Drop and give me 40 would become a background noise heard in the din of Fort Leonard Wood everywhere we went.

The next day, after what seemed like 6 hours of exercise and waiting in lines, Sergeant Franko called each one of us into his office to have a "talk" with us. Sometimes he would yell at people, sometimes guys would drop for 40 and other times people would leave his office crying with him yelling "YOU AIN'T GONNA MAKE IT PRIVATE!!! PACK YOUR BAGS!!! MOMMY'S WAITING!!" Honestly, the "pack your bags" stopped my heart more than his yelling. I was used to people yelling but when he yelled "Pack your bags" my heart dropped and I froze. This dude didn't have to create trauma just activate it.

I entered the office by doing the cute little footwork they taught us (I was a dancer no problem). He talked, I looked, he told me to stare straight ahead. He said; "JOHN!! Your last name is John?! That's a first name, who fucked that up?" I said it was changed from Greek Sergeant! He said "GREEK?! The Greeks were Warriors John the Greek, are you a warrior John the Greek," "I'M GONNA BE Sergeant!!!!" "Right answer Private John! Am I gonna get 100% out of you Private John?" "I certainly hope so Sergeant." "HOPE SO!? What the fuck is hope so? Drop and give me 40 JOHN!" After critiquing my form he said, "GET THE FUCK OUT OF MY OFFICE PRIVATE JOHN. That damn name makes it sound like I'm looking for a personal latrine. Bye Private JOHN!!! Next!!!"

To be honest, what existed of my ego was so deep down behind so many walls he was going to have trouble finding it. In hindsight, I think he sensed that. I'm sure I wasn't the first person he'd seen in withdrawal.

As I mentioned earlier Basic Training was my first true detox. I don't think that I had drawn a clean and sober breath since I was around 13 or 14. As the days passed my anxiety grew but thanks to all the exercise and energy burns it quickly dissipated. I was tired but that didn't stop me from wanting a drink.

I heard talk about the PX having 3.2 beer but we couldn't access that until we were done basic training. Basic lasted 8 weeks; then engineer school. Aside from a few really bad colds and the cough medicine we got for it, there wasn't much mood-altering available. A couple guys were huffing stuff but that was bad news; I considered it a tool for the garbage heads. I would just have to stick it out and persevere. It felt a lot like it did when we were hungry as kids; you just had to wait it out.

CLICK CLICK BOOM

I'm not sure exactly when it happened but one day, about 3 weeks in, something just clicked and my mindset changed. It could have been after my body detoxed but it might have been when the brainwashing started taking hold. I was growing more and more interested in their killing machine agenda. Maybe the fact that everything we shot at or attacked had to do with people. We shot at human silhouettes, we shot at the doors on trucks, we threw hand grenades into houses and fired anti-tank weapons at anything that moved; we even got yelled at when we missed. Regardless, it was all a perfect fit for my anger and rage. The fact that I didn't care about anyone and that I wanted to die made me very dangerous. I was exactly what they wanted and I was feeling it. At some point during my training, I became some sort of a "gung ho" monster. I wanted to be first at everything we did as a group and sometimes I even repeated obstacles when I finished early. I'd be "killing it" and I'd catch Sergeant Franco watching me while pretending he wasn't. That's how I knew I was doing it right; just like my father watching me in the bars.

On the last day of basic, the Sergeants ordered the Beer Truck to come to the barracks. It was essentially an ice cream truck converted into a beer bar with hot dogs and burgers (pretty sure the Army invented the food truck). If you haven't ever had 3.2 beer it's like drinking air with half the alcohol of beer. You get really bloated before you get drunk but since we hadn't had any in 2 months we did get a little loose and silly. We were only allowed two each; I gladly helped the lightweight's finish theirs.

Once Basic was over we started engineering school and then our Military Occupational Specialty (MOS). Mine was pretty cool. We worked on everything from diesel generators to tank engines but mostly dozers, scrapers, graders and cranes. We had to learn how to drive them all too; that was cool. It took me back to those innocent times playing with Tonka trucks in the dirt as a child.

I chose my MOS because my uncle Norman (also my godfather and a Vietnam Vet) was now a supervisor at the Alban Tractor/Caterpillar plant outside of Baltimore. It was his idea that I do this MOS and then come to work with him. I freakin loved heavy equipment and I wasn't a bad mechanic except for the time I almost blew up a Detroit Diesel only to be saved by a Sergeant with a clipboard. I could write a whole book about the Army from the war games to the inter-company brawls at the Animal House bar on post. I even had a few smart-ass run-ins with the MPs that I usually had to be told about the day after.

During this whole time, Sergeant Franco was still watching me out of the corner of his eye, always checking my form and energy output. We had a really cute Greek second Lieutenant that liked to talk to me because I was Greek. (Females were just beginning to train with males at the time.) She outranked all the sergeants and they were attracted to her so it pissed a few of them off when she gave a "puke" like me special attention.

I knew how to work people so I figured as long as I could charm her into my fan club then I would have a failsafe. (A very common awareness for the abused.) I don't think she was Franco's type so it didn't seem to bother him. I think he found the other Sergeants getting mad about it pretty funny. I was able to use my charm with her for a bit of leverage. It was insurance against any of these DI's trying to actually kill me. They may have had no ill intent at all; maybe it was just a "somebody wants you dead" scar left over from my family.

After being torn down physically and emotionally for a few weeks there were 4 of us that eventually became exactly what they wanted. It was obvious we had bought what they were selling. We bought into the whole ready-for-war mentality as well as adapting to the military structure. We wanted to be tested to prove our metal.

Danny (from Kentucky) and I became fast friends during basic. He even saved me from the MPs a couple of times. We went from trying to find the easier way around obstacles to diving face-first into the biggest mud puddles we could find. (All while Franco kept watching.) I went from catching him staring at me to see what I was doing wrong to catching him being surprised and even a little proud of my performance. He tried not to let me see the latter but we both knew what was happening; I was becoming a little soldier badass. I loved it so much I even started to seriously consider Ranger School.

Thanks to my old alter ego "Butch Cassidy" I was also pretty damn good at the range, with the exception of that forest fire I almost started with a LAW (Light Anti-tank Weapon). Butch Cassidy had entered the modern era but the wind left his sails when they told us that there probably wouldn't be a war in South America thanks to Reagan. That disappointed a lot of us. Almost as fast as the fervor switched on to train hard, it switched off. (That was around the same time I resumed drinking.)

HARDER

I might have been an obnoxious little punk when I was dealing but now I was actually dangerous thanks to my military training and conditioning. I had just spent 6 months being taught to target and kill humans and now I was being sent back to a reality I didn't like.

One night I let some random girl at a club punch me in the stomach as hard as she could so it became a thing. It never hurt but the guys doing it would sometimes move me back a few feet. It seemed to be great fun for the girls; a conversation starter for sure. My hair was short for the first time in my life so it made me a little stealthy to the preppy girls. (No one knew I was a hippy anymore; but I still was, on the inside.) I looked harmless now but I certainly wasn't. I looked just like you might expect, like I just got back from boot camp (or a Middle-Eastern terrorist camp).

I now had something that very few of those rich kids and other dealers had; a lot of experience outside of Maryland. I was also armed with the confidence I gathered, along with the tools of destruction as a government-certified soldier. Coming home from the military gets you a lot of attention from the ladies. It's like they now knew that I was more of a man than the other boys, a tough guy even, ready to die for his country. I did walk differently and I was even more intense than I had ever been. I also had a new Delta Demon tattoo. (Tattoos weren't exactly in vogue at the time so they started a lot of conversations.)

While I had entered the reserves to eventually transition to regular army I didn't see that happening until someone started a real war.

The Sandinista National Liberation Front was in control and things were calming down in South America. US involvement was limited to special ops: Granada hadn't happened yet.

I wasn't big on God but I did notice that something spared me from being a full-time peacetime soldier (Grace?). I went to church every Sunday while in basic because you could smoke on the way and because God was all anybody had. I realized I literally may have dodged a bullet by being forced to join the Reserves first (thank God). All I knew was that even though I only weighed about 140 pounds no one on the street was going to mess with me. I was angry as ever and now I was less afraid to die for what I believed in. I wasn't afraid of getting shot by anyone because I had already accepted the possibility of my death. I knew those soft little civilian cops were certainly not going to stand in my way or control me. I was Federal property and I had a legion of brothers on my side.

RIGHT SIZED

I always had a great work ethic. I knew that if you wanted security of any kind you had to have cash in your pocket. That meant having some kind of job be it legal or not. It was my experience that you could never count on anyone else for your security needs. Dealing was no longer an option because I was of legal age. Now I also had the Army to answer to. That meant there was a whole new set of laws that I could be prosecuted under.

Getting a job at Alban Tractor/Caterpillar would take some time. Two months of training was not enough to feel very confident as a diesel mechanic and I didn't have the tools. The CAT jobs were highly revered by people with a lot more experience. I would have to wait for my uncle to slide me in on my potential and army service.

I heard through a friend that a local deli in Cockeysville was trying to start up a pizza business without much luck. I decided to stop by to see if I could make a deal with the owner. We met and he agreed to hire me as their pizza man on the spot. I agreed to work almost every evening except for Sunday (because they closed early). Everything in the pizza area would be my baby but he would assist me by preparing the dough in the morning.

It only took me about a week to improve their business and within 2 months I had built their pizza sales to more than 4 times what they were. It was a fun place working with a great group of folks. We had a blast from trash ball battles in the kitchen to partying out back. Typical of the hospitality industry there were often sexually charged exchanges behind the counter. I liked exotic women and the Deli was probably one of the most multicultural businesses in the area.

As the pizza man I had my own fridge and the evening crowd didn't mind drinking a few beers as the day came to a close. The drinking became earlier and earlier but nobody cared because everybody partied in the early 80s. It didn't hurt that we had a liquor store 4 doors up.

One of the managers we'll call "M" was actually a fairly big dealer and even more of a partier. He would actually have shipments of Sinsemilla mailed to him from Hawaii in sealed pineapple juice containers. I know this because I witnessed the smell of those packages being opened from their vacuum-sealed bags. There was also plenty of coke, regular weed, hash, and Rush (a form of industrial deodorant that people huffed). We all became fast friends but probably no pair closer than Melanie and I.

Since we both lived on the same side of town Melanie started giving me rides home when she worked nights. I hadn't gotten a car yet so she helped out a lot. She often went to work earlier than I did so going in together was rare but we always got high on the way if we did. I became friends with both her and her husband. We all partied together at the quad they lived in. Melanie and her husband were a few years older than I but she always had weed and I always had the beer. Since we were headed in the same direction it worked great; we kept each other high and laughing.

Melanie and her husband had a 7-year-old child but they were struggling to make another one. They both seemed to make that really clear to me: In hindsight maybe too clear. Melanie began to flirt with me even when her husband was around and he never seemed to care. He seemed to know all about our rides home too. I just saw them as really friendly people and sexuality was much freer than it is now.

SUPER NOVA

I knew that unless I was dealing drugs joining the service would be one of the only ways that I could save enough money to get a car. In those days people like me didn't get credit (even at 20% interest): There certainly wasn't going to be a cosigner in my future.

A couple of weeks after I returned from Basic Training my grandfather heard that I had gotten a job across town so he let it be known that he was selling his 1972 Chevy Nova. The car was only 10 years old at the time and he would sell it to me for $500. The deal required 1/3 of my military savings. I got liability insurance for a couple hundred, the tags and an inspection for another $100. I now had my first real car on the road: the first thing I'd ever owned besides some clothes or a stereo. To me this meant that I would never be homeless again; there would always be a place to sleep and I could keep my stuff in the trunk.

I honored that car; named it Michelle. I never drove her drunk (my father taught me that). In fact, if I knew that I was going to party I would just hitchhike out and leave it home. That or I would leave it where I was and just hitchhike home the 20 miles or more. All I knew was that I wanted to get drunk and I didn't want the car holding me back. I never once slept in it, nor did I ever pass out in it. It was a very valued commodity to me but like anything good in my life it didn't last long.

One night Brian and I went to help my sister move to her new place on Wyanoke Road. I was feeling down because a girl I was interested in had other commitments. I was also a little handicapped because I had 7 stitches in my hand from a work injury at the deli (probably too high). I remember Brian trying to cheer me up by saying; "You don't know happiness until you know sorrow." Probably the deepest thing that dude ever said in his life. I felt like I knew sorrow so I was waiting on the happy.

There wasn't a lot of partying or anything during the move; just me, Brian, my sister and a few dinghy strippers. Since you never knew what those girls were up to in the bathroom all I can say is we weren't doing much partying. We might have had one beer when we were done. Our plan was to save the partying for when we got back to my house.

We were heading North on Charles Street getting ready to turn onto Northern Parkway towards Pikesville when out of the dark, came a Volkswagen station wagon without any headlights on, BAM!!! Head on!!!

The car filled with sparks from the steel-on-steel impact. Their little car bounced off us and went down a 15-foot embankment where it struck a small tree. I tried to open my door to run down to the other car whose horn was now blaring. I had a visual of a person knocked unconscious or dead, leaning against the steering wheel. My door didn't open. I yelled "fuck" because I knew my car frame had been bent. I jumped out through the window, bad hand and all. I went running down the hill to check on the people in the car (my army training I guess). I greeted one of the four 16-year-old kids with his back to me staring at his car with his friends still in it. He then tried to walk up the hill, saw me and started shouting some incomprehensible sounds. Then he started with the sign language.

After he hid his pot Brian helped me get the other 3 kids out of their car. They were all deaf. No one was seriously hurt, just a lot of shock. I stood there heartbroken, staring back at the car that I worked so hard to get knowing it was gone (along with my backup home). My liability insurance meant there would be no help fixing it so this kid would have to pay. The insurance company did nothing to fight for me despite the fact that the 4 deaf kids were drunk and out after the city curfew.

It became public knowledge as the news later broke that there was a big deaf kid party disturbing the rich people 3 blocks away. It had been raided for underage drinking by the cops. These kids were actually fleeing the scene of a busted party with their lights off on purpose (the cops noted it in the report). Just my luck, the little rich kid driver was the son of a local judge. It would be back to hitchhiking and bumming rides from Melanie and anyone else that I could find until I could get my car fixed; if I could get it fixed. It seemed the rich were screwing the poor once more. These rich people were gonna have to pay somehow.

Sadly the Nova never got fixed as it was eventually totaled. My intrapersonal scripts played louder; "Nothing good ever happens for me and when it does, someone always fucks it up," and "No good deed goes unpunished," for helping my sister. My perspective on evil began to change but not how you might think. I began to consider that evil only existed in people. That what we called evil was just the manifestation of selfishness and self-centeredness; that the cosmos had nothing to do with it. Evil was the fallout from people putting themselves first and not caring how they affected others. I was getting even angrier.

I returned to hitch-hiking back and forth to work. Now I could drink all I wanted without ever considering my level of sobriety. Many hours were spent walking down the side of some road or highway drunk while mired in self-pity and victimization. I started hanging out at the bars more often after work and getting drunker than ever. I began to drink a lot more vodka. I figured it was cultural for me having Russian blood and all. I'd order it with a bad Russian accent too, "Wattka!!" I began to care less and less about getting home at night because it wasn't my home, it was hers. I would break into empty apartments, crash on people's sofas and sleep in 24-hour business hallways. Bridges were a nice place to get out of the rain but I even slept out on the grass next to the highway if I had to.

I remember one night I tried to hitchhike back to Pikesville a little late. I stayed at the bar too long and most of the roads were empty. I walked two miles to the highway exit on 83 and Padonia roads where I tried unsuccessfully for about an hour to catch a ride. I got so tired around 3am, I decided to cross the street and catch a nap. Just kidding! I crossed the street to pass out in the grass.

The next thing I remember was a cement truck passing by me at about 6am shaking the ground where I lay. I was 12 feet from the road. I woke up to the light of dawn, seeing lots of cars and all the normal earthlings driving to work. I got pissed off when I realized that I had just committed to dying for this country and these people didn't care if I was dead on the side of the road. I thought, this is how you people act? All these people could see me lying out here on the grass and not one of them stopped to see if I was OK or even dead. "ASSHOLES!!!! FUCKING ASSHOLES!!!!!"

I walked back into Cockeysville and as fate would have it I passed the old apartment where I used to climb balconies. I could see through the sliding glass window that it was empty. Since I had about 6 hours before I had to be at work at the Deli I figured a nap was in order. I climbed up to the third-floor porch and popped the lock on the glass door. While there I reflected back on how my sister and I managed food there in that kitchen as well as my early abandonment experiences.

I pictured how I used to stand on the high chair to make my special Mac & Cheese with hot dog pieces. I looked into the fridge and it looked just like ours, empty. These apartments had free heat so I turned it up, laid down and took a nap. I woke up, washed my semi-bald head in the sink and sat on the floor of what used to be my bedroom. One of my mother's old boyfriends had built a wall splitting the master bedroom into two rooms so that my mother had a room alone without my sister. My sister got the window and I got the dark square corner near the walk-in closet. The wall was gone now but I could still see it despite all the brilliant light that seemed to be flowing in now. Around 2:30pm I headed off to work to get something to eat.

TIME TO BRAGG

I did OK getting to work without my car for a while but I became a little careless about being there on time. I was rocking their pizza business and we all knew it. I understand now that they had to give me a hard time for being late because it was bad for morale but I didn't care. I did good work for them.

The evening managers were my party friends and the girls were my flirt buddies. It was the early 80s; everyone spanked each other on the ass and said perverted stuff. We would often accidentally-on-purpose bump crotches and asses when we squeezed through the sandwich line. Sometimes we would even pet each other where the customers couldn't see it; hell sometimes we pet each other when they could, nobody cared.

Since I needed a ride and Melanie was going that way we carpooled more often; almost daily after she started working nights. We would have very deep conversation about her family and their desire to have another kid without any luck. Her husband and I were on good terms and again, he didn't seem to care what we did. I figured he had a girl on the side and it was the 80s. The three of us even partied together on a few occasions. I was a hip young man but I was not worldly by any means. I was clueless to any possible schemes Melanie and her husband might have had.

Melanie and I were having sex in the car at least once a week, sometimes more. There seemed to be no barrier to our involvement but still no talk of difficulties between her and her husband. It wasn't my problem I wasn't the married one. That was their business. (In hindsight I am certain he knew.)

I worked at the deli the night before I was to leave for my Army Reserve annual two-week summer camp. Obviously, Melanie and I had formed an attachment and we wouldn't be seeing each other for several weeks. So on this night, she decided that she would come into the house with me, to the bed. My mother and Sandy were in the next room asleep. They had probably had sex and passed out already.

Bringing a female into my room was never a problem. Growing up everyone in the house brought people home. My first girlfriend to spend a night was my Skateland girlfriend Jenifer around age 13. This would however be the first time that Melanie and I had sex in a bed. We did it 4 times that late spring night. It was pretty intense.

I got up the next morning at 5 am. Melanie was long gone. My mother agreed to give me a ride to my U.S.A.R. station: Probably why she was asleep early.

My Reserve unit/company was the 818th Maintenance Division on Green Spring Ave about a 10-minute ride from the house. I had my BDU's (camo fatigues) on and I was looking good. I had hidden two small ½ pint bottles of Black Berry Brandy deep in the center of my duffle bag so they wouldn't be found or get broken. I wasn't sure if I would get away with it or not. I was a little nervous pulling up because military rules are much more complicated.

When we got to my unit I got out of the car, put on my hat, grabbed my duffle from the trunk and turned to walk up the hill. "What in the hell?" All I saw was people carrying booze and government hand trucks fully stacked with cases of beer and liquor. People were carrying 4 and 5, ½ gallon bottles of liquor at a time. There were hundreds of people going on this trip and almost every one of them had some form of booze in their hands. I was pissed! Pissed I only had these two little bottles.

My Lieutenant stopped me and asked; "Why aren't you in your dress greens Private John." My response was simple. No one told me to. I had only been to the unit a few times as an active member. There were about 6 chartered buses sitting there on the lot full of people in their dress greens. I said, "I thought we were going in deuce and a halfs?" He said "No, change of plans but you can't go on the bus dressed like that. You'll have to ask one of the Sergeants (in their camo) if you can drive with them in their personal vehicle."

At this time the Army in my area was still mostly black. One of the black sergeants felt sorry for me so he said "You can come with us; you got any beer or anything?" I said, not as much as I want. "You can share ours but you'll have to buy a case." He walked me over to his conversion van; I put my stuff in the back and was ushered inside.

The last time I went for a ride with four black guys in a van it almost cost me my life (my scars were tingling). In that moment it didn't feel like I had any choice in the matter this time either. I really needed a beer now. I entered the van that had 2 big coolers filled with beer. The two side doors closed like before but this time I was handed a beer. I was in the van with 4 old-school sergeants that had a ton of real war stories but most of what they talked about was girls and partying. This army summer camp van trip thing might be OK after all; I would even get paid money for this ride.

We must have gone through about 3 cases of beer on the 500-mile trip to Fort Bragg. Soldiers know how to hold their pee but we did stop a lot for the old guys. We got to Bragg and went to our row of barracks. The rest of the guys were outside in their civvies by now and drinking their butts off. We were later than most because we stopped to visit a Sergeant's mother on the way. Pretty sure they bought weed there too.

Carolina was Stroh's beer country and it was cheap. The Sergeant was with me when I entered so people started asking questions about why the white boy didn't have to ride on the bus. They kept most of their comments to themselves because the Sergeant was a 1st Sergeant and a Vietnam Vet. He asked where my locker was, we found it and then he asked me (not ordered me) if I would keep his cooler in my locker. He said he would be by occasionally to grab a beer. My job was to keep it full. "No problem sergeant."

We had to do our training and war game stuff but we had a great time. It was the furthest South I had ever been in my life. (Did I mention we drove past the park where I was sexually abused?)

Somewhere along the line, I had gotten into this habit of foot-racing people for money and pride. A good portion of my life was spent surrounded by black guys that thought they were faster than me in the 100-yard dash. We were partying when one of the people I had beaten before started egging me on to race another soldier. They were teasing him saying "The white boy could beat your ass" even though no one else ever had ever beaten this guy before. The two of us weren't betting but they were. It was a very polite exchange.

We all went out to the big muster field and prepared for the showdown. I had seen this dude around but we didn't know each other.

We were going to race but there was a very clear white guy, black guy race tone being set. Not in a negative way though; it just was what it was. The two of us were more concerned about Bragg-ing rights.

I admit that my competition seemed very confident and he was about 2 inches taller than me. We got set. Someone yelled go and we took off. We were neck and neck. Over the years I had learned a very odd way of using my mind to speed up my legs without considering the ground. I called it my afterburner. I kicked that in but so did he. We ran, 50 yards, 100 yards, teasing each other the whole way. "You still here man?" "Right here bruh! I'm not going anywhere and neither are you." Heavy breathing now. 150 yards, 200 yards, "You stopping?" "No!" "You?" "How far we gonna run?" Now 300 yards, "I'm done! "Me too!" and we just coasted to a stop and shook hands.

We turned around and he said "Oh shit we got a long walk back," I said, "I ain't running want a beer?" "Oh yeah, you got the Sergeants cooler, can't wait." I looked down at his shirt to see his name. It was Joyner. Yep, his cousin was a college track star at the time, another was the fastest guy in the NFL and one would later take home a medal in the 84 Olympics in track and field. Some people knew her as Flo-Jo. I think he would have won because I smoked a lot and I was getting tired, and about to quit. I think he still had more in the tank. The bets never paid out, we made sure of that as we walked back. It was our race and it wasn't about race. We became the fastest white dude and black dude in the company. We never raced again; probably because neither of us wanted to lose.

YOU CAN'T RUN

I returned to work shortly after returning home from Bragg. The Deli was very supportive of my service and I even got some accolades and a few good full-body hugs from the girls. Melanie was really happy to see me. She met me back in the kitchen with a sneaky kiss. We both knew that our last night was something special. There was never any hint from either side that we would be together in any greater capacity than how we were. We really just liked each other as friends and party buddies, but that was going to change over the next few weeks.

Melanie started leaving earlier and we started having fewer rides together and therefore less sex. I questioned if her husband and she had talked about us. She said her marriage was fine and that everything was really cool. I had plenty of other irons in the fire so I just moved on. Kimberly was going to hook me up with a friend of hers as soon as she dumped her current boyfriend. (Having two girls in your life that are emotionally unavailable takes talent.)

I left the Deli job shortly after returning home from Fort Bragg. I don't remember if it was because I was distracted by the new girl Dawn (Kim's friend) or just drunk and late all the time. That era was very foggy for me. (You may have noticed that I had a habit of removing things from my life that kept me from being with the people I wanted to be with and drinking the way I wanted.) The Deli was a BS job and it was just on the wrong side of town. I do remember calling in sick a lot when I had a chance to party or be with a girl I was interested in sexually. Dawn was nice and she was the kind of girl that you could settle down with; a "keeper." Her boyfriend was fooling around on her and she wanted something serious. While serious relationships weren't my thing I was starting to consider it; despite my conditioning it seemed more natural.

A couple months after I left the Deli job I stopped in to say hi. I saw Melanie sitting at a table, now grinning ear to ear. She always had a great smile when she was happy or high but she was really glowing now. She gave me a big hug and said, "I got something to show you" and she reached for her purse: She pulled out a picture. She said, "I've been hoping to see you so I can show you this." It was a sonogram picture of a fetus.

I guess I was initially a little slow on the uptake so all I could think was that I was happy for her and her husband. I knew that they had wanted another child for years with no luck. Maybe it was denial or maybe just a blonde moment for me but it wasn't until she asked me if I was happy about it that I even thought twice. My quick wit engaged and I said, "That's what you wanted right?" She said you have no idea how much and gave me a big hug. Everyone else in the store was listening in on the whole conversation. I said "I'm glad you're happy do you need anything from me. What does Brian (her husband) think about it?" She said he's very happy about it too. She hugged me and said thank you.

CHAPTER THIRTEEN
EMOTIONAL BANKRUPTCY

42 YEAR KARMIC DEBT

It was the 4th of July 1982. I was now seeing the new love of my life for the moment. She wasn't my first Dawn but I really did like her. OK, I'll admit it, I was infatuated with her. Sadly I still wasn't the only guy interested. It seems Dawn had yet to break from her philandering boyfriend. Since my friend Kimberly didn't approve of him she let me know that she was plotting to oust him and position me.

Being with Dawn usually meant Kimberly orchestrating the time for the 4 of us to get together. Kimberly (my dance partner and currently Brian's girlfriend again) would tell Dawn that I wanted to hang out. She would meet up with Dawn before our double dates making it look like a girl's night out. The problem with this particular planned date was that Kimberly had forgotten to tell Dawn about the plan in time. Dawn went ahead and accepted plans with her current boyfriend for the 4th. I was a little letdown and pretty disappointed with Kimberly.

We knew we were gonna party and have fun anyway no matter what but I was still a little bummed out. Regardless of all my past liaisons I still believed in my head that I was a monogamous person at heart. It was just too much of an emotional risk to want someone that didn't want me too. I really just wanted, maybe needed, a female that wanted me for me. I wanted a female that wouldn't abandon me, yet here I was alone on another big day. Even though it wasn't anyone's fault or intent, I felt the old scars nonetheless.

When I returned from basic training I moved back in with my mother at the apartment in Pikesville. The complex had a pool so the plan was to get shit-faced drunk at the pool and then go to the harbor to see the fireworks. There was another older lady, a friend of mine (probably in her mid-30s, a MILF, I might have invented that) who lived across the parking lot from us. I'm pretty sure we first met at the strip show. She was always interested in hanging out with me but for some reason she never showed up at the pool. That was OK though because the other love of my life was there. Yep, my true love, the one that never let me down: A 1/5 of vodka. It was up to the Russian gal to keep me company during the fireworks. I thought that since Dawn was with her Bo it was only natural for me to be looking for chicks at harbor place and then later on the dance floor at Hammers. Vodka didn't mind sharing me in a threesome.

A few months earlier Brian had let me know that Kim wanted to have sex with both of us at the same time. Brian had told Kimberly he was up for it but once she said she wanted to see us kiss that notion was thrown out the window with an "Ewe, in your wildest dreams, gross!"

Well, I was pretty drunk that night but there was still no way I was doing anything with Brian. It was understood that it would just never happen. No one knew about my abuse as a child yet but people knew I could get pretty touchy on the issue of anything gay. That was a certain "no-go." (It should be obvious that homophobia can form as the result of prior male-on-male sexual abuse.) Unbeknownst to me Kimberly and Brian had been working out the details of her fantasy without my input. Everyone else in my life had used me for their own ends so why not my friends?

I got so drunk that afternoon that I started going into one of those self-pity crying jags about how I wasn't able to see Dawn and how my life was so f-d up. I didn't so much cry as mope with a bottle of Vodka at the pool. At around 5pm I started feeling 3rd wheelish; probably because Brian and Kim kept making out. My mother and Sandy were out for the 4th of July. I hadn't seen them in days.

I remember I was sitting in the living room next to Kim with Brian on the other side. I did a huge bong hit and leaned back. Brian stopped kissing Kimberly and pulled down her top. He said look, that's your side and this is my side.

We quickly went from having sides on the couch to having ends in the bedroom. Kimberly was in heaven. I remember finishing what I was doing and passing out. Brian and Kimberly could go all night so people just started ignoring the two of them, I had for years. I was passed out with the music still playing really loudly in my room. Brian was on top of Kimberly on the floor with me sprawled out naked on the bed.

All I remember was the bedroom door being opened and then closed and hearing my mother's shrill screaming voice. "GET THEM OUT OF MY HOUSE," I screamed back to her; "Stay the fuck out of my room." She screamed, "Lower that damn music. I want them out of my house." She immediately threatened to call the cops. I passed back out.

Next thing I knew Brian was waking me up telling me the cops were in the living room. Brian and Kimberly were dressed by now but I wasn't. I put on my jeans to go deal with the cops. In my eyes I wasn't doing anything wrong. It was legal for me to be drunk at 18 and it was legal for them to be having sex. (OK, maybe not for Kim and Brian because of their age difference.)

I walked out into the living room hearing my mother say I want him out of my house to the cops. I've had it with this shit she said. My brain was still foggy but I remember thinking, it's the damn 4th of July, what the hell are you doing here woman. One of the cops, a big black dude, said sternly, "You got to go!" I said, "I live here, I pay rent." The cop asked, "Is your name on the lease?" I said, "Yeah, as a tenant." He said, "You can take that up in court but you got to go for now," almost pushing me towards the door. I shook him off and said, "NO!" Then in a slow signifying manner I said, "First I'm going to get my shoes, some socks, a shirt, maybe two and then I'm allowed reasonable time to get anything else I need that belongs to me." The cop said, "Alright then let's get your things."

The three cops followed me back to my room. I blocked them from entering by sitting on the edge of the bed near the door; I knew I couldn't shut it for their safety. Most of the bongs and stuff were set behind the arm of the sofa bed. Still signifying I tied my shoes really slowly and moved really slowly around the room. The two male cops moved back to the living room with my mother while the female cop watched me with her hand on her gun. (At that moment I started feeling all those old scars of E-1's old cop boyfriend and the orphanage threats. It hurt in the center of my chest.)

After I had taken my time gathering my things it was time for me to take the most important thing in the room, my second 1/5 of vodka for the day. (Come on, it was the 4th of July. You need more than a 1/5 for the 4th.) Suddenly I realized I had a problem, I couldn't find the bottle's top. Thanks to my earlier arrest I knew that open container was illegal in Baltimore County.

By now the male cops were back in the room and standing on each side of me getting ready to hurry me out. (Apparently, my mother had ratted me out and told the cops about the weed and bongs.)

The black cop, the sergeant, saw the bottle in my hand and said in a smart-ass tone. "You take that this will be the easiest DWI I've ever had." I looked the white male cop in the eye, like what's with this guy, turned and looked the black cop in the eye and then said. "I don't drive you fucking asshole." He then said, "You take it outside and I'll get you for open container." I looked him in the eye, then looked the other cop in the eye, smiled at the female cop in front of me, leaned back and drank almost half a 1/5 of vodka all the way down in about 6 seconds. I remember seeing the stunned look on their faces and then thinking. How did I just do that and how come I had no reaction to it, not even a deep breath.

Brian and Kimberly had made it down to his car by this time. I remember suspiciously staring at that bottle as I walked out of the room, wondering if someone had put water in the bottle; they hadn't. The female cop followed me down the steps.

My older female friend from across the parking lot came outside and did the worst thing you can do to a drunk drunk. She made me the victim by shouting "What did they do to you?" She was actually trying to defend me and she started asking the female cop what the problem was.

Well, the pity must have set me OFF! I turned, looked to my third-floor bedroom window and saw the black cop holding my 32-inch Toke Master bong. So I did what anyone would do at that moment. No, remember I don't run. Instead, I yelled at the top of my lungs "FUCK YOU! YOU! NIGGER! FUCKING! PIG!" The female cop said, "Be quiet!" I shouted "FUCK YOU!!! BITCH!!! PIG!!!! FUCK YOU!!!" Now I was ready to leave; at least now seemed like a good time.

Brian and Kimberly quickly ushered me into the back seat of the car. I had already seen the cops running down the steps of the building at full speed. I got in the back of the car. Brian started it but by this time the guns were drawn and pointing at the windows. (We didn't have any weapons.) The cops were saying stop the damn car and Brian was saying, "We're leaving man, we're leaving, just let us go, you just made this guy homeless, he's upset." I told Brian in a calm voice, "No dude stop, let me out, they're taking me with them." I got out, went air-born onto the hood and the cuffs went on real tight. All the while Brian was trying to talk them out of it. At least until he was threatened with arrest. I went to jail that night but at least I had a place to stay.

The next thing I remember was waking up in a cell facing the gray steel wall and hearing other people in the little cell block of 6 cells chatting. When I asked where I was I was told I was at Garrison Precinct. I overheard the other guys talking about probation violations and I thought, oh that sucks, they're keeping you. I was used to hangovers and headaches but all I could think was I needed some hair of the dog that bit me.

As I came too I started moving around trying to remember what had happened. Sadly there were no friends to help me remember. Shortly after I stood up I was asked, "What are you in for man?" I said arrogantly, "Man all they got me for is disorderly contact, I'm walking today." I remember the other guys being happy for me because their probation violations had them on their way to Baltimore County Detention Center. Pretty sure there were 5 guys when that day started. Person after person got their charging papers which told each what was happening to them. One after the other they also started getting bail hearings. After about 20 hours they were all gone and I had still not gotten a bail hearing or any charging papers. I started getting worried because disorderly conduct usually meant a quick release.

Once the bologna sandwich dinner was served there really wasn't any reason for them to come back into the block that night. They don't give you food unless you're staying. I knew that a shift change would happen at 11:00 so I began to worry that they had merely forgotten me, you know, the small-time guy in on a disorderly conduct charge. I think it was about 9:30pm when I got my papers. It was 23 hours after I was booked; they had purposely waited until the last minute.

When they finally gave me the papers I started reading them. Yep, my name then all I could see was CDS Distribution Felony, I knew that meant 10 to 20 years (when you're in jail you automatically think the highest number, the worst case scenario.) If you also have an anxiety disorder and you're starting to withdrawal, you think that you're going to die in jail. The second charge CDS Distribution and Manufacture 10 to 20 years and a disorderly conduct, 0 to 2 years.

FORTY-TWO years is what you think at that moment. Then you add that to your age; 60, I'd be out at 60 (I wasn't up on the good behavior time thing yet). At that moment it becomes hard to tell if you're shaking from fear, anxiety or withdrawal. The fun part is that none of that matters; you just get an instant panic attack. It looked like I found that forever home I was always looking for. I thought, I'm in the adult orphanage now, can't leave here either.

I think it would have been better if there was someone else in that cell block but there wasn't. There would be no sympathy or distraction, just me and my anxiety (now panic). The withdrawal symptoms were coming on fast. The realization set in that I had once again been abandoned by the very person that started those feelings of being unwanted long ago. (When something negative happens to you over and over again it starts to look like evil.) It started up again the minute she threatened to call the cops. That was her new, "Get the fuck out!" That 7-

year-old kid that was threatened to be sent to the orphanage was sitting there in that cell with no one to look out for him once again. As if I wasn't shaking enough from the withdrawal the AC was so cold my teeth chattered.

When they gave me the charging papers they clearly outlined for me what they said happened. Beyond the sex, nudity, booze, drugs and the name calling there was the interview. You see while I was being processed the cops had gotten a search warrant for my mother's house. The searching was so intense that they had apparently torn the posters off the walls looking for drugs taped behind them. They took the sofa and bedding apart looking for cocaine, marijuana and anything else that they could find. All they found was a few pot seeds being germinated and a few flower pots with dirt. In my closet, they found an old broken Baltimore County Board of Education triple beam scale that I paid someone to steal from our science class years earlier. Basically, they collected anything and everything that might incriminate me.

I get it, I pissed them off that night but they were putting me, a soldier, out on the street without due process. They wanted to make some charges stick so they even called over to Cockeysville and got the low down on me. After that, they even vacuumed the rugs looking for drugs that might have been dropped into the carpet (they wanted me bad).

It seems that after shot-gunning down a large amount of vodka a curious thing happens to a person. Something you don't usually see coming. It's called a blackout. Not a brownout, a full-on blackout. (That's how much booze it takes to medicate trauma.)

It seems that my drunk little smart-ass self still believed in this thing called justice; at least while I was being grilled. (I learned about the interviews from the charging papers and the transcribed recording that I still have today.) Did I mention that I was a heavy smoker too and that I needed a cigarette that they weren't ever gonna give me?

As I'm reading the papers it's all beginning to come back to me. While being interviewed one of the cops tells me that they're in the process of searching my room. I knew the liquor was legal and I also knew I didn't have any drugs to speak of. I knew Brian well enough to know that when the shit started he took or hid everything he could. I hadn't dealt in some time and you can trust me when I say that people know where their drugs are and how much they have. Pretty sure that most of those bongs had been cleaned out in search of a resin buzz long before the 4th. The only resin in them probably came from Brian's pot that night.

Seemingly out of nowhere one of the cops says, "So where do you get your Coke?" I was stunned because as you know Coke was never my thing. While it was compact and easy to move the margins were too small unless you were importing it. Crack wasn't even out yet. I laughed at him. He said, "Tell us about the triple beam balance in the back of your closet; you know the one with the white powdery substance on it." Now I was miffed and drunk, half thinking they were trying to frame me or something.

I had actually forgotten about that scale even being in there. It was broken but poor people don't throw anything away. They were actually suggesting that the dust on it, from years of being unused was Cocaine. Knowing how stupid they were I figured I'd be stupid too I guess. I said, "Oh yeah, Coke! Good fucking stuff man. Yeah, I make more money in a month than all three of you assholes put together make in a year." Pretty sure that hurt their feelings but I am certain it pissed them off more. Remember, all I thought they could actually prove was a measly disorderly conduct. I wasn't a bigot; trust me, people know it when you are. It's Baltimore; they knew I was just pissed and trying to set them off or get them to hit me if I could. It was almost a year since basic training but I was still army tough and even angrier than when I went in. Their bull shit actions that night made me hate cops even more.

Did I mention the tape and the under-oath thing? Of course, they didn't write down the part where I said I've never dealt Coke or any hard drugs. They remembered the "I made more money than them" part though. They then radioed the people doing the search, suggesting they look harder. They wanted names. I told them, "Joe Fuckyouself" did it. I later learned that they were there searching that room until almost daylight (another reason for waiting on the charging paper).

Sitting there in that cold cell block shaking I read those documents over and over again. It was all I had in that cell area. No TV and no one to talk to or to ask questions to. It wasn't until about 23 hours and 55 minutes in that I was given my first phone call. You had to call collect and the only person that I somehow knew the number of was my alcoholic Uncle Norman who was also my supposed Godfather. Thanks to his nasty new wife June he was no help at all (abandoned again).

I remember looking around the cell to figure out how I might kill myself and be done with it. (Traumatic memories often trigger homicide and suicidal ideations.) My withdrawal was really getting bad. I was used to feeling shaky around 4 or 5 in the afternoon because I drank every day. At this point, I was drinking at least a case of beer a day or a 1/5 or more of vodka. Thanks to the army I was a lean 5' 10" and 135 pounds. I drank my dinner most nights. Not on purpose though, I would just forget to eat because I was so intoxicated.

I did finally get my bail hearing. For context the week before this happened, a man in the Woodlawn area had barricaded himself in his house and shot at police. His bail was later set at $5,000 (in 1982 you could still buy a new car for that). I went before the commissioner, a poor, now homeless person with no real means and he set the bail at $10,000.

I knew they wanted to keep me in jail as long as they could and after reading what I read I knew they did it to teach me a lesson. No one I knew had that kind of money for bail. Like most poor people I would be staying in jail until court. I remember thinking that no one I knew should pay the $1000 to bond me out because I couldn't earn that kind of money in a month on the outside. It wasn't worth it. The army only paid me $551 a month when I was full-time. Minimum wage jobs were under $3 an hour by now; that's about $120 gross a week, 4 weeks wouldn't make me $500.

Listening to some of the other detainees on that first day I learned that there was a thing called bail review that occurred 24-48 hours after your bail was set if you couldn't pay it. So that was all that I could hope for. I didn't know where I was going and all I literally had were the clothes on my back.

Unfortunately for me, July 4th was an extended weekend for the holiday so the court system would be observing the holiday schedule by being closed an extra day. I was returned from the bail hearing to that little cell block back at Garrison Precinct, alone. I remember going in through the door and being led by a black cop that I thought might be the guy I cussed out. We didn't say anything to each other but he was the same size.

I was to spend the next 3 days in the cell block alone. I had gone to the bail review but the judge thought that holding me as long as possible was a good idea. Despite lowering everyone else's bail he kept mine the same. He even threatened to raise it.

Once again I was seriously considering killing myself because I knew what happened to pretty little semi-white boys in jail. Having already been abused and raped I would not be experiencing that again. It was going to be a fight to the death. Even though I was little guy, I was hard and tough thanks to the army. A fight to the death was probably in my future. I knew that poor people never really got equal justice. Newsflash! It doesn't matter if you're white-ish only poor-ish.

It was around 72 hours in when I remember sitting on the floor of the cell block curled up into a little ball; freezing and shaking from withdrawal. The best way I can describe it is feeling like a sponge that was drying up and shrinking inwardly. My heart was racing, I was breaking out in sweats when I wasn't freezing; I felt like I was going to puke but I couldn't. I began to think that I wouldn't have to die in a fight; that I was going to die right here on this cold floor. I'd be one of the stories you heard about on the news where the prisoner mysteriously dies in custody.

After feeling that way for hours I started screaming for a doctor. "I NEED A DOCTOR!!!" Over and over and over again. I would shake until I would pass out on the floor. At times the concrete felt good on my face. The cops would come in and look at me and as soon as I woke up and asked for a doctor they would just turn around and walk out without saying a word. I felt like they wanted me to die. I thought that I would. I thought that maybe it was for the best. I mean, my scars told me that I had no real worth and that I didn't matter. Now I had proof. There was nothing and no one to argue against it except for the fact that I was still the property of the US Army.

When the guys were still in that block with me I looked over to see one scratching out a name on the cell wall with a plastic spork. (The jails invented that one.) He was one of the probation guys. I asked him what he was doing and he said "My father told me that if you write your name on the jailhouse wall you'll be back to see it again. I wrote this here a year ago."

I never put my name on that wall but I thought about it. Bathroom graffiti was big in those days. We didn't have an internet we had stall walls for our memes. Instead of writing my name this once devil-hating atheist spent 10 hours writing GOD in 2-foot-tall letters. It wasn't a testament, I'm pretty sure it was either a plea for help or a message to me from beyond.

There wouldn't be any lawyer. After pestering the police and screaming I want a lawyer when I wasn't asking for a doctor they gave me a paper to fill out to apply to the Public Pretender's Office. Since the long holiday weekend was slowing things down that wasn't going to happen and I wasn't making bail anyway. A cop came into the cell block, looked shocked at seeing me in my condition and stated that I would be moved to the Detention Center in an hour. I remember him looking back and saying, "You'll be able to see a doctor there."

I don't know why I didn't die in that withdrawal (Grace). I now know that I have a genetic heart condition known as Hypertrophic Obstructed Cardiomyopathy and that it should have killed me. Maybe

Grace was keeping me alive but why? (HCM is the condition that led to high school sports physicals after young kids started dying of heart attacks.) Perhaps something did care for me, maybe my dead father. I was too ill to think that deep in those moments. I had not showered in days and could taste the salt on my skin from sweating and crying.

I'm not going to bore you with all the details of the detention center but it was worse than you would think. I did get some clothes there. They gave me a couple pairs of underwear, a couple T-shirts and a splendid blue jumpsuit that snapped up from the crotch to the chin. Already it seemed the state was taking better care of me than my family. (There was no Greek side of the family to turn to by now. They had abandoned me the minute my father died. I was the white chic's kid now.)

I was taken to the 4th floor of the detention center. I found out later that that was where all the people doing an undetermined amount of time were placed. It was full of wonderful people from murderers to rapists to pedophiles to the guy that once tried to land his plane in Memorial Stadium at the end of a game: Fascinating fellow, I nicknamed him Crash. I was so curious about him that I questioned him the whole time. That kid that wanted to be a psychologist at 10 was always interested in the machinations of crazy people (thanks to E1). He was in there this time for threatening to blow up the stadium if the charges against him weren't dropped. He may have been "out there" but he started giving me his food tray when he was on hunger strike so that made us friends.

OUTSIDE INTERFERENCE

I had been in jail for a week when the first visiting day came. When I got seated in the booth with the phone the only person that I saw sitting there on the other side of the glass was that girl that wanted me dead my whole life. She was no stranger to jail and certainly not to things police related. At the time she was dancing and tending bar on Baltimore's block (the red light district). Before we picked up the phones she just looked at me like dude this sucks. I could see in her eyes that she knew our upbringing had more to do with this than anything else. She knew it was Evil One's doing. She said, "Ma told me what happened, I got some of your things out of the dumpster; she's such a fucking bitch. She's here do you want to talk to her." I just sat there staring stunned at the question.

My sister waved her over and she stood behind her. She started crying. I remember getting mad and yelling softly so she could read my lips, "What are you fucking crying for? I'm the one that's fuckin in here thanks to you. You don't have the right to cry you fucking bitch." I mouthed the words to my sister, "Get her the fuck out of here." She said, "MA! GO!"

I knew that bitch mother of mine well. She wasn't crying for me she was crying because she was being confronted with the result of her own failed parenting and selfish self-serving ways. She was probably worried about appearances. That was her best trick, feel better at other people's expense; make it all about her all the time.

A couple days later I was in the cell block playing spades when the guard in the glass booth called JOHN!!! This was only the second time they had ever called my name; the first was for the doctor's call. Of course when your last name is John you have to wait for your first name because they may just be calling some dude named John. "Emmanuel John your lawyers here." FINALLY, I was gonna talk to a lawyer, after almost 2 weeks of being locked up.

I remember my first impression of the Public Pretender (defender) was not good. He was just what I expected, a fat civil servant in a bad knit suit of some kind; in the middle of summer. All I remember was the "let's get this done so I can go home" look on his face. He asked simpleton questions and just like you can imagine he tried to get the poor person to plead guilty to a crime he didn't do. "With a guilty plea we can get your sentence down to like a year or two," he said. I got agitated and said "I wasn't dealing. They have no evidence." "Well, they have a lot of stuff from the scene after the day-long search they did." I said "It's bullshit!! I've never sold cocaine and there were no drugs in the house." He said their still running tests I'll see what I can find out.

I returned to that cell block thinking, yep, these guys are my new family. I was used to people not wanting me around and wanting me dead and gone, why not. Then the guy in the booth called my name again. He said, "John your lawyers here." I said, "I just saw my lawyer" (because I was now managing the jail). He said, "You want to see him or not?" I figured the dumb fat pretender forgot something.

I went through the series of locked doors but this time I was taken to a better room. The guard opened the door and I thought that's not him. This guy was the lawyer opposite of the first guy. Great hair, a beeper, an Armani suit and he said "I'm here on behalf of your lawyer Howard Cardin, your sister hired us but they wanted me to come down here and let you know that we are going to get you out of here, this case is bullshit and you shouldn't be here." (Even as I am sitting here today writing this almost 40 years later I tear up thinking about the emotional shift that occurred at that moment. Was I being rescued by my sister?)

The lawyer said, "Your sister told me to tell you not to do anything stupid." I was thinking about a lot of stupid stuff too. Not just suicide but how to get to a mental health facility and not jail. My plan was to take a run at the judge if he sentenced me. I thought that if I tried to kill him right there in court they would have to have me evaluated. Maybe I could get that section 8 that Crash was trying for.

The good lawyer said, "We could try to get you out on bail but you only have a week or two until court, it might not be worth the money. Can you make it in here for two more weeks?" (I was planning on years so yeah, I got this. Jail was easier than basic training.) I was pretty happy, even happier after he gave me a cigarette and told me he was putting $20 in my commissary account to buy some more.

I was taken back to my cell and all I could think was that the little girl that wanted me dead most of my life was probably actually saving my life right now. Grace was real and she might be a stripper from the block. God works in mysterious ways, right? Out of all the stuck-up people who said they cared, the only one that came through for me was the one they all said was the biggest mess.

I was a different guy after meeting that lawyer. I was still facing 42 years in my head but when I told the guys in the cell block who my lawyer was they educated me real quick. You see Howard had recently become very well known, not just for his soon-to-be Senator brother either, but for a case called Peanut King. Maurice King was one of the first real drug KING PIN dealers busted in the US. He ran a huge criminal drug operation in East Baltimore, often using young kids to sell and deliver drugs on Mopeds. (Maurice "Peanut" King was just released about a year before the authoring of this book, 39 years after his sentencing.) While King went to jail for 39 years he was originally threatened with both capital punishment and several life sentences. Howard got famous and all the DAs hated him for it.

I always felt different and separate from most of the white boys. I just thought it was from being poor and disadvantaged. I knew I was Mediterranean but I know now that I'm also Middle Eastern and Jewish. When I look back at my childhood my father was always close to people of color (not just black people). He was destined to be a part of the underbelly music scene as Mr. Blues. You can't sing the blues if you're a rich white guy.

Despite my brush with the black cop I grew up around black people and felt closer to them than to white people. If I had a dollar for every time I was called "my nigga" I could have paid my own bail. The only color I ever saw was white and they never let me in their little club. The reason I bring this up now is because while in jail I gained the moniker, "Inside out Oreo." Oreo is a derogatory name for a guy that is black on the outside but white on the inside. In jail, I was "Reverse O-re-O."

Trust me when I say I accepted that name with pride because it was as though I had now moved up the pecking order in the black inmate population, even above some of the actual black people in the building. I do have a different tone when I speak but I think that what people hear is the poor and hungry part; something all poor people can identify with. While it might not look that way on the outside I could feel those same scars of socio-economic differences and social rejection deep down on the inside. (Privilege ain't white it's green.)

I remember looking out the window of my 4th-floor room in the Towson Hyatt one night (by Hyatt I mean jail). It actually looked down upon the school where I was busted in for possession 4 years earlier. You know the school where my weed was sprawled out on the table in the Vice Principal's office? The place of my first expansion and possibly the real start of my drug dealing empire; the place I carried a gun. When I say it looked down upon it I mean the school building was literally 75 yards from my jail cell window. (That there is a special kind of Grace.)

One night when I was staring out that window I noticed that if I put my finger in the grates and put my face on the metal I could see the HOJO's restaurant (Howard Johnson's for the kids). It was about a quarter mile away but I could still see people going in and out. It was a Saturday night and boy did I miss getting stoned on Saturday nights. The weekend usually meant good times for me because I got good and drunk. Saturdays also meant chasing females so I was missing that too. I was wondering if I would ever have sex again or ever be in love. My experiences taught me that sex was my only real value in life; now I couldn't see any purpose at all. (I would rip off someone's genitals if they tried anything in jail.)

So one sober Saturday night around 9:30, while looking down on the people going into the Hojo's restaurant I started making comments about it out loud to the cell block. I couldn't understand why any free person would willingly make the choice to go to HoJo's on a Saturday night. Yeah, I got the breakfast thing, even the breakfast after the bar thing but Saturday night? HOJO's? 9:30? I editorialized loudly to the cell block (because I knew that none of them would be going there either) "What kind of fucking people go to HOJO's on a Saturday Night?" From behind me I heard, "HOJOs?" One guy actually jumped up to see what I was talking about. Another yelled, "What's HOJO's?" I think he might have thought it was a whore house. We all laughed at the stupid people for going there when they could go anywhere, not realizing the irony. You know, us stupid people locked up in jail laughing at the free people for their choices.

A week later I found myself looking out that same window on another Saturday night. By now I was becoming quite curious about the goings on at HOJOs. I said, "Man that is just weird, there must be something going on in there." I heard from behind me, "Yeah that is weird, people need to get a life." Because, you know, us people in jail have a life.

By the time the third week came, I just said fairly quietly. "Man, I'd like to go to HOJO's." Then from behind me, "Yeah man me too. I'd love to go to HOJO's!" Another guy yelled, "Yeah man, we should all go there and crash that party." I said, yeah for sure, thinking I might have a new life by then but only if my sister's rich lawyer friend saves the day.

Court hadn't happened yet and I didn't trust rich people or lawyers and mine was a rich lawyer. My father warned me about them too. It was a lawyer that actually screwed my sister and me out of our father's inheritance by changing his will on his deathbed.

While in jail I was able to talk to Brian and Kimberly on the phone and even my old buddy Wormo who was back from Panama for a while. They gave me a lot of encouragement. It was important to me that they actually took the time to write letters. The girl Dawn had written me a few letters too, that helped a whole lot. She wished that she would have been there, that maybe things would have gone differently. She was right but I didn't blame her. She still had a chance to be my savior, if she was willing to date an ex-con someday.

While I was in jail I was still in the Army. I had a weekend Reserve drill scheduled and was not going to make it because they weren't going to let me out to attend it. There is a form of AWOL (absent without leave) that happens if you miss the drill without notifying them. So I was going to have to call my unit to let them know of my status. I reminded the jail staff that I was government property and that they had to let me make contact so they took me to the jail social worker who let me call.

The person that answered the phone asked me why I was calling. I said, "To let you know that I won't be making drill this weekend." She said you'll have to speak to the Lieutenant. I thought owe damn, all the way up the chain to the guy that yelled at me for not being in my dress greens.

He picked up the phone "This is Lieutenant Daniels" (there was no Lt. Dan yet but I thought that odd looking back) "How can I help you." "This is Private John calling sir." "What's up Private John why are you calling me?" I said, "Well sir, you see sir, I'm not going to be able to make drill this weekend sir." "NOT GONNA BE ABLE TO MAKE DRILL? WHY THE HELL NOT!!!" "Well sir, you see sir, I'm incarcerated, sir." "INCARCERATED!!!! What the hell did you do? I'm gonna need some confirmation on that Private." All I could think was what, you think this was something someone would pick for a lie? He said, "I need an official from the jail to call me and let me know that you're in there." "She's right here with me Sir, do you want to speak with her?" "No, she has to call me from the jail herself." I'm still trying to figure this procedure out today because I could have easily had my sister or some female do it. The army was still using rotary phones in those days so there were no caller ID boxes. "You need to call me the day you're done with your court stuff Private John. You can't be on probation and in the army." Yes sir.

I went back to my cell block on the 4th floor to stare out the window and consider how cool going to drill would be. I remember days when I would just stare out that window at my old school where I pulled the gun and sold drugs. There was a long sidewalk that went down Kenilworth Drive behind the school that I used to walk and skateboard on. I remember looking out the window and thinking how much I just wanted to be able to walk in one direction for 100 yards without turning or hitting a wall. (When you're in jail the simple things seem to be the greatest losses. I also missed the sun on my face. You never feel the sun in most detention centers.)

FEEL THE HEAT!

It was the end of July in not-so Mary-land. I was heading to court to face my charges and to hopefully get this travesty of justice righted. I was aware enough to know there might be some Karma at play but the charges were still disproportionate. Forty-two years for being a smart-ass was a little excessive. I didn't make the booze legal and I certainly didn't neglect and abuse myself. I took some ownership in these events but I didn't deserve 42 years in jail for being drunk, stupid or even a drug dealer for that matter (a drug that's almost legal now).

I probably didn't deserve to be in jail for a month either but that's just the difference between being poor and not poor. People argue all the time that race is a factor when it comes to sentencing but those people haven't looked at the correlation between poverty and prison sentences (wonder why). There weren't any rich black people in that jail either. People that choose to focus on racial inequalities miss what is right there in front of them; wealth disparity is the real problem in our legal system. We all know it but still nothing; they distract us by making it about color.

Are there more poor black people? No! A greater percentage may be poor but there are still many more poor white people in the US. All poor people have a greater mortality rate and jail sentence length. If you're poor you just swallow it, just like being hungry. No matter your race when you are unable to make bail you don't come in the front door of the court house you come in the back door or underground. Usually in a jumpsuit that makes you look even more guilty.

During my time at the Towson Hyatt I never once felt the sun on my face. Everything was indoors. A person could be placed in that jail for up to 18 months without ever feeling the sun. In some areas of the country it's longer than that. The point being I went from an underground gate at the jail to an underground door at the courthouse. I never got to feel that sunlight I was longing for.

When you're poor and you don't make bail you sit in the back of the courthouse until it's your turn or until you meet with your lawyer.

Luckily I did meet with the private lawyer in the back before the guards paraded us jump suited guilty looking handcuffed men into the courtroom. My lawyer told me that he was trying to get my clothes sent back so I could at least not look like a convicted criminal.

They didn't give most of us our clothes to wear because they thought we were all just coming right back. At the last minute I got to change thanks to my lawyer who was even able to get the cuffs removed after I was taken into the courtroom. Why? Because my lawyer was a high-dollar lawyer and the other guys had Public Pretenders. Lacking trust in people meant my "go after the judge's throat plan B" was still being entertained and now I would have both my hands free.

One of my clearest memories was that this high-priced lawyer was saying things I thought would piss off the judge. Like: "Mr. John has been wronged here Your Honor. Yeah perhaps Mr. John was drinking too much and saying questionable things but none of that is illegal. He wasn't bothering anyone before this all started. He was passed out naked in his own bed. Perhaps he was mad at the cops and said some mean things but he was being tossed out onto the street again by a woman that had done this to him his entire life."

Howard knew my sister's sentiments about our mother and he played on that a little too. He said, "He just lost his father a few years ago and he has spent a lot of time on the streets trying to survive. He joined the Army to try to change that. The stuff that was found in his bedroom were the same things that you might find in the average teen's room these days (knowing the judge had kids). We are asking for all the charges to be dropped and for Mr. John to be released as the police department lab has yet to provide any evidence of these charges. He has already lost a month of his life, all without any evidence to support these drummed-up charges."

The courthouse fell very quiet as the judge seemed to consider the case. You could see the justice system actually being held accountable for its actions by someone that knew the law. That silence was quite probably the loudest noise I've ever heard in my life besides Sergeant

Franco. I remember getting nods from the other older inmates in court suggesting that my lawyer was crushin it. There were people in the courtroom that actually came in just to watch Howard work.

The judge looked at my lawyer, not me, and said. You make a good case Mr. Cardin but I am not going to drop the charges. I am going to postpone this case for one month and we are going to give the police lab a chance to put up or shut up. (Was I going back to jail until then,,,, this pause lasted a long time too). Does Mr. John have a place to go, an address? Yes, he's going to stay with his sister. She is here in the courthouse today Your Honor; I think his mother may be here too." "Well then, I am going to release Mr. John on his own recognizance and we will meet on August the 16th. Bailiff, take Mr. John back to the back and get him processed out as soon as possible. His sister is waiting for him; we've held him long enough." I was actually a little pissed they were letting me out now. Oh sure, the rich lawyer comes and you all think it suddenly seems to be the right thing to do.

The other inmates gave me the thumbs up as I went back to get processed. Afterward, I exited the front door through the lobby of the jail. My sister asked me if I wanted to stop and see my mother. I said, "Fuck her!" My sister said, "Yeah, that's what I was thinking too, I told her we would try to call her later." I asked my sister if I was actually staying with her because the court statement might have not meant anything and I was not going to assume I wasn't homeless. She said, "Yeah, you have to, Howard said." I exhaled.

I remember stepping out of the front door of the Detention Center and seeing that long sidewalk I had stared at so often. It was a hot and humid summer day in Baltimore, about 98 degrees. I felt that sun hit my face and I just paused. I inhaled that muggy air like it was bacon and eggs cooking; I thought I could actually feel my now pale face burning in the sun. I started running down that sidewalk about 50 yards, just long enough to break that big-house limitation; I looked up and waved bye-bye to my window. My sister laughed and said come on get in the car. She had a yellow 78 Camaro with a black stripe down the middle. I'd be riding in style, half hanging out the window. FREE AT LAST, FREE AT LAST, THANK… (Wait! Do I thank God? Grace? A stripper?)

I had made a decision several weeks back that I would not need to use any drugs or alcohol to enjoy my life ever again. It was plain to see that I could not control my mouth when I was drunk. I watched booze take my father and it wasn't going to get me too. For the first time in my life I didn't want to be like him. Free would be enough for me from here on out.

NO MENTAL DEFENSE

My sister lived on Wyanoke Road in Pen Lucy, a poor black neighborhood in Baltimore (the neighborhood Tupac was afraid of). It was one block above 39th Street and a couple of blocks from the old stadium; the very same Memorial Stadium that crash crashed his plane into. The same stadium where my abuser would take me to see ball games while thinking about doing perverted shit to me as a child. It was also the same stadium where I met people like Brooks Robinson, Paul Blair, Johnny Unitas, Burt Jones, Boog Powell, Reggie Jackson, Lee May, Jim Palmer and dozens more.

As we drove down Bologna Ave my sister pulled off to the right to go to the liquor store. I was just going to sit in the car and wait. All I had was $9 left over from my jail commissary and I might need that to eat. My sister asked me if I wanted anything and I said, "No, I'm good," sitting in the sunlight and fresh air was enough. I had no intention of drinking any time soon. My sister said, "Come on Mann, I'm buying."

Well hell yeah! Free booze was my 2nd favorite weakness. That's how quickly my mind changed. I remember going back to the cooler where the beer was (my sister didn't drink beer). What did I get? Of all things, a six-pack of Michelob Light. Why? Because I was a little heavy at 135 pounds? No, because the people on the commercials and TV shows drinking Mic Light weren't getting locked up. I walked up to the register and she asked, because she knows me, "Is that all you want?" I was speechless, so much love. I said, "What do you mean?" She said,

"Get a case if you want, hell you just got out of jail Mann, I might even have one with ya after all of this shit." I got my old standby case of bud tall boys but no vodka; that would just be asking for trouble. Maybe I just had to keep away from that stuff; maybe it brought out my Russian or something.

That my friends is how fast an addicted person's mind can change. No matter what motivations you think are in place to keep them sober it can all change that quickly. All the mental defenses disappear when the conditioning gets triggered. For me, it was even more than that. My sister had never really offered me anything so it was an act of love I wasn't going to miss out on. That's the scar of desperation for affection.

STRIPPED OF EVERYTHING

My sister had a three-bedroom apartment in the hood. She rented two of those rooms to people she worked with; you know, at the strip club. They were the same, "Who knows what they're on" girls that we helped move in just a few months before, on the night I wrecked my car. All clearly great omens for the future right?

Some guys I knew thought I had hit the party dude jackpot. It was the 80s and AIDS wasn't a straight or female thing yet. Here I was moving in with 3 bisexual strippers. I was also unknowingly moving into one of the favorite after-work party houses of Baltimore's Red Light district. When I entered the house I felt like a soldier returning home from war. Suddenly we were having a get-out-of-jail party with people that faced the chance of jail every day (usually while just trying to earn a living and survive the way poor people do). There were hugs and drugs and booze and nearly naked broads from 18 to 28 in and out of that house at all times.

After sleeping in jail for a month with a bunch of stinky dudes you could've just put me on the floor anywhere. Somehow my sofa bed from my bedroom had ended up at my sister's along with my dressers and some clothes. I remember thinking Dam, she was really coming through for me. I knew there was going to be a cost of some kind. Boom!!! I instantly became the butler/maid. I would have to clean and cook until I got a job. My army training was going to pay off because I could scrub a floor like no one I knew.

I vividly recall that first night back on the street. Brian and Kimberly came down that night to celebrate and like usual Brian brought some good pot. I remember that after drinking only ½ a beer and doing a single bong hit that I felt really high. (If you aren't aware addicts do a lot of math. I remember thinking that I could make that case of beer I got last a month if I only drank one a day.)

It was a busy night on the block so all the girls had to leave by around 8 or so. Sadly within 3 hours my tolerance had returned and I ended up drinking about 12 beers that night. Brian, Kimberly and I just hung out and talked about my jail experience and my bitch mother catching them screwing.

This wasn't the first time Brian had witnessed my mother's wrath firsthand. Brian had always tried to help me when I was on the street. His mother wouldn't let me stay with them on their farm so he actually lived with me in his car for about a week once. It might not seem like much but it was "inside." Brian also knew firsthand what being out on the street was like. He also knew what being taken in by a friend's parent felt like too. When I met him he was living with a dude named Aaron and his mother.

DO WHAT?

So what happens when you're fresh out of jail and unemployed? You do poor people's work. Any kind of work you can find. You do temp work where you get in a line to sweep floors for a day. You do any kind of dirty ass job you can, right beside other broke-ass people.

It was suggested by the girls from the block that I become a "runner" because there weren't any barker/bouncer jobs available at the moment. Being a runner was a simple job on the block. You went into the bars and asked the girls if they needed anything. The girls weren't allowed to be on the streets of the block because that supposedly made strippers look like prostitutes; cough! You can rest assured that all a girl had to do was walk outside and she'd get offers; sometimes from the cops.

It's occurring to me as I write this book that "running" didn't just mean going to get food and sandwiches it also meant going to get things like drugs or even outfits they forgot at home. If they wanted something they gave you money, you got a cab, you ran the errand then you got tipped, usually pretty damn well. (These girls were after all people working in the oldest hospitality profession on Earth, they knew how to tip.) If you were a cute young thing like me you got some extra offers as well; sometimes even an offer to hang out with them on their days off.

I had some great dinners, romantic boat rides, a wedding or two and even a few paddle boat outings on the harbor thanks to my new friends. Yes, I got laid plenty, usually in groups of three or more. (Like I said they were bisexual dancers.) Strippers really seemed to like getting to pick who they were with sexually because their job didn't allow for that. It gave them power they didn't usually have. Aside from all the debauchery we had some good clean fun. When you work in that industry the wholesome times seem to be the freakiest; the most intense.

Eventually, I did get the barker gig but that also included some running. I also made cash from the bars that didn't have barkers. As a barker your job is to stand out front of the bar and stop the bums from coming in. A barker also tries to entice those young soldiers and dudes with their Friday paychecks to enter. The barking thing is a lot like being a Carney. "GENTLEMEN WE GOT THE HOTTEST GIRLS ON THE BLOCK!! THIS IS THE PLACE YOU'LL TELL YOUR FRIENDS ABOUT. NO, DON'T GO DOWN THERE, THAT'S WHERE THEY HIDE THE UGLY FAT GIRLS!" If you barked at someone it usually meant that they were going to get served too because barkers/doormen did most of the carding in those days. The girls working the bar inside always had the final say but they could just blame the doorman.

The block felt like home in so many ways. It always reminded me of weekends with my father. Owners, Carl, Maria and Eddy reminded me of his friends. Since my sister was usually tending bar it actually was a family event. While I spent some time at the Circus Circus my favorite place was the old Gayety, three doors down from the corner of Gay and Baltimore streets. I stood out front but I also made my way up to the corner of Baltimore and Gay. (This corner was made famous during the 2019 riots when a black cop knocked out a black woman that had struck another officer. I remember seeing that clip 40 years later and thinking, hey, that's my corner.) The Gayety is gone from that location now but it's easy to recognize it because it's the same corner as the Baltimore City police department. In fact, the bar staff and select visitors parked their cars in the Judge's parking spaces at night. The only time anyone noticed was when the judges came down to party at the block. Trust me they did too and they didn't make a fuss either. They seemed to think letting the girls park there was some sort of tip from them. My sister's cars were parked there almost every night. I think people thought she worked for the judges; but in the court building, not the bar.

I didn't see much of my lawyer on the block but I saw every other politician, judge, lawyer and doctor in the city. It's not like they could tell people that they saw you there so all of us probationer types were quite safe. Working on the block and meeting cops was a positive experience. It was certainly the first time in my adult life that I saw cops as humans or felt like they saw me as a person (not since Barney's dad). We all worked together, we had a code, a set of best practices to keep things going smoothly.

For instance, a cop would walk up to the barker and say "How's it going? Is ____ working tonight?" The barker would say, "Let me see if she's here yet." I'd go in and give the cutthroat sign, people would put their clothes on, finish snorting the coke they had on the bar and I'd walk back out and say "Yeah she is, she wants you to come in and say hi."

Trust me, I wasn't the only one getting favors from the girls in those days. Many of those cops spent their entire careers walking that beat. Everyone knew everyone and everyone knew what everyone did; on the street and in their beds. In fact, I became such good friends with one of the cops that he actually gave me a nightstick for the unruly characters (A cherished memento I still have today).

HEARING BETTER

High times were in vogue but the wheels of justice were in low gear. I knew that I would have to go back to court but I wasn't very conscious of it. I returned to partying like nothing had ever happened. I felt quite vindicated working on the block; like the Universe was finally starting to make up for its mistakes. The court day in August came and went; it was pretty uneventful. I spent days getting nervous only to have the thing postponed again till September, then again till October. I also got a Cook/Pizza job a few weeks before court so I looked on the up and up.

When I went in to apply for the job it was at a college bar called PJ's Pub across the street from Johns Hopkins University. In a stunning turn of synchronicity and probably a helping of Grace, PJ's just happened to be owned by Paul and Jerry the now former owners of Giuseppe's. Even more amazing is that I applied for and was given the job before any of us even knew of our shared history. I walked in for my first day on the job to find Jerry who greeted me with a smile to show me the kitchen.

It was a fun job but I did start drinking there after work. How could I resist they sold my favorite 16 oz buds for $1.25. The math meant I could drink a case of beer at a bar for less than $25 and I could run a tab. My drinking there was mostly uneventful unless you count my getting into fights with the entire Johns Hopkins football team one night and the entire lacrosse team a week later. I still hated those rich fuckers; the same demographic that took my car from me.

By the time we went back to court in October Howard had become quite frustrated with the pro-bono case dragging on and on. He never asked for money from me but told me that my sister was taking care of it, to take it up with her. He was starting to help her in lots of ways; they actually became pretty close friends. Regardless he was still getting tired of wasting his time on this little no-pay case: he went off on the court again. I quote, "Your honor I do not believe that my client should have to suffer any longer due to the inadequacy of the police department lab; they are trying to turn dust into cocaine your Honor. How long do we need to give them before it's just not fair?" (I was thinking dude! Shut up! You'll make him mad at me.) The judge turned to the state and said, "Do you have any evidence to present today?"

You have to remember that during this time in America and especially in Baltimore, the system was going crazy trying to bust big drug dealers. It was the "War On Drugs." No one wanted to be the DA that couldn't prove a case. The state responded, "Not at this time your honor but I'm sure we will." Here they were, failing another hyped-up drug case and it looked bad for them, real bad. You could see it in all their faces, even the judge's.

I was freaked out about Howard yelling at the judge. The judge then turned to me, took a breath and said; "Mr. John, did you finish high school? (I thought back to Ms. Thomas my High School Vice Principal). Have you done anything to further your education?" I looked down and said, "No your honor, I joined the Army." He actually perked up a little. He asked if I was still in the Army with a shocked look on his face. I said it depends on the outcome of this trial your Honor. This new insight gave the judge all he needed and he said to my lawyer. "Please explain to your client what a one-year Stet Docket is." After we talked he said, "Do you accept the stet Mr. John?" I said I do.

What that Stet meant was that the case would be set aside for one year and if I didn't get into any trouble during that year the case would be disposed of. I remember actually getting mad thinking of all the trauma of being arrested, me pondering a lifetime in jail, homicide or suicide and having it all reduced down to a "be good and stop it." I remember shaking my head and thinking, if I had money I wouldn't have had to go through any of this shit.

After finishing up with the court I continued to rock the block bars, PJ's and Hammerjacks nightclub. After a year of living with my sister it came time for me to move on. Her drug use and emotional problems were getting out of hand along with everyone else's in the house. I was tired of being the Butler and my soon-to-be stepfather had a glass company that could always use some under-the-table labor.

NEW LIFE AT THE DELI

I was up in Cockeysville one day so I decided to stop by the Deli again. Somehow news had gotten around that I was locked up. Cockeysville's a small town and news travels fast. Most people that knew me from my dealing days figured I would end up there one day.

The greeting I received when I walked in the door this time wasn't quite like the return home from Army summer camp but there was a lot of interest. Melanie was sitting down prepping food at a table so I went over and sat down next to her after giving her a hug. She said I have something to show you as she pushed out her chair. I thought she was staring at the floor so I looked under the table but she was holding her belly. She was now showing. Again my first thought was that I was happy for her and her husband, they got what they wanted. She was quick to tell me when she conceived but I wasn't into baby math back then. She suggested she thought it would be a girl, she hugged me hard and I said congrats.

If I'm being honest I didn't really care if it was mine or not. If it was mine I thought I was happy to have given her and her husband that gift. During that conversation some of her comments made me think that she and her husband had actually set me up. Being used sexually was the story of my life. I noticed some of the other girls in the deli looking at me funny and all I could manage was to be a little cocky about it. I was not in the right place to raise a kid and I was still working on the block some. I thought if it's mine I'll meet it when it turns 18. (I know how that sounds but that's the truth. My damage never taught me the value of a child.) I had made a decision to let them decide what to do about the details of the whole thing. I was just happy she wasn't after any money because I didn't have any. (I can tell you this, the status of that child has never left my consciousness; to this day I still don't know the truth about her.)

My next visit to the Deli was after Melanie had the baby. She ran over to see me and asked if I wanted to see a picture of "THE BABY." My eyes caught the eyes in the picture and I was just stunned, breathless. It was like seeing a ghost. Something stirred in me at that moment. I still didn't have any proof of anything but people always say you know when it's yours. That's what I felt.

Years later I found out after my sister lost a baby that our family had an abnormal factor 9 blood clotting condition. My sister and her girlfriend at that time suggested that I needed to let Melanie know just in case. It was a genetic condition that affected the sons of daughters. I sat down with Melanie at a table during a visit years later and told her of the condition.

In the late 80s talk shows were doing a lot of paternity tests. I didn't know if it would ever come out or not. I asked her if I could write a letter for her to keep in case something ever happen to me. In case she told Nancy after I was already gone. She became quite stern with me and said "She will NEVER KNOW and I will take that to my grave. I don't want her finding some piece of paper after I'm gone either." I thought that was selfish but I felt like I had already given all my rights away years earlier. I knew I didn't have the right to upset a happy family so I once again left the whole issue in their hands; they were her parents after all. To be really clear here I'm not sure if they ever got a paternity test. I'm not sure they would have ever shared the "actual" results with anybody, either way. Her existence always made me feel like I was at least of some value to someone; that I had contributed to something positive.

DAMAGE

I soon found an ad in the paper for a room for rent in Reisterstown MD. It was an area just a few miles North of Pikesville where my mother and Sandy lived. My new place was actually on the same street as Sandy's parent's apartment; right next to an apartment complex owned by his uncle where we often did glass work.

There used to be an old joke. "Where did you find him, in the newspaper?" Well, that is where I found Arthur S and that's where he found me. Arthur was one hinky dude. He told everyone that he was a Psychologist but I later learned he had no degree at all, that he just worked with the homeless for years. Pretty sure that's how he got started renting out rooms in his house. You paid $17 a week for the room and $2 for a phone extension in that room. If you wanted a color TV that was $5 more. Just $24 a week and I would never have to be homeless again. If you behaved and paid your rent you could even pet the ferrets he kept in his bathtub.

When I moved in I didn't expect to find a new drinking buddy but I did. His name was Boyd, a for-real hillbilly from Staunton Virginia. Good old Boyd had a little Chevy truck but he also had 12 DUIs in VA and was about to go to court for his 13th.

On the average Saturday Boyd and I would buy a case of beer around noon. We'd drink that case by 6pm, take a shower then buy another case and head downtown to Hammerjack's. Hammer's was the Mecca of hair bands, heavy metal and punk but most importantly it had more dance floors than any bar in the United States at the time. Max capacity was somewhere north of 3000 people a night. While the beer there was cheap we'd usually knock off most of that second case before we ever arrived. Like most people we got to Hammer's, hammered.

On average I would drink 24, 16oz beers a day. Illicit drugs meant nothing to me at this time. I rarely considered the fact that I was self-medicating with alcohol but I obviously was. It took that much alcohol to keep my emotional scars on the inside. That's what it took to keep my soul from hurting.

My philosophy was, out of sight out of mind? If I couldn't see straight I didn't mind. Heavy use was the only way I knew to quiet those voices, lessen my past traumas and remove the emotional triggers associated with the damage. Alcohol was a great drug for pushing emotional injuries way down deep.

While I never liked people with money it really wasn't about their wealth at all. I actually despised anyone that didn't have to fight for their survival. It's a subconscious distain shared by a lot of underprivileged people. As a young kid, I remember going to other people's houses and seeing full refrigerators and thinking that they were spoiled. I was flabbergasted when I realized that there were actually people with freezers in their garages and basements.

As mentioned I wasn't a bigot, nor did I have the capacity to be a racist but I did have a problem with people that I thought didn't have to suffer like I did. It wasn't right that only some people had to struggle. I knew that misery loved company. Like E-1, if I was going to suffer I wanted everyone else to suffer too. I was taught that was fairness. Since I couldn't stop my suffering I wanted others to join me. (In today's terms it's a form of being emotionally toxic.)

The only way I could keep those wounds hidden and keep from acting out on them was to stay wasted. Alcohol was the only thing I could depend on, the only thing that actually worked; that actually did what it was supposed to do. Governments didn't work, people didn't work, churches didn't work and God didn't work. Alcohol did.

I never got the help a kid with my issues should have; not on any level. No counseling, no church, no consultation of any kind beyond my old Vice Principle Ms. Thomas. The only people that ever helped me feel good and valuable were my sex partners. While they were probably triggering old wounds from the past I still felt better when I felt physically close to someone. Sadly my emotional walls and resentments made that difficult too.

The people that made me feel wanted were given very esteemed places in my heart for doing so, an unchallenged loyalty. It was like it forged some steel bond that could never be broken inside of me. Even after they were gone I still held them close.

I would hold out hoping that old flames would come to their senses and realize what I had to offer; just like I did with my mother. When a connection ended I'd feel the loss of a lifetime. (This is why some damaged people become dangerously obsessed. They're not just fighting for the current relationship they're in; they're fighting for all of their relationships over time, every time one ends.)

As previously mentioned I later learned that my sister and E-1 had a conversation about my having been abused. My sister confronted her after a girlfriend of mine revealed it to her. She asked if she was aware that I was sexually abused by Robert Holcomb. (I didn't have a conversation about my abuse with my family until I was in my 30's.) For years I thought it was my secret but it wasn't, I could have gotten help.

For perspective, I grew up watching black and white westerns with hard-ass John Wayne, vengeance movies like Death Wish with Charles Bronson, Dirty Harry setting things straight and the great underdog Bruce Lee. Men didn't even hug in those days. Hell, there was even a standard distance for two males on a dance floor to observe, lest they be thought gay.

I am 100% convinced that despite my "great alcoholic genes" from both my father and mother's father, my dependence on alcohol was primarily the result of untreated emotional neglect and abuse, i.e. damage. That damage is why I felt alone, why I felt like an object and why I self-medicated. Essentially I was raised to be a person with no feelings, a person only on this Earth for others to use when convenient; bred to be a sociopath. I was taught that emotional pain didn't really matter. I was treated in such a way as to foment great hostility and to disregard emotions. Then I was trained to kill people in the US Army. It's easy to see that things were not heading in a healthy direction. I felt invisible, irrelevant and worthless and I saw no reason to give compassion when I received none myself. (Sound Familiar?) From a young age, I had thoughts that one day I would make them all pay; now I had the means. One day they would all shake in their boots and regret not caring for me. (This is our problem today.)

ONE MORE MOVE

I lived with the crazy wannabe doctor for a little over a year. I did pretty well paying my rent but there were a couple weeks when I was late. He didn't mind, he had a fee for that too. I started searching the newspaper again and found my next home. It was back near the city in Pikesville, about a mile from where I was arrested. The new place was a single-family home managed by a guy a couple years younger than me named Tony.

Tony was given a house to manage when his family moved to England for work. It seemed a little harsh to me that his parents would do that to their kids but Tony always suggested that he was given an option to stay. He was a good kid but still a little rich kid to me because he was basically given a house. He was however required to pay all the bills and upkeep on the house. That's why he decided to rent out the 3 upstairs rooms. The cost was $150 a month in 1984.

The Bedford road house was basically a farm on the edge of the city. It was only about an acre of land but it had 2 goats, 30+ chickens, 12 ducks, 6 meat rabbits and even a dog. Tony explained to me that he and another roommate were aspiring chefs in culinary school together. Like my father I liked to cook so I thought we would get along well.

On my first visit, I was told that anything in the kitchen was fair game to eat and that Tony and Keith would often practice making meals that everyone could partake in. If you didn't want someone to eat something you put a color-coded sticker on it. I remember being a little taken aback by the offer of free food. Could it be? What a blessing that was for a kid who spent a large part of his life hungry. The entire house was a sort of communal effort from the food to the care of the animals. We heated the house with a woodstove fueled by resourced pallet boards that we all took turns breaking down and cutting up in the garage. (We might have invented that.)

The refrigerator had room for my beer and there was public transportation a mile away. My future stepfather Sandy was a mile up the road for work and he came to get me almost every morning. I could even take the new light rail down to the city if I wanted a shift working door for my sister. Things started off great but as you may have predicted my relationship with alcohol became even more dysfunctional.

TAP ROOM CHURCH GIRLS

Tony only had one real rule that he asked me to observe. He told me on my first day that he didn't care about liquor but that since drugs were illegal he didn't want them in the house. He stated, "I don't care what you do outside just please don't bring them in here." That was no problem for me because I was only dating alcohol. Drugs meant nothing to me, they were unpredictable and you never knew what you were getting. In contrast, you always knew exactly what you were getting with alcohol. That reliability made it much easier to self-medicate with.

It was a cold December night and one of those rare occasions when Brian and I found ourselves feeling bored. Usually, there was some band or dance floor calling our names somewhere. It was on one of those slow nights that Brian and I planned to stay at the house and drink. Since no one was there we could drink freely and smoke outside if we wanted.

Females are usually a necessity when you're a 21-year-old male but it was a cold night and the fireplace was warm and toasty. Brian and I got into the habit of playing one on one quarters using a case of quart beers; "quarter quarts" we called it. It was about 7 pm when we decided that we should get some more beer so we decided to go to Rodger's Tap Room. Rodgers was an old dinky neighborhood bar that only locals seemed to notice. It was a lot like the Store Room but for kids in Pikesville. It was also the nearest place to find some horny women. Enter the church girls.

While at Rodger's we did some dancing and when guys can dance they end up with dance partners. After some mingling a guy at the bar started talking about how much great weed he had. It was cold and I didn't want to stand outside so I said. Party at my house! The girls cheered and guys saw the girls cheer so then everyone cheered, except for the bartender because we emptied out the bar when we left. (I know I know, right now you're thinking about Tony and his no weed policy. I wasn't thinking about it, I was drinking.)

My memories of that night ended up a lot like many other successful nights of drinking, vague. Some of it I never forgot, like the girls. While I couldn't remember their names, I never forgot what they looked like. I was trying to get the two girls I was dancing with at the bar more worked up so I was flirting hard. One was in the kitchen and one was in the living room. I had noticed that the three of us seemed pretty happy dancing together so maybe the three of us could have some real fun. (I always liked nice girls; their innocence reminded me of mine.)

It was probably about midnight when Tony unexpectedly returned to the house. I was in the kitchen with my new friend and some random dude when he entered. From what I gathered he was quite shocked. Apparently, he knew one of the girls in the living room from church. Someone yelled, "Tony's here!" As if to make sure he was welcome. At that moment I stopped making out with the girl in the kitchen and turned to find him standing behind me with his jaw on the floor. He knew this girl too. (Tony was the guy these girls never gave the time of day except in Sunday school.)

You have to understand that Tony was a good church boy. He worked every day and went to church a couple times a week. At that time he had never consumed alcohol outside of communion at church; it wasn't legal for him yet because of the drinking age change.

I saw Tony as an honest but very naive sheltered child. Pretty sure he was saving himself for marriage. He certainly was alien to things like red-light districts and jails. I don't think he had ever been in a fight in his life so confrontation wasn't his thing either. He was so gullible that he believed in Jesus; at least that's how I viewed him at the time.

I asked Tony to join the party, I offered him one of the girls but he just looked at the ground and walked back towards his room. He came out again a little later to find me and the other girl making out but this girl was straddling me on his sofa while we did. He blushed, hid his face and quickly retreated to his room after getting something from the refrigerator. He never said a word in objection to what was going on. (I had forgotten all about the weed smoking rule.)

The next day I woke up at noon and came downstairs. Tony was out back with the animals. He came walking in shocked to see me awake, I said hi and he quickly went into his room and shut the door. I really didn't pay him much attention as he stomped his feet like a petulant child. The next day I saw Tony again for a brief moment, said hi but he only gave me a muddled response. I said "Dude! What's up? Did I do something?" No response. This kind of silent treatment had no affect me; I majored in "emotional alienation" and the "withholding of affection" growing up. This happened between us one more time then on the 4th day I cornered him in his room.

"Tony, dude, what did I do? Why are you mad at me? Tell me what I did." Tony sat down on his mattress that was on the floor in the room (because it was cool then). I was standing about 6 feet away facing him. He very softly and respectfully said while looking up at me almost in tears. "Dude, I love my God, I've never questioned His existence, not once in my life until the other night." Suddenly my memory started to return. I had forgotten all about our late-night conversation after everyone left.

He said: "Dude, those two girls you were with were from my church. I went to School and Sunday school with them my entire life. I'm worried about them telling their parents about the party and their parents then telling mine. I don't want to have to go to England." That's how innocent and clueless he was. He actually thought these girls would run and tell their parents that they were smoking pot at his house.

I was getting confused about a lot of things he was suggesting. I asked, "That party is what made you question God?" He said, "No, what made me question God was when you started telling me that I was a gullible little boy; that I didn't know anything about the world and that God may have put you here in my life to wake me the heck up." He said, "I actually did start questioning why he would put you here just like you said, Why would he? Perhaps a test like he did with Job?" Essentially what I had suggested to him while drunk was that if I was such a nasty sinful person then why was God doing this to him? (I know, it's a special trick only wounded addicted people can use.)

Apparently, I had challenged his belief in an omnipotent God; that if he did exist and if I was so wrong that he should have spared Tony all this hassle because good people are supposed to be protected from evil. I believe my exact words were; "If God does exist then why am I in your life; maybe you need to wake up from your little dream. Why did God make it so that these two girls ended up at this house?" There was more back and forth but he finished with this. "I don't want anyone around me that is going to make me question my God. You have every right to doubt Him but I don't doubt Him and I don't want to."

Something mysterious happened at that moment. I suddenly saw my behavior in its true light, like I was standing next to myself. I tasted my own bitterness. I couldn't deny how I had acted but it wasn't how I wanted to be. I caught a side glimpse of myself in a mirror on his wall and for the first time in my life, Dr. Jekyll actually saw Mr. Hyde. It was actually a bit of a shock because I knew I could be such a good person when I liked someone and I did like Tony. My father had taught me kindness but it seemed absent. I felt like that gentle little kid that wanted to be a psychologist and help people was lost inside of me; this was some other guy, some demented altered version.

The truth is the person that convinced me not to become a therapist was the same POS that abused me. (His exact words were, "No you don't, they all end up shooting themselves in the head.") At this moment, in Tony's bedroom, that little kid (Dr. Jekyll) was staring at the monster that came out whenever that special blend of alcohol, hurt, doubt, damage, fear, criticism and rejection were mixed together.

Tony had delivered his message to me in such an innocent way that I didn't need to put up any defenses or denial (while sober). He was even giving me the right to be me and to believe what I wanted. He did it without making me feel judged. He just explained to me how he was hurt by me. I hated people that hurt people. Tony had done something that even jail couldn't do. He then asked me to find a new place to live as soon as I could. He provided a moment of clarity that would prove indispensable (Grace). Once again I was facing the street. Now it seemed that the only thing that I could still depend on (alcohol) was abandoning me too.

DYING FOR HELP

While I was willing to move as Tony requested I still had my rent paid up for the month of December and he knew better than to challenge me legally. I was so stirred by his account of that evening that I became quite disillusioned. I thought back to my old drinking buddy Billy R. I recalled him saying that he was sober but since he had a problem with the truth I really didn't believe he was. Since he missed a couple of party invites I decided to suspend logic and give him a call anyway. I needed something, even if it was going to be bullshit. I needed a distraction from my brain; something to talk me out of suicide. Brian was a follower, even a bit of a sycophant so I knew that I would never get a straight answer from his stoned ass.

I got Billy on the phone; I remember his voice was very animated and his tone was very upbeat. I asked him "Dude, do you really not drink?" He said, "Man I haven't had a drink in a year and a half." I then asked in a very serious tone, "Do you still have fun?"

My friend went on to tell me that he had been going to AA for quite some time. That he was hanging out with a group of young people our age and that they did lots of fun things together sober. He described a sense of camaraderie I'd never really known. He said they went camping together, white water rafting, bowling, and were now planning a skydiving trip. In my head, I questioned if these weren't just more of his tall tales so I just looked past the hype speak. He told me about a group of them getting thrown out of Denny's that weekend for laughing too loud and having too much fun. I thought; "Oh joy! That's what's left for me now. Oh my God, life really is over!"

Then came the turning point of the entire conversation. This was a Tuesday night around 6:00. He said he had a commitment that evening but said he would come to get me tomorrow and take me to an AA meeting. He said he had to get me early because he had to set up the meeting. I was shocked that he was being trusted with the keys to the very same church that I had actually paid people to steal candelabras out of just a few years before. The karma and irony were coursing through my veins and I said yeah dude that would be cool.

Then he said something that was completely unexpected. "Can you not take a drink until after the meeting? If you can't that's cool but it will be better if you don't." By now I had trouble making it until 4pm without getting the shakes. For some odd reason, I said yeah without even thinking about it. He said, "I'll take you to the liquor store afterward if you need me to. But I'll pick you up at 7:00."

I was so desperate for something I just trusted my intuition and agreed to that meeting even though I had a bizarre conception of what AA was. My only awareness of AA was from an episode of The Flintstones. Fred had joined FA (Food Anonymous) because he couldn't stop eating Brontosaurus Burgers and he was getting too fat. After Fred went to the meeting the members of FA would sneak around behind him and steal the burger from him every time he tried to eat one. You would hear those little tip-toe sounds dew dew, dew dew dew dew, then SNATCH!!! The member would run off with the burger and boom, crisis/relapse averted.

Hiding and taking booze was the only way that I thought you could ever get someone to stop drinking so I was a little confused when he actually said that he would drive me to a liquor store afterward. I thought it might be a trick but at this point, I didn't even care. I needed an excuse to not kill myself; I needed something. The truth is I was sick and tired of being sick and tired. I was done fighting this desperate battle to keep my emotional pain at bay.

I had no idea what AA was but the keep-away method did work while I was in basic and jail. I figured that I would have to tough it out once again. That was the story of my life, that's what life was, heartache, loss and suffering? It truly seemed life was just a series of heartbreaks, letdowns and deep-seated disappointments. Losing booze might be one of the biggest losses ever but it wasn't working anymore. I was actually going to have to give up the only thing in my life that did what it was supposed to do when it was supposed to do it. Alcohol was the only dependable thing I'd ever found in life but now it was failing me too. Nothing else made the hurt go away; it gave me a nightly reprieve from the scar noises and damage in my head. I didn't think there was any formula for fixing all the things that were broken in my world and in my heart. I was thinking that my life really couldn't get any worse. Death wasn't worse, this was hell!

Before our phone call, I was just going to kill myself and hope for a better set of parents next time in this cycle of torment; I couldn't have any worse luck. At a minimum, I would be done with this place for now. I knew I had made some bad choices and perhaps some were so bad that they couldn't be overcome. I caused some of my problems but most were inflicted upon me by others as a child. I didn't believe that my wounds could be healed.

I was concerned about the AA cult but even a cult might be an improvement. They couldn't screw up my life any more than it already was; I was already going to kill myself. (FYI, giving up on life is a common reason people enter cults.) I thought that since I didn't have any money that they might not let me in anyway. If the cult didn't work the next step was clear; death. Since it didn't look like we would be going to war any time soon that righteous form of death was off the table. My hope of dying for my country in the Army, dying for a good purpose was dashed too. I even considered dying for some protest or cause but I didn't have enough passion about anything social because, fuck people! I questioned if there was a message I needed to send to society before I left but there was nothing worth doing because humans were hopeless (sound familiar).

These are the thoughts that were going through my head when my friend arrived at exactly the time he said he would. He wasn't the most credible person I knew but his accuracy, even with the traffic, was an intriguing turn of events; it was different. (We didn't have GPS in those days so extra credit there.) We got in the car and drove all the way back to where he had just come from in Cockeysville. I remember thinking that this would be some full-circle stuff since I had actually tried to stay away from Cockeysville because I had gotten in so much trouble there.

More irony, the church he took me to was about 30 feet from where my drinking in public arrest occurred; about 20 yards from Max's radiator shop. I wasn't thinking about the irony but this was more than that, this was some cosmic shit (Grace). My brain was so foggy I didn't think about the historical parallels at the time I just put it all in the Cockeysville basket of problems. Looking back now it appears as an obvious presentation of Grace. It was like undoing a misstep of some kind.

Billy had the keys to the church just like he had said. I thought they definitely didn't know him. This was getting just a little too surreal. We went in and he started making coffee in two of the largest coffee pots I'd ever seen. We started setting up the tables and chairs. According to Billy it had to be done in a very special pattern or people would get upset. We put ashtrays on every other seat and set up a table full of literature. Once we were done setting everything up Billy grabbed a blue book and said, "Here, this is yours." I thought to myself "I can't afford it." "It's on me," he said. "Read it, it could save your life, it saved mine." I thought, Well OK then!

My next thought was I don't read. The only entire book that I had ever read in my life was The Shining and that was when I was locked up. Billy stopped and turned back towards me; he grabbed the book and went directly to the back. When I was in school the answers were often in the back of the book. I figured he knew how smart I was so he was going to do me a favor and save me all that reading. (I mean the book didn't even have any pictures.) I thought he was taking me to where the answers were, past the propaganda.

He read a quote that was attributed to Herbert Spencer (I was to learn later it was actually a guy named William Paley).

"There is a principle which is a bar against all information, which is proof against all arguments and which cannot fail to keep a man in everlasting ignorance—that principle is contempt prior to investigation." -Herbert Spencer.

My first thought was damn, Billy got smarter; he nailed me right between the eyes with that one. I had contempt for everything and everyone. I actually felt pretty righteous about it too after having lived through what I had. I'm sure he could see the defeat in my eyes. He said, "Just keep an open mind to what you read and what you hear tonight, this shit works." I knew how much Billy loved drinking and if he really believed it I was going to have to suspend my knowledge of the cosmos for at least this one evening. I would just put off killing myself one more day. Once again, things couldn't be made any worse than they were. I was going to kill myself; life doesn't get any worse than that.

Then something really spooky happened. These yuppie preppy type people that Billy and I had always hated started showing up with smiles and open hands. A month ago I wouldn't have shaken their hands but they were so smiley. It was freaky!!! They looked like old preppy rich white guys in their Polo and Izod shirts, their green golf pants with loafers and no socks. I thought I had died and gone to actual hell. I thought perhaps I had already killed myself and this is where I ended up for all my misdeeds: Without a drink in Yuppie preppy hell!

There I was a glam rocker with big hair, parachute pants, flip flops, silver jewelry, dangly earrings and a cutoff shirt that actually said Maniac on it; in winter. These were not my people. Since nothing good ever worked out for me I began to think that maybe only people with money could join this club. Maybe Billy wasn't actually sober after all. Maybe they only let a couple poor people in a year, to make coffee and clean up.

The two of us stepped outside to smoke but I think I just wanted to get away from some of these creepy preppy people. The parking lot started filling up with Cadillacs, Lincolns, Beamers and Benzes; I didn't even have a car. This was not going to work for me I just knew it. At least I was promised a ride to the liquor store on the way home.

Then they started assaulting me, no, not really, they just started shaking my hand and telling me to keep coming back. I was looking at them sideways thinking; you know I'm not rich right? (In my head I'm thinking I'm not paying any membership fees or buying any Amway stuff.) They kept shaking my hand and saying "Keep coming back." I was beginning to think that Billy had called them all and told them he was bringing me and that was why they were all being nice to me. Then I started to think exactly what a person with my history would think. I figured it out, they were all gay. Billy had turned. Maybe this was why he never came to my parties. Are these his Denny's people? Now I was thinking I could hitchhike home: What a bunch of bullshit. (Understandably I didn't trust older men with big smiles that wanted to be my friend.)

Suddenly I realized that I was not in hell. Holly crap I was in Gay God's country. I was used to hell, this was worse. I was sure that death was close. There was no way I could suspend enough logic to get this thing they called recovery. I was not going to be dumb enough for this to work on me. I was way too intelligent. I even heard a guy say there had never been anyone too dumb to get this program but there were plenty of people that were too smart. THERE IT WAS, they were showing me the door, I knew it.

Then, without any warning, all the sudden, an angel appeared. No! Not that kind of angel; the 80s kind with tight jeans and a tight low-cut blouse. This angel was a gorgeous chick named Beth. BETH??? Can you hear me calling you? I'M IN!!! Quit drinking no problem! For her? Piece of cake! Thanks to KISS I had a crush on that name Beth alone. Maybe it was a sign!

It didn't stop with Beth; the pretty women kept coming in the door and saying hi to me just like the gay guys. I remember thinking, so this is where all the hot chicks have been hiding out; with the gay guys in AA. Billy may have struck gold.

I had obviously competed for women before but these guys wouldn't be much competition for me. Even if the girls swung both ways I could work with that. My old roommates trained me well. This AA was beginning to look feasible after all.

Let's pause for a moment. I shared these thoughts to give you some insight into how the hyper-sexualized mind of an abused child prioritizes its worldview. I hope you can see how sexually abused people use sexuality to overcome sadness and loss. In my head, I thought I might be worthless in most areas but when it came to the sexual gratification of females I was the Master. I was standing there with a wrecked life wanting to die a minute earlier. My life was in complete shambles then suddenly without hesitation, I'm actually better than everyone else in the room (albeit if sex is the measure).

Sexually abused children have been taught through their abuse experience that sex is how the world values people; it stains (scars) their core. They believe that everyone prioritizes sexual prowess over everything else including emotional stability because that is their experience. It certainly was mine. Sadly hyper-sexuality is just one of the stains that sexual abuse leaves behind. Layer that with the fact that people from emotionally dysfunctional families face life with an all-or-nothing mentality and the choices become very limited. Many are left as an egomaniac with an inferiority complex.

As the meeting was about to start I noticed there was a group of young people gathered at the table Billy had chosen for us to sit. Want to guess who sat down right next to me? Beth. (Yay Grace!) I have to admit it freaked me out a little but I played it cool. I found out later that the old timers called it the "kiddie table," even though everyone was in their 20s. There I sat, right next to Beth and two seats over from her was a wealthy young lady named Janice in a full-length fur coat. Was my ship about to come in? Was Billy a genius?

Things were getting interesting then suddenly BANG BANG BANG, no, not a gun bang, but a Big Book hitting a table to get the meetings started. I lit Beth's cigarette for her; cause I had class. I didn't really drink coffee but I had one anyway; something I hadn't had since being out on maneuvers in Basic Training. Billy gave me a cup and said just fill it halfway. I thought it was because he didn't want me to waste it but it was so I didn't burn myself if my hands started to shake.

The guy running the meeting introduced himself and they shouted HEY JIM!!! It seemed a little cultish or maybe just a little Amway but Beth was into it so I was too. They went through the formalities of the meeting opening which included the serenity prayer, a prologue, how it works, the steps and the traditions. Every time someone introduced themselves they got the same HI ----!! They asked if there were any newcomers. I felt the eyes on me but all I could think was, there was no way that this whole group of people could shout "Hi Emmanuel" and I didn't want to confuse them, especially if they were a little slow. I wasn't really sure if I wanted these Brontosaurus Burger people finding me or my house so I used my old alias E.J. HI E.J.!!! KEEP COMING BACK!!! I knew Billy told them I was new but this "keep coming back" thing was actually beginning to make me feel like they wanted me around. It was almost unconditional. I thought to myself, when they get to know me they'll cut that shit out.

What if they actually did know me? What if this problem I had, was affecting other people the same way. Did they know who I really was inside? No matter, I still wasn't giving them any money; they looked like they had plenty. The group secretary said the basket was going around in order to cover expenses for the group like coffee and literature. He said, if you have some cash put some in the basket and if you need some, take some out. I quickly looked at Billy and he whispered, "You don't need any." I was suddenly beginning to question his knowledge of the program. I was up in my head thinking I still might come back without him for the cash and the chicks.

Suddenly the secretary said, "We have a special event tonight." I thought, damn it, I don't want to be given any more attention right now. Then the secretary said, "Peter K is celebrating 11 years sober." There were thunderous applause and Peter stood up at the front table. He said his name with a great smile and they shouted HI PETER!! (A coded gay reference maybe?) I was intrigued because he was one of the first people to greet me. I listened to him speak, he was sincere, honest, unabashed and he gave people hope. He told us what happened to get him sober and what his life was like now. I was waiting for him to bring up dues and fees but instead, he told us we had already paid all the dues we'd ever need to pay unless we decided to drink again. He believed to drink was to die spiritually.

Afterward, I was given phone numbers and told to call before I took a drink. My abuse experience had me questioning their motives once again. I had serious issues in that area, especially with men; it was an obstacle I would have to overcome if this was ever going to work. That is unless I could get a female sponsor.

Peter shared in such a way that he made the insane thought processes of being a drunk seem like it was OK and maybe even normal. All these hoity-toity-looking people seemed to agree. I was confused but curious as hell. I chain-smoked and gently sipped my way through that meeting but sitting still was very hard. I learned later this was my body wanting to get a real drink somewhere. I wondered if it was Beth giving me these heart flutters but it was probably withdrawal. As I mentioned Beth was always my favorite girl's name. All the way back in Jr. High when I had a crush on a girl named Beth and then I heard that Kiss song. This Beth looked just like the Angel in the video too. I probably looked a little like the guys in KISS, only prettier. Then I heard someone say; "You're in the right place."

While I was a devout atheist at the time the meeting hit me a little like that old V-8 commercial when the person hits themselves on the forehead realizing things suddenly made sense. Thock!! Suddenly I recalled how I once believed in this God that didn't currently exist for me. You'd think that having a name like Emmanuel may have led me down a holier path. That it might have been a sign but no; it gave me a complex instead.

I started to worry, what if I couldn't get with this God that abandoned me as a child? What if this God thing couldn't work for me even if I really wanted it? I truly believed that I might be too smart to get it. I also considered that my mind may have been too small to grasp such a large concept as God this whole time. Was I dumb? If I was dumb maybe I could get this thing? (These mind fluctuations aren't just a sign of withdrawal they're also a sign of emotional damage and instability.)

They kept talking about a Higher Power so at least that wasn't totally Christian but we were in a church. (There was however a guy named Ruby G that said he was a Jew with a Catholic disease.) I had been studying the Tao Te Ching for years and had been doing quite a bit of meditation. At least that's what I called it. It was a lot like tripping without the acid. When it came to a God I never really thought that I was God; life would have been easier if I was. I did seriously doubt that there was anything "all-loving" or "all-powerful" in the Universe. I certainly never saw or felt any evidence of that love growing up except when I was with my father or grandmother. Both of whom were taken away from me by this God.

Why did God take my father? Why didn't I have a real mother? Why was I abused? How come nobody cared about me as a kid? I didn't believe in a real heaven or hell by this time but if there was a hell I was convinced that it was living here on Earth. Heaven could thus be anywhere but here. That's the major reason death was so attractive to me. It was anywhere but here.

I remember thinking that these AA people seemed to have it all figured out; at least when it came to the alcohol problem. They seemed to have a really open-minded view of the God thing too. They also had this special way of knowing where the alcoholic mind was going before it got there. They were starting to look like the only people that might.

There was still one issue that seemed to give me a lot of doubt. They kept talking about 28-day treatment and I didn't have any insurance or anyone that cared enough to help me pay for it. I thought if treatment was required then boom, here we go again, me being cast out and abandoned. Here was one more NOT YOU EMMANUEL!! It seemed too good to be true so something had to spoil it. (My mind really did move around this fast. That's what happens when you take away the sedatives of a damaged and wounded person with an anxiety disorder. Everything speeds up and for a person not thinking clearly that's a bad thing; it results in impulsive and sometimes dangerous choices.)

After the meeting, we had to clean up the church but we had a lot more help. Before we cleaned up Billy took me over to the guy Peter that spoke. They all started writing down their names and telling me that if I needed to talk to call them whenever I wanted; before I took a drink.

They started asking me how I was getting to the next meeting. I thought that this was the only meeting in Maryland. My brain said here we go again, these gay guys and their ride offers. I met plenty like them hitchhiking late at night as they left the bars, but this was different because they were so upfront about it. Billy quickly rescued me by saying that he could take me to Springfield State Mental Hospital with him tomorrow night. I thought wait a damn minute. Is this a trick to get me admitted into the state mental hospital where the poor people go? Were they going to try to get me there willingly and then tell me I can't leave? Was this the alternative to the 28-day treatment? Actually, it didn't matter. It would still be a roof over my head and free meals; hell I might even get some much-needed counseling.

My friend drove me back to the other side of town and we talked about some of the things we had heard in the meeting. He dispelled a lot of my confusion and he even renewed his offer to take me to the liquor store. I thought it would be insulting if I said yes; besides, I had enough beer at home. He asked if I was sure, then he asked how much I had. I said a little, he said, "Good, you might need it."

CHAPTER FOURTEEN

GRACED

THE RIDE FROM HELL

On the ride home from that first meeting Billy and I talked in depth about the Higher Power (HP) concept. He explained how he was instructed to find his own HP and suggested I try doing the same thing. He directed me to get a piece of paper and draw a line down the middle. On the left side I was to write everything I was ever told God was; all loving, all-knowing all forgiving, all-powerful, He knows when you are bad or good; when you've sinned, he's forgiving, etc. Then on the right side of the paper, I was to put whatever I wanted God to be; anything at all, religion didn't matter. When finished I was to take the piece of paper, tear it down the middle and throw their shit away. I thought wait what? It can't be that simple to create a God that worked. I couldn't even fathom how a person was supposed to construct this list "of their own understanding." I didn't want to look stupid so I asked him what he wrote. He said, "My Higher Power likes loud rock and roll music, likes fast cars, likes chasing women and he wants me to have fun." I said, "I'll have what your havin." I was actually quite taken aback by the simplicity. This was an astounding revelation to me. I was pretty sure you had to get it from a book of some kind; someone had to authorize it right? Even the devil came from a book.

My life experiences suggested that I was supposed to meet other people's needs; that my needs and wants really didn't matter to anyone, especially not God. How was I going to now create my own God; one that cared about me, maybe even prioritize me somehow?

Even while I was dealing drugs I was meeting other peoples' needs. Because of my history with my mother, I wasn't even sure how to be important to anything outside of myself; I didn't know how to respond to it. (This is a major self-esteem scar; to believe one is not worthy of love is perhaps the saddest of all scars. It's so simple to remedy yet most violent offenders can't conceive of it. It's so simple for us to heal, yet there are people all around us that can't fathom it. I couldn't.)

If I was going to construct this higher Power I would have to understand personal value. I had learned from Sergeant Franco to fake it till I make it so I figured I'd fake being important enough until I proved I wasn't. Once again I'd try being open-minded and not contemptuous (as you can see it was hard). I really did like the sound of a personal God designed by me. I asked how I could get started. I assumed that I would have to start talking or praying to this Higher Power no matter what it was. I had a long list of wants that essentially consisted of a list of how all the other Gods had failed me. To start, I was instructed to ask this thing, this HP to remove my desire to drink from me. I was to start simple and not worry about all the details. I was told that until my mind was detoxed the details didn't really matter, that things wouldn't really make sense until then. "First Things First," I had to stop drinking. They said that not worrying about the details was called faith. I would however be asked to consider that if there was a God that was willing to do all of what I wanted, then what would I be willing to do in exchange? (This played to my sense of fairness.)

I have to admit I was hung up on the details. Those details had been my whole argument against God for years. I was instructed not to worry about it today, that the withdrawal was gonna kick my ass first. I was told that if I needed to take a drink that night that it was ok but before I did I was to try getting on my knees and asking my new "God" for help first. I was given permission to use Billy's God if I needed to. I was to ask my HP to take away my desire to take a drink and to do that every day until it was gone. It was suggested that I ask my Higher Power to help keep me sober and then thank "It" for the help if it worked. They called it research.

When I returned to the house I told Tony about the meeting. There was no letting me stay at this point but I thought he might have some

256

insight. He struggled with the open HP concept and I could see the doubt in his eyes but he was happy I went. I asked him a couple questions trying to find out if he knew about AA. I knew somewhere in my head I was going to be using not drinking as an excuse to stay in the house but that wasn't going to happen yet. There was no trust and rightly so.

I told him a little bit about what I heard and he said "I really hope it works for you." He meant it too. I found out later that he had been praying for this very thing for me for months. The Grace of other people's prayers cannot be explained but it cannot be ignored either. (Grace alert! My threatening of his beliefs ended up confirming them.)

Then I did something that still astounds me to this day. I went upstairs to my room, opened the door and saw the unopened beers sitting in between the window and the storm window: I didn't take one out. Instead, I sat in bed, then kneeled in bed and said. "Hey Billy's God, could you help me not take a drink and take away my desire to drink. I don't know if you care about me or not but I could use any help that I can get. Dad, if you can hear me and God can't can you ask him to help me not take a drink." I laid down and tried to read some of this Big Book that I was given but I wasn't ready to read the whole thing. I knew it would be hard so I recalled a lucky number that I had had in my head since my early childhood. I never really understood why I called it a lucky number because I never had any luck or won anything with it.

I figured I would make a deal with the Universe. I told myself that if there was anything in this book or this program for me, if there was anything supernatural it would prove itself on page 55. I thumbed to the page and began reading. I started getting chills down my leg. I have to admit I was freaking out. My damaged attention span required that I read the same sentences over and over. The sentences weren't making sense, partly because I was forgetting them and partly because I just couldn't believe how personal to me they seemed. There were two lines that struck me the most. "In this book, you will read the experiences of a man who thought he was an atheist" and "His change of heart was dramatic convincing and moving."

You'll have to read the page to get the full impact but the page was so on target for me that it seemed like proof of God or at least something mystical. I couldn't question the miraculous nature that this number 55 had been in my head most of my life and I didn't know why. If I had chosen any other number in the entire book it wouldn't have hit me between the eyes like page 55 did. Now I had chills covering my entire body. I felt a presence in the room with me; like someone was watching me. (Was this Grace? God?)

What I retained most from reading that page and from the meeting was that these people knew how I felt, how I thought and what I was afraid of. They seemed to know how my mind worked; about the hurt, shame, frustration, depression, mental anguish, fear/anxiety and even the self-loathing. They also understood the implausibility of it all working but that didn't stop them. They expected miracles! My first miracle happened that night because I didn't take a drink and didn't want to. Before I fell asleep I asked my friend's God and my father to talk to God for me again, asking to remove my desire to drink.

The next day I started reading the book from the beginning as originally instructed. Reading was as hard as I expected it would be. I would read a sentence and before I could get to the end of the sentence I would forget what the first part of the sentence said. It took me about 10 minutes to read one paragraph. I could feel my brain coming apart just like in the jail cell but I kept reading and believing (faking it).

The next day was December 12th (12-12-1984). (I didn't know it then but it was also the sobriety date of the founder of AA in 1934. Exactly 50 years earlier.) I had to go to work that day. I recall having no idea of what to drink in the morning because I usually just had a beer. That was all I ever bought from the store so it was all I ever owned. I grabbed a cheap knockoff soda I had been offered a hundred times before. I went out front to wait for my ride to work with my book in hand.

After Sandy picked me up our routine was that we'd drive down to SoWeBo (South West Baltimore) and pick up his friend and employee Paul. Paul was a real alcoholic. He was 42 at the time but looked 62. He carried a playmate cooler with him everywhere he went that he called his briefcase. It was never more than 25 feet away from him. It always had the same thing in it, seven PBRs (Pabst Blue Ribbon beers). I worked with Paul on and off for several years. I only saw him eat food 2 times.

Paul and I had a really odd friendship because Paul knew that I was going to be him one day. He knew that my relationship with booze was just like his. He actually did a double-take when he saw me reading the blue book as we drove. I think he knew but he asked "What's that?" I sneakily showed him instead of saying it out loud. His response was; "Nice people." He said, "I tried that once in the hospital. It wasn't for me." I didn't want to be Paul.

I read that book every chance I got; in the truck on the way to jobs, on breaks, during lunch, every time I wasn't supposed to be working and sometimes when I was. There wasn't much said about it. People knew my history. My soon-to-be-stepfather Sandy was a nice guy but what could he say. His best friend was an alcoholic like nearly everyone else in the commercial storefront glass business. Most of them actually lived near Paul in SoWeBo. Paul's hands would start shaking in the morning so we left most of the heavy lifting until after he drank his lunch.

That night Billy showed up again; right on time, again. He asked, "Did you take a drink?" I said nope! He said, "That is awesome, you've been reading the book?" "Yep, I even talked to your Higher Power last night." "Awesome!" I also explained how I talked to my dead father; he thought that was great too. I have to admit that the concern and validation was odd. I wasn't used to it at all. We drove up to Carroll County to Springfield State Mental Hospital to do what was referred to as an "Institution Commitment." It was something that Billy had been doing every Thursday night for months. Basically, he would set up the meeting and outside groups from around the area would come in and speak with the residents.

In case you're wondering they didn't want to keep me. That required paperwork. I remember hearing patients share and being a little dismayed that the residents of a nut house seemed to have their heads on straighter than I did. There was a guy there they called Hairspray. I asked why they called him that. They said he used to drink Aquanet. He'd spray it in the plastic lid and drink it because it was 60-proof. I was beginning to realize that I was now among professionals; serious drinkers. Another guy there was fixated on Nyquil's shot glass, saying it was there because it was 100 proof. He loved that they never carded people for it. (Were these guys telling me of my future if I kept drinking?)

There was a line that I heard over and over both in the literature and from the people in the meetings. "We aren't a glum lot. We absolutely insist on enjoying life." My problem was that I didn't think enjoyment was possible but I was still going to fake it.

So I went home again that evening with my book still in hand and started to read some more. This time I didn't need Billy's God but I did start communication with God through my father. My father knew what a struggle it was to not take a drink so I knew he would understand without a lot of dialogue. I also felt like he owed me since he'd abandoned me by dying. He was in essence a professional drinker but he never gave me any advice at all about something he did every day.

The OUR FATHER WHO ART IN HEAVEN took on a whole new meaning during this era. The AA members always said the Lord's Prayer at the end of every meeting. Either the OUR FATHER was just what I needed or the whole thing was just the old LSD trips talking. I didn't care. They said, "Don't analyze, utilize."

While some people think that you have to remove all temptation I'm not so sure that's the case. Quitting alcohol and drugs was then and I believe always will be a conscious choice. Probably a choice a person has to make every day in the beginning. I knew in my heart after just two days that it would be easier to not take another drink than to try to get that first day all over again. I asked my father (now in heaven, not hell) to help me. I was a practicing Taoist in the army so I viewed God as more of a Native American, mother-nature, Spirit of the Universe sort of Power.

I took their Big Book everywhere I went. Billy continued to come and get me almost every day for 3 months with the exception of Tuesdays because of a jail commitment he had. I couldn't go because I was still on probation. I found a meeting called the Rockdale group that was 3.5 miles away. I walked that 7 miles every Tuesday. Why? Because I was too proud to ask for a ride and as a Hitchhiker I was used to walking.

Instead of walking home with liquor I actually started buying groceries. I remember those paper bags that would sometimes rip but I did it anyway. It felt normal and right somehow to be walking with groceries instead of a case of beer. I almost felt proud that I was doing the right thing in taking care of myself. There was a sense of humility in doing what all the other stupid people had to do. I was happy just trying to be a "stupid people."

I don't know if it was Grace or if it was the power of suggestion but I didn't drink. Something very strange started happening. Those withdrawals and DTs that I had had nearly every day for two years and in jail never quite presented, ever! You heard that right. Somehow, miraculously, the physical symptoms disappeared. Grace came in and the craving to drink was removed. The biological and scientifically proven signs of withdrawal didn't happen. I was staying sober the whole time with 7 ice-cold beers in the bedroom window. They stared me in my face every night when I went to bed and every morning when I woke up. Instead of being tempted by them I actually felt reassured by their presence in case I decided to change my mind. You may call it tempting providence but those old AA drunks called it being sure. They were not shy about telling people to go drink if they weren't; they called that research too. I wanted to be that sure.

One Saturday night after a meeting in Towson we all went out to get coffee and ice cream. We were sitting there about a ½ hour. I was sitting next to a big window. I looked up to the lights in the distance and I got chills all over my entire body; from head to toe. I was staring up at the jailhouse window that I looked down from with ridicule. Curious about those stupid people on that FATEFUL night. I was now one of those "Kind of fucking people that goes to HoJo's on a Saturday night at 9:30." And I loved it! I now knew exactly who those people were that I saw. I knew exactly why they were coming here. I could have even been sitting with some of them at this very moment. That's GRACE!!!

BUT! BUTT!

By this point, I knew that drinking wasn't a viable option but I hadn't committed to total abstinence. AA's only requirement for membership is "A desire to stop drinking." You don't even have to be sober you just need a desire to not drink. No one mentioned drugs at any of the meetings. In fact, speaking about drugs was highly discouraged; singleness in purpose they called it.

The reality is that beyond smoking other people's weed I hadn't used drugs in quite some time and I didn't care to; I certainly never craved them. The only time I smoked pot prior to attending AA was with Brian. AA seemed unconcerned with drugs but they didn't believe a person could be sober and recover while using other mood-altering chemicals. Since I didn't really believe people could be chemical free I imagined that many of the members were in fact using weed; I believed people needed to use something to cope with life.

For Christmas that year my sister's "friend" (lawyer) gifted her with a really nice corner suite on the 8th floor of the Brookshire Hotel for a week. It was a place for all the lonely hearts from "The Block" to bond together over the holiday. It had an amazing view of the harbor (at the time). The plan was for a 24-hour, 4-day party with all the best talent from Baltimore Street. Christmas fell on of all days, Tuesday and Billy would be busy with his jail commitment.

The poor stripper girls had one major problem. They couldn't find any cocaine so they called on old faithful. As you know I didn't sell coke but I sure knew who did. Not only did I know a guy that sold it, I knew a guy that liked to give it away to hot chicks. He didn't even ask for sex for his coke, all he wanted was to party with hot women. (Sadly he did so much of it that I don't think he could do much else.) He made me an offer a long time ago at the Deli saying, "You can do all the Cocaine you want, all you have to do is bring the women and I'll hook you up."

M was a man of his word. It was just a year earlier when one of my scariest nights of overuse occurred. M was hosting a Christmas party that included many of the employees from the Deli. That party had pretty much every drug that you could imagine, including many edibles with different drugs in them. Alcohol was my love but when I used Cocaine I could love alcohol longer.

His Christmas party had rolled on like you might imagine and I became so intoxicated that I needed some air. I went out for a walk to keep from puking. There was about 4 inches of crunchy snow on the ground. It was a clear cold night in Maryland so I decided to stare at the stars. I began to stagger as I tried to look over my head at the sky. I lost my balance and landed in the snow. I lay there gazing for some time before I passed out. I had rolled over actually placing my face on the snow. I can only assume I was passed out for about 20 minutes when I heard a car pull up and park. I heard a girl tell her boyfriend that there was someone lying in the snow not moving. I could hear him cautiously walking in that crunchy snow toward me but I didn't move. By Grace, he softly yelled, "Hey dude are you OK?"

I started to move and sat up knowing that I didn't want him to call the police. I had to prove I was OK. I responded, "Yeah dude I'm good, REAL GOOD!!!" He said, "Do you need any help?" I said no and told him clearly that I was OK. He said OK back and then began to walk away. I yelled back "Hey dude! MERRY CHRISTMAS!!!!" He said "Merry Christmas dude."

By the Grace of something, they came when they did. By their Grace, they bothered to see if I was OK. They had unknowingly woken me up from what could have been my death. You see I laid there in that snow so long that I actually damaged nerves in the left side of my face; I still have minor paralysis there to this day that keeps me from winking my left eye. That "snow nap" also damaged the muscles in my face causing it to droop slightly. It was only a matter of time until that reduced temperature on my face reached my brain. Add to that the hypothermic nature of heavy alcohol use and I was very lucky (if it was luck and not Grace). In my dark days I saw luck as even less real than God because I didn't have either. My face-plant made for a great party story and it gave M and I a bond for life. It was proof we knew how to party.

Fast forward, I called up my friend M and said, "I got 10 dancers that want to party at a suite at the Brookshire, you interested?" He said oh yeah and he came to pick me up in his van. I had no idea how much coke he was bringing. We got up to the suite and it was hopping. Tons of booze and weed but I was sober. I would only be drinking soda. No sedatives for me, my focus was on the girls. There was a big glass dinette table. M asked "How long do we have" and he was told 4 days. He walked over to the glass table, reached into his coat and proceeded to dump about a ¼ pound of cocaine on the glass table. (The dancers were stunned and that's saying something.) He said, "Have at it." In those days dancers all had rolled-up bills in their bras when they were on; if not they were sticking out of their G-strings. I knew then I would be using free cocaine along with the free weed. I didn't need to bring anything else or pay anybody because I brought Mr. M.

While I did lots of other things that night I didn't drink. I probably should have. I remember countless trips to the soda machine for myself and to buy mixers for the girls' drinks. I remember the machine going empty and all that was left was Dr. Pepper (not a good drink mixer). When I say that I should have drank I say that because I got too amped up on the coke and weed. I stayed up for days.

There was a Christmas party at my sister's God mother's house. She was married to a Greek named Gus and she was cool so my sister and I went there that Saturday night after days of hard partying. (I still didn't have a drink.) Interestingly alcohol was the only thing I asked God/dad to help me not do. I remember being so strung out and wired that I clenched my jaw for days; it ached well into the New Year.

I remember people at the family party being proud and shocked that I wasn't drinking. (How ironic and confusing is that?) I was up on coke for days with whores and being congratulated on my recovery (they were all personally familiar with my father's struggles). Their praise validated everything I was thinking about drugs being OK.

Billy came and got me for a few days in a row before New Year's which was again on a Tuesday. He asked if I took a drink and I said no; he didn't ask about the drugs. We went to several meetings together that weekend and I felt like I was still on track despite my adventure. It started to look like drinking would become a thing of the past. I had proven that I wasn't a part of any "glum lot." As mentioned earlier having fun "sober" was one of my biggest concerns. Fun was proving to be a non-issue. In fact, I may have just had one of the best few days of my young adult life and I did it without booze.

When people blame you for their feelings you start to feel responsible for their feelings. That was the script that both my mother's neglect and my abuser's perversions laid out for me. As backward as it sounds abused people perpetuate the scripts that they're given during their trauma. My training was to put others' desires before my needs, even when their feeling good was at my expense.

RESOLUTIONS

The party invites didn't stop just because I wasn't selling drugs or drinking. People didn't even ask if I was dealing they just expected me to have drugs. The way I related to others was transactional so I believed that was how everybody related to one another. Because of my experiences growing up my reflex was to monetize myself. I had to rationalize a reason for people wanting me around; a reason beyond self (still a faint scar today). Since I didn't believe I had personal value as just a friend or person I always sought a motive for their invites. I never questioned why anyone else was there; they were all regular people and I wasn't. In my head, I was a thing, a commodity only. I never even considered that I might be invited because I was smart, funny or friendly.

Untreated abused, neglected and damaged children become adults that can't recognize their value as people or as individuals. This creates a lot of social anxieties. When there is no, "Why they would want me," conclusion; the scar just screams THEY MUST NOT WANT ME! That was my mindset. I always searched for some quantitative reason why people wanted me around. Since no one in my family ever seemed to why would others? I had no sense of innate value; I was robbed of it by neglect and abuse.

Regardless of what I thought that New Year's Eve an old friend from school called me to invite me to a party that he was having (because we were friends). It was near Skateland; 100 yards through the woods on Sherwood Hill near the graveyard. I prepared to not drink by bringing a bottle of fake champagne for the midnight celebration. I wouldn't need much else because there would be a few females there.

We started partying around 8:00pm. There was a little basic refreshment but that ran out once people started mixing the family booze with anything they could find. People thought it was pretty cool that I wasn't going to drink; they even encouraged and supported it (wonder why). As luck would have it the cotton mouth arrived early so guess what? No, I didn't drink alcohol. I started drinking my sparkling cider. It was a new thing so everybody wanted a taste. I only had one bottle and it was gone by 9:30. I decided to make a trip to the Village Inn to get some more or some alcohol-free beer for the midnight celebration. The group wanted more beer and since I was legal I'd be getting it. They gathered up their one-dollar bills and some change to get a case of Coors beer (my mistress to Budweiser).

There was a rare line at the Village Bar that night and the guy at the counter was a grumpy old man, more interested in his beer than the customers in line. I got up to the front and asked, "Do you have anything alcohol-free?" In a hoarse old grumbly man voice, he said: "WE DON'T SELL WATER!" Instantly without a moment's hesitation and with no mental defense. I said; "Do you have LA" (LA was Less Alcohol beer).

He said, "WE DON'T SELL WATER." Getting angry and feeling insulted I said, "Give me 3 cases of Coors."

There wasn't a moment of hesitation in that transition from alcohol-free to 3 cases of Coors. Why? Because I was high that's why. There was no thought of any of my struggles that had existed over the past several years, no thought of Tony, or jail, of AA; nothing. No mental defense.

Why three cases when they only had enough money for one? Simple, one for them, one for me and one for the party so that the one for me would be left the hell alone. That's how fast things shift in the addicted mind. If you love someone that can't stay sober that is exactly what takes place in about half of their relapses: The other half are very well planned out.

I noticed one thing occurring that I probably wouldn't have had it not been for the AA meetings. I became aware that the second case was running out long before it did (more math). I decided to stash some of my case so people would just think that we were out and go back to their bong hits. I hid two beers in the crisper, two beers in the freezer, two beers behind the toaster and even two beers in a bedroom behind a bed. Some of you know what I was doing. For the rest, I was "protecting my supply" because it was after all New Year's Eve. Why two beers? Because that way I could pay off the person that saw me retrieve them; distract them from thinking there were more. Thanks to AA I was very aware of how obsessed I was; they called it powerlessness.

There was something else going on at this party, she was a girl we all called Thunder-Thighs or Whale Tail (a nickname she reveled in.) She wasn't that big she was just a tallish Amablonde with strong leg muscles. Billy, Wormo and I had all dated or slept with her. I don't remember who she was with first back when we were 16 but when we were around 19 I do know that Wormo gave her the Clap from Panama, then she gave it to me and Billy too I think. I was still a little "pissed" at her for that "trick." If you've ever been drunk in your life you know what happens next. You lower your standards and try to hook up with people you wouldn't otherwise hook up with; even exes. This New Year's Eve would be no different and she had a car. We flirted, kissed and played around in the same bed where she got a payoff beer. About 1:00 am I tried to get her to take me home. She said she would but said that she couldn't stay, that she had to work the next day (knowing I don't do fast sex). She was however really keen on us getting together afterward. I returned home drunk with no thought of Tony or anyone else. I grabbed a beer out of the window and went to sleep.

COMING TO

The next morning is still very vivid to me now. I raised my head about a foot up off the pillow, recalled the booze, saw the beer can, remembered trying to hook up with ole thunder thighs again and boom, I fell back into the pillow.

I know some of you are thinking, standards? STD's? You were just with a bunch of whores in a hotel room bingeing on Coke the week before. Yeah, you're right, but I still never caught anything from a dancer. (FYI, the high-end girls take care of their money makers and get tested often, the average girl may never get checked in her lifetime.)

I didn't just wake up that morning I had a revelation. When I lifted my head I was able to see how, in the blink of an eye I'd given up all my aspirations and goals for the future in just a split second. I had traded what I wanted most, for what I wanted now, for instant gratification. I could clearly see my powerlessness. They said there may come a time when there would be no mental defense against the first drink. They warned me of this very thing just not about the role drugs could play in it. The most important point is that they were right about the booze. While they didn't care about drugs in those meetings they did talk about total abstinence. In that moment it was quite clear to me that the drugs took away my mental defense against the first drink. It was obvious that the drugs impaired my thinking just enough to set off the very mechanism of compulsion that made it impossible for me to not buy that beer. In that instance, I learned just how powerful alcohol really was and just how Powerless I was over it.

CHAPTER FIFTEEN
DATING GRACE

JANUARY 1, 1985

The first day of the year is usually when people begin their new year's resolutions. I don't know if it still counts because I never really set a goal for changing my life that New Year's Eve. The truth was I spent that night up to my old tricks. What I am sure of is that I woke up that day and believed that I was done drinking; that I was done with all the mood-altering chemicals, everything. It was like breaking through to a new level of enlightenment and having a spiritual awakening at the same time. I was suddenly certain that victory over alcohol would not occur while using other drugs. Any attempt I might make to rationalize chemical use would undoubtedly be total bullshit! My intuition strongly suggested the party was over.

My view of mood-altering chemicals as a whole was that I had used up all the fun that they had in them. All the potential respite and needed escape they might offer had been exhausted. It was as if they weren't meant to handle the amount of torment I was experiencing. I didn't think that I was gonna be cheated out of anything by not drinking and using because I knew that I had taken them for all that they had to offer and then some. (People that don't have this moment keep using more and more until they die.) I suddenly believed that the rest of any time I might spend using chemicals to feel OK would only lead to more catastrophe and heartache: I had had enough of both.

I figured I'd just be pressing luck I didn't have if I kept trying the same old failed solutions. Just like the people in my life the chemical that I loved, needed and relied upon had abandoned me too. I now felt even more alone than before I fell in love with alcohol. Like being in a bad relationship I thirsted for something that just didn't exist. I was left to consider if my new present mindset was the result of the prayer I had tried asking that my desire to use be taken away. While the desire to use was gone, my need to treat my emotional struggles wasn't. Having just lost the preferred method for escaping those feelings I was going to need something. This newfound clarity and awareness was either a dose of reality or a helping of Grace.

The last years of my use were a lot like the movie Ground Hog Day. Day after day after day of repeating the same old nightmare of waking up to a world that sucked, getting money, getting my supply and getting drunk, over and over again, every day. Whenever I would wake up and see the clock the pain would turn on. The chemicals were like a snooze button that just went off again and again. Every day looked exactly the same and there seemed to be no end in sight. Continued use would amount to nothing more than the Dr. Jekyll and Mr. Hyde dichotomy of good intentions being eclipsed and maligned by the neglected, damaged and altered me.

If there was any hope it was going to take a lot of help, a lot of work, a lot of magic, a lot of support, a lot of time and a lot of Grace. It would take all those things that no one close to me ever gave me; all those things the world had seemingly denied me. The reality was that their 12 Step suggestions to build a relationship with a Higher Power were my last hope; the only path I saw. If it didn't work for me my only option was death; my final solution to life. Miraculously the thought occurred to me that I would "just not kill myself one day at a time." Before I off'd myself I would try the AA program just to prove it didn't work for me either; prove that I was forsaken.

SPOILER ALERT: IT WORKED

If I would have killed myself I would have gotten the wrong guy. At the writing of this book, I have not had a drink or drug in nearly 40 years; I don't even use caffeine or nicotine. I spend my time between my private practice clients and my writing. While my love for learning may have been obscured by calamity in the past I now find it to be one of my greatest joys and my primary passion.

I would like to tell you the story of how I was able to perpetuate the Grace I was given in full but that will take another book. Sufficed to say I worked the AA program very hard. I did lots of things they told me not to do but I did everything they told me to do. Countless men and women helped me along the way with their knowledge, love, experience, strength, hope, and yes, Grace. I have hundreds of examples to share with you and I'm working on that now.

Since my first institution commitment with AA, on my second day in AA, I have volunteered in jails, institutions, hospitals, treatment centers and in the program itself. That is what I was taught. I do it because someone did it for me; out of gratitude. Those people and their Grace saved my life and I owe them. I am fiercely loyal to the people that extended themselves to me; the people that saved me from the altered me. I heal others in their names.

In essence, loving people (in and out of the programs) taught me how to care for myself, for people and for systems that help people. They showed me things about "good people" that I wasn't exposed to in my early life. Their compassion and grace toward me taught me my worth. For this reason, I have dedicated my life to helping others find their value. Graceful people relieved so much of my suffering that I want to pay it forward. I now make the sacrifices for others that no one seemed to make for me as a child. The spirituality and love that I experienced was so powerful it turned a budding sociopath into someone that nurtures people emotionally every day. (Grace?)

I went back to school, lots of school, but before that, I started studying for my GED test. At the time I was receiving unemployment benefits and that agency funded a drafting course for me at a local community college. That course was canceled at the last minute but I then had a credit at the school. That school just happened to be (by Grace) the only school in the region that offered a Chemical Dependency Counseling Certificate. The book I was studying for the GED test aided in my entrance exam preparation. I did so well on the test that I was able to start school without a GED (I attained my GED a few months later, getting my test scores on Thanksgiving Day).

One of my first college classes was English 101. I hated English but it appeared that my writing skills and style came so naturally that my teacher allowed me to forgo the last few weeks of the class (We didn't use the Oxford Comma). That teacher (and many to come) inspired me and pushed me to consider writing as a career. His encouragement did a lot more than that. Unknowingly he broke down my own conceptions and stereotypes about who I was and wasn't.

In total, I've attained five college degrees, including two Masters. One is a Masters in Social Work the other a Masters in Instructional Design and Human Performance. (It may also interest you to know that I attained a Minor in Philosophy of Religion as well.)

All my help didn't come from AA and school; there were other people too. By Grace, I found people that knew how to nurture and encourage. They helped me trade in my seat at the office for a place on the Dean's List; a place I stayed for every semester of my educational career. One of my proudest educational achievements was completing my last degree with a 4.0 GPA. Another joy was learning to read and write Chinese (now working on Sanskrit).

Every step of the way there have been moments of pure Grace both Universal and Individual. I've had great teachers and great mentors. I've had the perfect supervisors, offering the perfect opportunities at the perfect jobs, for me.

Life has been an amazing circus ride of heartache and opportunity. In the first 8 years of my journey, I was able to become a stepfather figure to a little girl born a month after the one I never got to know. In an odd twist of fate, the two girls born a month apart and on opposite sides of a big city were in the same classroom 8 years later. The little blessing that Grace brought into my life to help raise, taught me that I couldn't escape Universal Grace. She taught me more about love than any other single individual I have ever known. Not just by loving me unconditionally but by letting me love her the way I should have been. She showed me that I was capable of the same levels of love that everyone else was. That relationship taught me that we all deserve and are worthy of unconditional love; the fact that she wasn't my blood magnified that lesson.

Thanks to my scars the journey to find romantic love has been extremely difficult. The stains that sexual abuse leaves behind make it very hard to choose and bond with people based on "who" and not "what" they are. I thought loving my partners meant making them feel good. (It's unavoidable if you grow up being told you're why other people aren't happy.) I did a good job making them feel good until they made me feel bad by triggering my damage. When the relationships were threatened I felt every event of abandonment I had ever experienced in my lifetime; all at once. I often forgot about my needs and obsessed over theirs until I became so drained that I would then demand from them what they didn't have to give me. My "picker" is probably still broken but that doesn't mean my heart isn't full.

There may be times when the truth is better left unsaid but not left unheeded. Fearing abandonment I've even endured physical abuse by a woman because I believed we were "supposed to be together." I am happy to say that by Grace she and I have healed a lot of the damage we experienced together but that still doesn't mean we are good for each other as partners.

At age 60 I find more fulfillment focusing on my own spiritual needs while loving others the best I can. Not being married or having kids has allowed me to be there for humanity. That's a far cry for someone that didn't believe in humanity. I think that aiding humanity is the only reason I've remained on this Earth-walk. I know I can reduce suffering: I do it every day.

I can still see my scars but they don't haunt me or limit me like they used to. I know now how I'm damaged. (Removing the chemicals was a must.) Sometimes my scars are sad to see because I know they could have been lessened with a little bit more compassion and some professional help.

Since January 1, 1985, I have been able to experience some amazing things in my life. The list is far too long to detail but what I will say is that for a kid that didn't feel important or valued my personal experiences have proven the opposite.

I continued dancing and for many years my dancing gave me the limelight that many people often crave or perhaps even fantasize about. Having people enjoy my creative expression and what I have to offer as a person has left me so grateful that I wouldn't dare ask for more. It's as if the desire to be relevant, wanted and needed has been satiated. That stain has been lightened and is now so faint that it's hard to trigger.

The greatest pleasure I've known has come from helping other people. I spent my first 20 years in the field working almost exclusively with alcoholics, addicts and their families. During that time I remained part of the program that saved my life; a program that allows me to live a life of service on a daily basis.

I have sacrificed a lot to help others but it was all worth it. I didn't get paid much but I got rewarded every day. Instead of being in prison I've worked and volunteered in them. I worked in the Baltimore City Public School System as a Student Assistance Program Counselor motivating kids like me to persevere and succeed. I worked with people in the sex industry, in domestic violence and as a family counselor. I worked educating clergy and church elders to improve services for parishioners. I worked within the gay and lesbian communities too but mostly with poor black kids in Baltimore City.

Early on in my career, I managed a Drug Prevention tutoring grant. I conducted one of the longest-running drug dealer therapy groups in the nation. I created a Children of Substance Abusing Parents Therapy Group Program for 3rd to 5th graders in the first elementary school-based health clinic in the nation (with Johns Hopkins Hospital). I spent years as a lobbyist for ATAM where we worked to improve drug treatment in Maryland.

I spent seven years working in one of the largest adult and adolescent outpatient drug treatment programs in Baltimore City. Instead of being locked up in Baltimore County I became the clinical director of the County's DWI treatment facility (a minimum security jail). I left there to work with The Associated Jewish Federation of Baltimore just after 9-11. There I began authoring and teaching professional seminars and educating the public on the needs of the addicted. That prompted me to begin writing my first book, "Addiction: Why They Use" (A handbook for anyone that loves an alcoholic or addict.)

In a moment of twisted ironic fate, I was hit by a drunk driver while on a motorcycle. Months after I healed I left the Federation with a strong drive to live out my childhood dream of being a psychotherapist in private practice. I did just that, at one point having three offices around the Baltimore metropolitan area. Were it not for my disgust of the health insurance industry I might still be there today.

In 2012 I moved my world to East Tennessee to focus on my writing. I started doing pre-surgical psych evaluations for a while then in 2014, I wrote, "Addiction: Am I Powerless (Self-assessing; a User's Guide to the Truth). I worked in residential foster care for a brief time then wrote "The Pacification of Humanity: Exposing the Ideological Contagions."

I didn't plan on opening a practice in Tennessee but I saw people suffering needlessly. In my practice I work with people I think I can help; usually people with Anxiety, Depression, Trauma and Self-Concept issues. I also treat people with compulsive issues related to addiction, porn, food, sex and gambling. Besides doing trauma work, I also love doing couples and family therapy.

Over the years I've worked with the poorest of the poor, celebrities, sports figures, bands and teams of all kinds. I've even worked with a lot of those nasty rich people who I now know have serious problems too. They say if you love what you do you'll never work a day in your life and they're right, it never feels like work.

My childhood dream is a reality. The little kid that wanted to be a therapist has become one; a good one. The little kid whose heart wanted to help others before it was damaged now does just that. Because of my career and my other books, I literally have people contacting me from all around the world asking me questions about addiction and other societal issues. Unconditionally helping random strangers on the other side of the planet for free has been a validation that few will ever know. I now know I wasn't put here to be abused or neglected. I know that I have a gift of insight and the ability to nurture others that is sometimes otherworldly.

I've had many people tell me my empathic and intuitive skills are off-the-chart. Those skills may have benefitted me when I was having lots of sex and dealing drugs but they were meant for healing. My clients and I both share and experience my gifts together when these insights of unknown origin present. It seems we each heal just a little bit more when they do. My family therapy teacher was right when she told me I was a natural and that it would be a shame for me not to be working with families. It may be because I'm bright but I think it's because I know the value of caring like only those who were robbed of it can.

Be their wounds from; neglect, damage, abuse, anxiety, anger, depression or trauma I work hard to help my clients heal their damage. Some of my most valued moments occur when I get to help parents be more whole, more loving and more aware of their children's needs. I know that when parents are healthy and work together their children thrive.

The emotional detachment that my family seemingly cursed me with has actually become a very valuable tool for maintaining a clinical perspective. Having been cheated out of many of the simple things in life has placed them at a much greater value in my heart. Uncovering the value of our own ability to Grace each other seems to be quite healing for everyone involved.

When it comes to God/god/Higher Power my relationship has evolved substantially. My Taoism has remained with me since my days in the service. I learned to speak, read and write Chinese so I could read the Tao firsthand. In connection with my love for all things Asian, I practiced Wushu (Kung Fu) for many years in order to increase my self-discipline and manifest my true self in the physical world. (I've even trained with Shaolin Monks.)

All told, I have practiced many of the world's most populous religions and I have gained something valuable from every one of them. At one point in the 90s I maintained spiritual leadership status in 7 different religions (I would name them but I don't want to slight any). Sufficed to say that I wasn't doing it to lead anyone I just attained the status through devotion and practice. I believe now that each and every religion has a unique strength and a secret for comfortable living. (The one thing they all have in common is Grace.)

I now possess many of the strengths and insights gained from those religions (at least when I'm paying attention). Having been a practicing Yogi now for the past 18 years, I'd say that the religious framework which best categorizes my current awareness seems to be Advaita Vedanta. I love that it connects the "world of physics" and the "world of the spirit." I don't believe they are separate worlds only that we have divided them because we have been conditioned to do so.

What my spiritual practices have given me is a peace inside that most people rarely experience regardless of how wealthy or healthy of an upbringing they may have had. The truth is that aside from wanting to heal others I am now so comfortable and whole that I yearn for nothing (I'm not rich, barely middle class). I have no unquenched worldly desires, no bucket list; only the occasional triggers and compulsions related to my old scars. Sadly they do still pop up when I least expect them to and usually at unfortunate times.

My scars rarely present as any form of discomfort for anyone other than my cat. With that being said I am still very aware and diligent about my physical presentation. These are leftover scars and damage from being objectified and objectifying. With all this in mind, I'll add the caution that people who have been emotionally damaged are not people you want to push too far when they're unhappy or spiritually ill. That's when they'll need your Grace the most.

As I stated at the beginning of this journey I was not writing this to sell books or to be known. I really did it to open both your eyes and those of a hypnotized clinical community to a more effective perspective for treating emotional injuries, i.e. damage. The treatment of damage has been so focused on trauma that the lesser pieces often go unresolved and untreated. Treat the damaged parts and the trauma will resolve.

As a society we've become lazy, thinking that treatment providers need to fix all the emotional problems we now face. Professionals have unwittingly taken the layperson's attention away from their own role in their healing and belittled the true impact of their acts on one another. Our failure as a society to do our part is why I think we have people acting out in the public square more now than ever before. Those people need you. The clinical world has been led astray from treating the human spirit but it is the spirit that becomes emotionally ill. Professionals have stopped teaching communities how to help each other. This leaves many scarred people in the shadows like ticking time bombs. Damaged people explode in the public square because they need to be more relevant to the people around them. They explode because no one acknowledges their pain. Individual Grace (your Grace) can help them heal before they feel the need to show us their damage; I'm proof.

SAVING GRACE

Another motivation for me to write this book was to show you that statistics can be beaten when our Grace is involved. The random acts of kindness that you may personally create can save lives and make other lives worth saving. Those seemingly small acts of love that people extended to me saved my life. I don't think most of them even know it nor have they seriously considered their role in my success and healing. (This book is also a thank you to them.)

Saving me was not why they did it but their Grace did make my life worth saving and maybe even some of yours. Was it God working through them, possibly; it was certainly love working through them and many people believe God is love.

A friend, mentor, sponsor and spiritual guide of mine named John Finney shared a poem with me. A poem that his grandfather; the creator of the blood bank and a historical figure from his Princeton football days carried with him in the trenches in WWI. To me, it speaks to the power of love and Grace.

DEATHLESS (Ella Wheeler Wilcox, {first two stanzas})
There lies in the center of each man's heart
A longing and love for the good and pure;
And if but an atom, or larger part,
I tell you this shall endure—endure—
After the body has gone to decay—
Yea, after the world has passed away.

The longer I live and the more I see
Of the struggle of souls toward the heights above,
The stronger this truth comes home to me:
That the Universe rests on the shoulders of love;
A love so limitless, deep, and broad,
That men have renamed it and called it—God.

It doesn't matter to me whether it is love that saved me or if that love is a manifestation of God in people. It doesn't matter to me whether God made love or Love made God or even if Grace made them both. None of them belong to any one entity or religion; all are a product of human generosity, compassion and selflessness. (I simply see Grace as the opposite of all the things that cause damage.) As a yogi (nearing 2 decades now) I know that God is in you and God is in me. Love is in you and love is in me. Grace is in you and Grace is in me. All we have to do is let IT out. That's how we make more Grace. That is how we find the state of Grace we seek; we make it. The easiest way I have found to produce Grace myself is to forgive the wrongs done to me. (That does not mean I subject myself to further damage.)

I've had great loves and great losses. I've seized some days and yearned for others to pass. As suggested I am working on the book that outlines my journey from sociopath to social worker, from Psycho-to-Therapist. I wanted to combine the two books but as I wrote and recalled the trauma of my past the damage seemed to multiply.

It was extremely emotional to relive this pain in great detail. I definitely paid quite a price having to stop writing several times to recoup my emotional stability and treat my scars again. I was even worried that I might regress in some areas but thankfully it resulted in more of a release. I'm not sure I would do it again but I haven't seen who benefits yet. (Please let me know.) I do know that during the process I've experienced more Grace and healing than I've ever known. My hope is that it will help you experience more Grace too.

DEFINING GRACE

In its purest form, Grace is often described as something positive that is undeserved; not due. I used to believe that too but now I see Grace as a positive force in the Universe that we're just not very good at tapping into. It's like there's a form of love that we're just not very educated about; like we're afraid to risk hoping for it. It's as if we believe that since there isn't enough of it we should somehow reserve it for the worthy. I'm convinced that holding it back reduces the supply.

In this book, I exposed Grace in many different forms. While I'm still learning about it I know this. We can make as much of it as we want and there is no limit to how Grace-full we can be. In some respects, Grace is the ability to give compassion without determining if it should be given. It seems we are even more Graceful when it's harder to give. It's most impactful when we can sneak it in on people without their knowing where it came from; when we can give it anonymously.

In this book, I also provided many examples of how a person can be damaged by abuse and neglect. What I experienced as a child fostered an abnormal view of the world; the "hurt" corrupted my thinking and hardened my heart. These experiences warped my worldview to such a degree that I didn't think that there was any hope for this mess they called humanity. As a child, I was convinced we couldn't be righted. My soul was so tortured at times that I wanted everyone else to suffer and struggle too: I thought it was only fair. I was left feeling so irrelevant that I dreamed of ways of making people notice me; to stand out. I hurt so badly that I wanted people to pay. This is what we see in the news because the easiest way to get noticed in the modern world is by doing something negative.

Thankfully, while unhealthy, the sexual and chemical means I found to get attention and be relevant distracted me enough to keep me from taking out my anger on innocent people. The Grace I did encounter along the way resulted in tiny interventions which altered my course just enough to redirect me. When I look back now I know that had these small acts not sustained me enough emotionally, for even those brief periods of time, that you would know my name for another reason.

I was trained to hurt and then trained to kill. The hurt, hurt so bad that it hurt not to hurt others. I used chemicals to medicate my desires to take revenge on humanity. Perhaps it was even Grace that made those chemicals available to me. Had I not been able to buy alcohol before age 21 to medicate with I probably would have exploded too; because that's what hurt people do. I promise you that many of the addicted people we see around us, on the edge of death, are medicating similar levels of damage and neglect too. I think we can provide them with enough Grace to keep death distracted long enough to save them and society.

The damage we endure in life creates a form of ignorance within us, ignorance about ourselves and others. It takes years of positive energy and help to unlearn the scripts that our negative experiences program us with. What I hoped to provide was evidence of how these small acts of compassion and Grace can make all the difference. Much has been omitted from this book. I now know that experiencing Grace is not enough. We have to build upon the brief breaks that life, people, God and the Universe gifts us with. We have to create more Grace to give each other more Hope.   MAY WE ALL SUFFER LESS!!!!!

Printed in the USA
CPSIA information can be obtained
at www.ICGtesting.com
JSHW010359170923
48402JS00003B/11